A TIME TO GATHER

Also by Bruce Feiler

The Search

Life Is in the Transitions

The First Love Story

The Secrets of Happy Families

Council of Dads

America's Prophet

Where God Was Born

Abraham

Walking the Bible

Dreaming Out Loud

Under the Big Top

Looking for Class

Learning to Bow

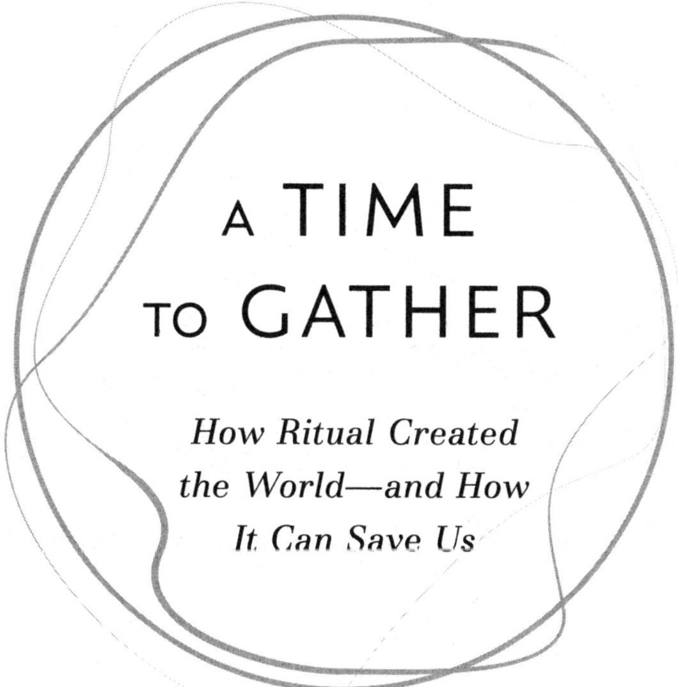

A TIME TO GATHER

How Ritual Created the World—and How It Can Save Us

Bruce Feiler

PENGUIN PRESS // NEW YORK // 2026

PENGUIN PRESS
An imprint of Penguin Random House LLC
1745 Broadway, New York, NY 10019
penguinrandomhouse.com

All photos courtesy of the author except for the photo on p. 207.

Designed by Amanda Dewey

LIBRARY OF CONGRESS CONTROL NUMBER: 2025037254

ISBN 9780593656433 (hardcover)
ISBN 9780593656440 (ebook)

Printed in the United States of America
1st Printing

The authorized representative in the EU for product safety and compliance is Penguin Random House Ireland, Morrison Chambers, 32 Nassau Street, Dublin D02 YH68, Ireland, https://eu-contact.penguin.ie.

For Linda, Tybee, and Eden

HOME

To everything there is a season,
and a time for every purpose under heaven:
a time to be born and a time to die,
a time to plant and a time to uproot,
a time to kill and a time to heal,
a time to break down and a time to build,
a time to weep and a time to laugh,
a time to mourn and a time to dance,
a time to scatter stones and a time to gather them

ECCLESIASTES 3:1–5

CONTENTS

A TIME TO GATHER

Introduction

THE RITUAL RENAISSANCE

How Ritual Created the World—
and How It Can Save Us

Sometimes our deepest pain gives rise to our greatest creations.

Missy Holliday and her twin sister, Michelle, were born into a large family in a small town in southwest Ohio—population 1,486. Their mother was the choir director at the Presbyterian church; their father was the mayor. "My parents made it very clear to us the importance of serving the community."

Missy earned a nursing degree from Good Samaritan College, became a critical care specialist, married, and moved to Indianapolis. On the weekend of Super Bowl XXV, in January 1991, Missy returned home to spend time with her family, especially her little sister, Dee-Dee, who confided that Friday evening that she would soon be getting engaged.

"I'm far from perfect," Missy said. "But Dee-Dee was as close to a perfect person as I can imagine."

The next morning, Dee-Dee kissed her sister goodbye and headed to work at a nearby restaurant. "A few minutes later, her boyfriend came running in. 'Dee-Dee just hit a tree!' There had been snow the night before. Dee-Dee slid on a patch of ice and slammed into a tree, broadside."

Missy rushed to the site and climbed into the wreckage. "She had no broken bones but was unconscious. 'Call Air Care!' I told my dad." While Dee-Dee rode in the helicopter, Missy drove forty-five minutes to the University of Cincinnati Hospital. "I kept telling myself, *She's going to be okay.*"

But when the attending physician appeared, he was grim. "I need to tell you: Things don't look good."

"I ran out of the emergency room screaming," Missy said.

Dee-Dee lay in critical care all evening, her vitals stable. "She looked like she was sleeping." But her brain showed no activity. At midnight, doctors performed the first of two required brain death tests. Dee-Dee failed. The next morning, they performed the follow-up.

"At six a.m., this physician walked through the door. He was new. We hadn't met him throughout the most exhausting night of my life. And he was completely impersonal. 'Dee-Dee is brain-dead. What do you think about donating her organs?'

"My parents didn't hesitate. Of course Dee-Dee would want to donate her organs. She was the epitome of selfless.

"But I didn't hesitate either," Missy said. "I was angry at how heartlessly he handled something as beautiful as donating an organ. I told my parents that I was determined to find some light in this day of darkness. I would find a way to make sure that no family ever felt this hopeless again."

Walking through the door was the hardest part.

At dusk on a late-August afternoon, I walked through the front door of our family's home in Brooklyn after my wife, Linda, and I dropped our identical twin daughters off at college. Our bustling roost had become an empty nest in the blink of a tear. Those twenty fingers and twenty toes at the center of my life were gone.

I was homesick in my own home.

And it wasn't just my children—all my relationships seemed asunder. In a matter of months, I had lost my father, was losing my mother, had quarreled with my siblings. My marriage needed to be redefined; my family needed to be rethought; my friendships needed to be remade. I was hardly alone. All around me, people were leaving relationships; quitting jobs; googling strange, unknown diseases. It was as if everyone were passing through the same unfamiliar doors into the same uncertain worlds, where they felt unsettled, uncomfortable, unsure. Everyone I knew seemed to be experiencing a kind of existential homesickness.

I thought I was prepared for this moment. For years, I had been thinking and writing about the destabilizing times when our lives are overtaken by change. Lifequakes, I call them. The transitions that shape and reshape our lives—from childhood to adulthood, singlehood to couplehood, healthy to sick, married to divorced, loving someone to losing that someone, counting the days until your sister gets married to signing off on donating her organs.

Yet this moment felt different. It was less individual, more relational. Less personal, more interpersonal.

I belong to the tribe of groupkeepers. I'm the emcee of the family dinner game, the moderator of the family meeting, the commissioner of the family Olympics, the collector of the family stories. I'm also a groupie of group spectacles—Super Bowls, World Series, Oscars, Grammys, horse shows, dog shows, world's fairs, state fairs. In my thirties, I wrote a series of books in which I visited spiritual gathering places around the world; in my forties, I hosted a television series in which I went on pilgrimages in India, Japan, Nigeria, France, Israel, and Saudi Arabia.

What I've learned from a lifetime of participating in these social flywheels is that each of us goes through periods when our we-I axis gets thrown off. When we become so consumed with ourselves that we become disconnected from our groups; when our groups melt away and we feel completely adrift.

Part of this plight rests with our culture, which has elevated tending your I to the apex of life and relegated tending your we to an afterthought. We bask in self-love, celebrate me time, put ourselves first. But as valuable as that instinct may be, we now overvalue it to such a degree that we undervalue a key source of happiness and meaning—our relationships, our communities, our kin.

All humans go through times when we feel out of sync, out of touch, or out of step with those around us. This uncertainty often escalates in moments of addition or subtraction. When someone joins the group—a baby, a spouse, an in-law; when someone leaves the group—a death, a divorce, a coming-of-age; when someone destabilizes the group—gets sick, retires, sets off on a new path.

A hallmark of being alive is that when we experience such moments of unbelonging, we take steps to reaffirm our belonging: We gather, we honor, we weep, we mourn, we feast, we dance, we listen, we share. When the group becomes tender, we tend the group. We all become groupkeepers. We turn to ritual.

Which is why, a few weeks after walking through my front door, I decided to walk out again. I would go in search of clues in the world of ritual for what still holds us together in a world where everything is pulling us apart. We're a generation into the epidemic of loneliness and widespread hand-wringing over isolation and polarization. Is there any wisdom, proven across time and culture, that might help restore our sense of unity and connection? Are there things that everyone agrees on and absolutely anyone can do to restitch our fraying world? Is there a cure for homesickness?

Dee-Dee Mitten saved four lives on the day that she died. Her heart went to a teenager in Cincinnati, her liver to a woman in Columbus, one kidney to another woman in Ohio, the other to a one-year-old girl. But through her sister, Missy, Dee-Dee indirectly shaped millions of other lives.

Soon after Dee-Dee's death, Missy quit her job, moved with her husband back to Cincinnati, and went to work as a transplant coordinator at LifeCenter Organ Donor Network. What she found was a field exploding with growth but rife with mistrust among families, hospitals, and transplant support groups.

Since the first organ transfer in 1954, when twenty-three-year-old Massachusetts native Ronald Herrick donated a kidney to his identical twin, Richard, the field has blossomed to include livers, hearts, lungs, and eyes; nearly two hundred thousand transplants now take place every year, a figure that doesn't include faces, skin, or bones.

For two decades, Missy worked grueling, twenty-four-hour shifts, jetting around the country procuring organs, balancing grieving families and time-stressed surgeons, all while raising four children of her own. "Let me tell you, the emotional toll of doing this very intense work is enormous." But all the while, she felt something was missing. "The most important ingredient is the one that was most absent: respect."

Then one day Missy turned on the television to find the funeral of a police officer slain in the line of duty. Rows of uniformed officers lined the streets; motorcycles flashed their lights; bagpipes played; a color guard folded a flag for the bereaved.

"I knew right away that a ceremony like this would have helped my family, and that a legacy like this is what I owed my sister. We all needed a meaningful way to honor the gift of life."

They needed a ritual.

As soon as I stepped into the world of ritual, I stumbled into a startling paradox. That paradox begins with a fundamental truth: ritual works.

Humanity is made up of overlapping groups—families, tribes, villages, nations, cultures, clans, religions, teams; these groups are held together by shared conventions, among them language, food, music, and play. A central feature that connects these conventions—and thus these groups—is that they're entwined with ritual.

Rituals are messages we send ourselves about ourselves. They're the first human technology—collective, multimedia pageants that force us to identify the values we most cherish, the beliefs we most prize, and the pleasures we're willing to sacrifice for the privilege of belonging to the group. Rituals are the single most effective tool in holding any community together. They are "the social act basic to humanity," in the words of the American anthropologist Roy Rappaport.

Human beings have practiced ritual since our earliest days wandering the earth. A generation of young scholars has found that our oldest ancestors held collective rituals, from celebrating their bounty to burying their dead. These discoveries, dating back more than three hundred thousand years, mean that ritual preceded civilization, society, and religion. Organized religion did not invent ritual; if anything, it's the other way around. The act of narrativizing and routinizing these universal experiences is what built universal religions.

One reason we can be confident that ritual was present at the dawn of humanity is that ritual has deep roots in the animal world. In 1914, the English biologist Julian Huxley described the courtship ceremony of the great crested grebe, an elaborate, rhythmic dance in which birds elevate their bodies out of the water, arc their intertwined necks, and pat-pat their webbed feet across the surface. Such gestures are not instrumental, Huxley wrote; they are purely communicative, designed to appease aggression, establish bonds, and convert a "useful action into a symbol and then into a ritual."

In the century since that groundbreaking study, scientists have identified similar behaviors among buzzing bees, courting fiddler crabs, dancing dolphins, singing whales, weeping elephants, and many others. In 2016, a team of eighty primatologists, publishing in *Scientific Reports*, showed that "panting, swaying, screaming" chimpanzees collect stones, carry them to specific trees, drum them on trunks, and pile them into cairns, in startling, ritualized conduct that the researchers likened to "behaviors commonly observed during human rituals." Long before humans embraced ritualized activities in times of uncertainty to reduce tensions and build trust, animals used them for similar ends.

Instead of fight or flight, you can also fete.

Humans took this biological inheritance and turned it into a cultural imperative. If ritualization among animals is instinctual, ritualization among humans is intentional—cultural fill-ins for our biological weaknesses. Humanity's greatest invention is symbol, which the American anthropologist Leslie White called "the basic unit of all human behavior and civilization." Rituals curate symbols into meaningful experiences that form the alphabet of intimacy and the grammar of coexistence. No human society ever identified on earth has been devoid of such acts.

So what *is* a ritual?

Well, that question turns out to be controversial. As early as 1968, the British anthropologist Edmund Leach wrote, "There is the widest possible disagreement as to how the word ritual should be used and how the performance of rituals should be understood." The term includes both religious and nonreligious activities, traditional and modern, prescribed and improvised; the practice of ritual overlaps with play, performance, and parties.

The word itself comes from the Latin *ritus*, which means "a ceremonial act," but its roots trace back to the Indo-European *rta*, which is Sanskrit for the melding of art and order, beauty and truth. In some ways it may be easier to identify what ritual is not. When I asked ChatGPT, "What's the opposite of ritual?" it listed the following words: *disagreement*, *discord*, *neglect*, *dullness*, *insignificance*, *thoughtlessness*, *impropriety*, *indecency*, *corruption*, *misconduct*, *wrongdoing*, *deviance*, *crudeness*, *haphazardness*, and *bad manners*.

Count me on the side of ritual!

Still, we can agree on some basic definitions. Rituals are a family of human activities that have certain central ingredients. First, they are *acts*. "Ritual is first and foremost a doing," writes Canadian scholar Barry Stephenson. With ritual, seeing isn't believing; doing is believing.

Second, they are *shared*. Rituals are acts of communal co-narration. All of us engage in personal gestures of self-soothing, from sipping a cup of tea in the morning to offering words of gratitude before sleep; these gestures rise to ritual when done with the intention of connecting us to a larger group or higher purpose. Meditating for a better test score is affirmation; meditating for a better world is ritual.

Third, rituals are *unnecessary*. Huxley's observation that ritualization among animals serves no instrumental purpose applies to ritualization among humans, too. You don't *need* to bend down on one knee to get engaged any more than you *need* to wear black when someone dies; yet both of these voluntary behaviors have become all but involuntary.

Rituals are unnecessities that become necessities.

Consider a simple human gesture: Handwashing, for the most part, is not ritual because it serves a utilitarian purpose; handshaking, by contrast, is ritual because it serves no such purpose. Its role is to send a prosocial message: *I trust you; I'm not carrying a weapon; we can form a relationship.* An obvious exception proves the point: Handwashing in Passover seders, Catholic Eucharists, or Buddhist offerings is no longer merely utilitarian but has been elevated to symbol. It's ritual. Similarly, ringing the dinner bell is not ritual, it's practical; ringing the chemo bell is ritual; it's the nonpractical, nonessential expression of communal joy when a patient completes treatment.

Supper is not ritual; the Last Supper is.

There are four main types of rituals. The first type is civic rituals—coronations, inaugurations, national anthems, "All rise, here comes the judge." The second is calendric rituals—cherry blossom festivals, maypole dances, midsummer bacchanals, Thanksgiving dinners. The third is daily rituals—bowing, saluting, tipping hats, kissing cheeks, namastes, grace.

In this book, I focus primarily on the fourth category, the periodic, collective rituals that mark meaningful changes in a human life—rituals around having a baby, becoming an adult, falling in love, losing a loved one. Some observers call these events *life cycle rituals,* using a term borrowed from biology, though they don't particularly happen in a cycle. Scholars label them *life-crisis rituals,* which is even more problematic. Having a baby is destabilizing—trust me, Linda and I had two in thirty-two minutes—but it's hardly a crisis; the same with falling in love or becoming an adult.

The most popular term is *rites of passage,* an expression coined by the German anthropologist Arnold van Gennep in 1909. But that name has also outgrown its usefulness. Van Gennep limited the term to the "big four" life transitions—birth, puberty, marriage, and death—and insisted that these events must happen in a fixed sequence, even though they are clearly more plentiful and nonsequential today. No one lives life "in order" anymore; we all live life "out of order."

I prefer *life ritual*; it's simple, easy to understand, and value neutral. Some life rituals are celebratory, others sad, some voluntary, others involuntary. Most feel like a combination of all these elements and more.

Just as civic rituals mark changes in our society, calendric rituals mark fluctuations in our year, and daily rituals mark variations in our days, life rituals mark oscillations in our lives. They stabilize our we-I axes.

Okay, so that's the first piece of the equation: Rituals are central to human life. What, then, is the paradox?

For a hundred centuries—that's ten thousand years—in every culture ever studied in every corner of the world, humans have marked moments of uncertainty in their lives with collective, ceremonial life celebrations. Every century, that is, until this one. After proving definitively that rituals work, we've decided as a culture to turn our backs on them. I see evidence everywhere I look.

Let's use the big four as a benchmark:

Birth.

The centrality of both giving birth and holding birth rituals has been declining steadily around the world for decades. The fertility rate in the United States has dropped by more than half since 1960, and declined even more sharply in Europe, Asia, and large swaths of the global south. The frequency of birth rites has gone down even *more* precipitously. The baptism rate in Catholic churches has fallen by two thirds in seventy years; in Southern Baptist churches, which christen toddlers, the baptism rate has halved in just the last two decades.

Traditional birth rites are becoming a thing of the past for more and more families.

Puberty.

Adolescent rituals are in complete disarray. While Americans have never embraced coming-of-age rituals to the degree of other cultures, the ones we have adopted to ease the transition to adulthood are in rapid retreat. Among Jews, bar and bat mitzvahs are down 20 percent since the 1980s; among Catholics, confirmations are down 65 percent since the 1960s; among mainline Protestants, they're down 80 percent during the same period.

Other familiar metrics of maturity and independence among adolescents show similar declines. The percentage of sixteen-year-olds with a driver's license—a common benchmark of freedom—has dropped 50 percent since 1980; the share of teenagers who've had sex has halved since 2000; the percentage of teens who even go out without their parents has dropped by a third.

While adolescent get-togethers have declined, adolescents themselves have grown more unstable—anxiety, depression, disordered eating, and suicide are all up—and adolescence itself has grown longer. Puberty happens earlier, separation from parents later. Half of Americans in their twenties still live at home. No wonder an entire new category of life transition, adulting, has been invented in the last generation.

Marriage.

If growing up is in disarray, falling in love is in shambles. In 1960, 95 percent of Americans over forty had married at least once; four in ten Americans told surveyors that anyone who remained single was "sick," "neurotic," or "immoral." Today, the percentage of American adults who are married has dipped below 50 percent for the first time. Most of us are immoral! The number of adults who've never married, meanwhile, has doubled, reaching a third of the country. Even those who do marry are shunning religious weddings; only one in five Americans marries in a place of worship, a figure that's fallen by half this century.

But it's not just marriage that's in free fall; all forms of intimacy are. People walk 15 percent faster than thirty years ago and spend half as much time talking to people they bump into. Dating is down, as is sex. Two thirds of men under thirty in America are single, with half saying they have no interest in relationships. Young women in the US boast about "self-partnering," going "boysober," and other "celibacy rebrands," while young women in South Korea, where the average number of children has fallen sevenfold in six decades, have started the 4B movement, or the "Four Nos"—no sex, no dating, no marriage, no babies. Through social media, the movement has spread quickly around the world.

Friendship is also down. The percentages of Americans who have ten, six, or even one close friend have all dropped by a third since 1990, while the percentage with no friends has jumped fivefold. This collapse in social cohesion has occurred as more and more research confirms the value of friendship. A six-year study out of Sweden showed that having a life partner did not reduce your risk of having a heart attack or coronary disease, while having a friend did; a ten-year study out of Australia found that older people with friends were 22 percent less likely to die during the decade under examination than their friendless peers.

Even collective eating, a backbone of civil society, is dwindling; American adults now consume half of their food from solo snacking instead of shared meals with family or friends.

Death.

Perhaps the biggest change around rituals is happening at the end of life. In 1970, 5 percent of Americans were cremated; today that number nears 65 percent and is projected to pass 80 percent by midcentury. Even more startling: only one in four people cremated has a funeral and only one in six a burial. In a country where cemeteries are considered sacred spaces, only a third of Americans today are interred. Poet and fifty-year veteran mortician Thomas Lynch calls this turnabout "the single greatest change in our funeral practices in our generation or, I'd venture to say, in the last couple of centuries."

I'm hardly the first to notice this wholesale drifting away from ritual. In the 1950s, the historian Mircea Eliade warned that the decline of religion could lead to the disappearance of shared rituals; in the 1980s, the sociologist Robert Bellah cautioned that radical individualism has weakened the "ritual and moral 'structure' that orders our freedom and binds our choices into something like habits of the heart"; in 2000, the political scientist Robert Putnam referenced rituals in *Bowling Alone*. But even these seers, I dare say, failed to anticipate the inflection point we're at today, which, to quote Hemingway, happened "gradually, then suddenly."

The decivilizing of society has led to the dissolving of rituals.

To add one more figure to the mix, I ran a comparison of the total number of traditional life rituals the average American would have experienced in just their nuclear family at various times in our history. Factoring in longevity, marriage age, and family size, the number of life rituals involving birth, coming of age, getting married, and dying dropped from nineteen in 1800 to twelve in 1900 to eight and a half in

2000 to seven and a half today. The frequency at which Americans attended a life ritual of a family member went from once every year and a half in 1800 to once every nine and a half years today. Considering that most of us also attend the ceremonies of close friends, the decline in those relationships means the actual numbers are even lower.

We are clearly in a celebration recession.

Looking at all these figures, it's hard not to conclude that life rituals are in systemic, irreversible decline. It took us ten thousand years to establish cultural norms around how we mark collective life transitions. It took us fifty years to dismantle them.

But this assessment leads us to the final twist of the paradox.

Alongside this wholesale recession in traditional life rituals, we're also experiencing an equally stunning recovery in nontraditional life rituals. We're in the midst of a sustained period of inventiveness around life rituals that is unrivaled in the long history of such behavior. And this change is not coming from the top down; it's coming from the bottom up. Freed from conventional expectations about how to live and empowered to write their own life stories, everyday people are creating an astonishing array of reimagined life rituals.

Just a small sampling hints at the breadth: gender reveals, NICU graduations, first-day-of-school photos, first cell phone celebrations, first gun parties, cancerversaries, soberversaries, trauma release ceremonies, gotcha day ceremonies, sanctity of life ceremonies, gratitude circles, mastectomy circles, psychedelic circles, end-of-life doulas, end-of-company doulas, achievement grinding in online gaming culture, blessingways in online tradwife culture, purity balls, daddy-daughter dances, mom proms, silent retreats, scream clubs, cacao ceremonies, sound baths, parole apologies, crafting, croning.

One hallmark of these celebrations is that they address life experiences that organized institutions long ignored—not just marriage but divorce; not just birth but stillbirth; not just menstruation but menopause; not just fertility but infertility. These shadow rituals, as I call them, are the heartbeat of life cycles liberated from centuries of stagnation.

Let's look again at the big four for a taste of how these changes are playing out.

Birth.

In 2016, I wrote an article in *The New York Times* about how YouTube birth announcements were supplanting traditional snail-mailed or emailed ones. Today, those videos seem tame, overtaken by social media memes like "Showing my spouse my pregnancy test," "Baby names I hate," "Registry hauls," and "If you're watching this, I'm in labor" videos. Forget one-off pregnancy rituals; today every kick, bloat, and morning heave are cause for ritualized posting.

But it's not all joy and flexing. Evite created a new product line called Parenthood Journey Invitations, templates that honor the one third of parents who create families in alternative ways. Examples include IVF showers (*Made with lots of love & a little bit of science*), surrogacy showers (*Pin the tail on the uterus*), egg showers (*I'm freezing my eggs and want to celebrate with you!*), adoption showers (*Ryan was so worth the wait!*), and rainbow showers for babies born after pregnancy loss (*After the rain comes the rainbow*). There's even a BaBy-Qs Backyard Ribs & Bibs with a diaper fund QR code for families who are stretched financially.

Puberty.

Some modern adolescent rituals are glittery and fun—promposals; homecoming asks; National Signing Day, where student athletes announce what college they'll be taking their talents to; Senior Skip Day, where graduating classmates play hooky and hang out. But many new rituals honor emotions that were long hidden away—not just college acceptance videos but college rejection videos; not just friendship bracelets but awareness bracelets for mental health; suicide bereavement camps, where children who've lost a loved one find comfort in shared pain; lavender graduations, where communities honor LGBTQ students and their allies.

Marriage.

Novel commitment ceremonies are also booming. Some offer a twist on familiar themes—*Game of Thrones* goth weddings! *Little Mermaid* scuba weddings! Others take forgotten traditions and update them for the present—jumping the broom, handfasting. Still more apply new solutions to timeless problems—GoFundMe campaigns for your honeymoons, painting your Venmo handle on your #JustMarried car, AI vow writers, stepchild adoption ceremonies.

In one viral video, a tuxedoed groom stops his nuptials to invite his six-year-old stepdaughter to the altar. "It's not really a tradition in the Catholic Church," he says, "but not only do I marry your mom today, but I accept you as my daughter." He then places a ring on the girl's finger. "I know you've been wanting to call me Dad for a long time. I want to give you this ring as my commitment that I will always be there for you—and that I love you."

Death.

With funeral homes losing their monopoly on grief, startups are rushing to fill the gap: death cafés, Death Over Dinner circles, the Silent Book Club of Death, write-your-own-obituary gatherings, build-your-own-coffin classes, write-a-letter-to-a-dead-loved-one salons, picnics where grave hunters cook the recipes they find on headstones and then eat the results alongside the graves where they're displayed. Living wakes are thriving, as are farewell celebrations for those who choose assisted dying, even funeral surprise parties, all of which feature guests saying nice things about the soon-to-be-deceased while they're still around to hear them.

This innovation is not limited to life rituals, of course. Just think of the breakthroughs we've seen among civic rituals (Earth Day, breast cancer walks, Pride parades, marches on Washington); calendric rituals (Friendsgiving, Dry January, Galentine's Day, Giving Tuesday); and daily rituals (gratitude circles, intention setting ceremonies, meditation meetups, digital detox dinners).

Sure, some of these rituals might seem superficial, insignificant, or even silly, but are they really all that different from the ones you grew up with? Canned cranberry jelly! Stork balloons! Matching, ill-fitting pink satin bridesmaids' dresses! Either way, the consequences are profound: After following a more or less stable playbook for centuries for how to navigate collective life transitions, we've summarily thrown out that playbook overnight, leaving families in flux, institutions scrambling, and individuals with more freedom to chart their own course but also more responsibility to figure out what they really want.

Contemplate for a second just one more statistic: If you broaden the lens and add together the number of births, deaths, graduations, marriages, cancer diagnoses, lost jobs, and retirements in America alone every year, the number is fifty million; globally, it's one billion. That's three million potential life rituals every day around the world where individuals could be connecting—or reconnecting—with those around them. In the paradox of modern ritual, the old rules for such occasions no longer apply, but the new rules haven't been written.

Will there be new rules at all? If so, what on earth will they contain?

Once Missy Holliday decided to build a ritual around organ donations, she quickly realized that she needed some guidelines. She started with how to serve the family.

"You're just being told that your child is not coming home and now you're being told to say goodbye. Families would ask me, 'What do you want to take?' I would say, 'I don't want to take anything. I'm here to tell you what they can give.' My goal was to flip the script even for a second from 'your loved one is not going to live' to 'your loved one is going to save lives.'"

But how could she pull off such a ritual in the middle of a busy hospital? "In the past, families would say goodbye to their loved one in the ICU. But the gift of organ donation does not happen in the ICU; it happens in the OR." Missy zeroed in on the transitional space between the two, the hallway. To convert that sterile environment into a sacred space would require the help of another sensitive group, the hospital staff.

"I wanted families to understand how powerful their gift was. For professionals to stop caring for their other patients to pay tribute to a patient who was already dead would be an amazing sign."

Her final constituency was her own colleagues. "It's easy to get burned out when you work around tragedy. Sometimes we're so busy helping others grieve that we forget to grieve ourselves."

After years of planning, Missy was finally ready. In December 2016, at the same hospital where her younger sister had died, Missy debuted her creation. The donor was placed on a gurney, his family gathered behind him. Missy had set up a Spotify account and asked the family what song the donor might like. They chose "Annie's Song" by John Denver. Missy placed her cell phone alongside his ear and pressed play—"Let me lay down beside you, let me always be with you"—as the attendants pushed the gurney into the hallway.

The sight was breathtaking. More than a hundred doctors, nurses, and support staff—everyone dressed in matching blue scrubs, their backs straight and their eyes fixed—lined the corridor, shoulder to shoulder, in an awesome display of compassion and human dignity. Each staff member held a flameless candle in blue and green, the colors of organ donation.

As the gurney processed down the solemn arcade, the attendants nodded and the family choked back tears, until the cortege paused exactly five feet from the swinging doors of the operating room. One by one, loved ones bent down to kiss the forehead, stroke the cheek, or cradle the face of their husband, father, brother, or son. With their goodbyes said, the family watched as the donor proceeded toward the cradle of his gift.

Missy's gift to her sister was also complete that day. She called her ritual an honor walk.

But Missy's gift to the world was just being wrapped. Before that initial walk, she put her last rule in place: No one was allowed to take photographs. But she made an exception for the wife of the donor, who before her husband left the room, stepped into the hallway and snapped a picture of the heartrending tribute spread out before her.

That night the widow posted the photo on Facebook.

There are three possible explanations for what's happening with life rituals.

The first is that the celebration recession is the big story here, and it reflects not just the long-term decoupling of society from religion but our larger disinterest in spending time with one another. We haven't simply outgrown life rituals; we view leaving them behind as a sign of progress. Just because our ancestors threw three-day weddings, held ornate funerals, or sent their adolescents into the wilderness to smear themselves in feces, drink cow blood, and mutilate their genitalia, doesn't mean we have to. Life rituals are barbaric, backward, and beyond repair.

The second possibility is that the celebration recovery is real but not real enough to stem the tide of the celebration recession. A few new rituals here and there is what Wall Street calls a "dead cat bounce," a fleeting recovery after a substantial fall that does little to dent the larger trend. A Renaissance faire throuple commitment ceremony may be buzzworthy, but it's hardly a replacement for the social benefits of a wedding.

The third option may be the most intriguing. Yes, the celebration recession is real, but it applies largely to institutionalized, top-down rituals that no longer speak to the majority of people today. The ritual revival is the headline here because it represents the green shoots of a movement by everyday people to wrest control of their life transitions from out-of-touch institutions and remake them for modern times. It's as if we've all become Laertes in *Hamlet*, who, after watching the priest refuse to host a funeral for his sister, Ophelia, because she died by suicide, lashes out, "What ceremony else?"

Today, none of us wants ceremony familiar; we all want ceremony else. We're all eager to cope better in the face of change. And if these green shoots can take hold, we will be witnessing less the death rattle of ritual for all time and more the birth pangs of a ritual renaissance, which, as the term suggests, involves the death of something old; the return to something older, in this case the earliest human longing for ceremony; and the rebirth of something new: a revitalized road map for turning feelings of aloneness into feelings of homeness.

To figure out which of these possibilities is most likely to prevail, I spent the next two years going on a round-the-world ritual road trip, attending rituals on six continents in sixteen countries. These rituals included a mass baptism in the Vatican, a tribal bride-price negotiation in South Africa, an adolescent tooth filing in Bali, six weddings in a day in Las Vegas, and ten funerals in a week in Ireland. I went forest bathing in Chile, sauna and cold plunging in Copenhagen, sound healing in Bangkok, and joined a grieving and weaving circle in Brooklyn.

In addition, I collected the life stories of more than a hundred ritual designers in twenty-six countries. These entrepreneurs of meaning include a Pentecostal priest in Nigeria who runs a fertility prayer circle, the creator of the Purple Pundit Project in New Jersey who leads LGBTQ+ Hindu weddings, and the founder of the Be Ceremonial app in Canada that helps "create your own rites of passage."

Finally, I interviewed scores of experts, plunged deep into the literature of anthropology, and read through more than five hundred academic studies at the cutting edge of neuroscience, evolutionary biology, and applied psychology. My goal was to create a field guide for modern ritual and, perhaps, a framework for repairing our fractured world.

Missy's phone blew up immediately. *We want to do an honor walk! What do we do in this situation? How do we handle that scenario?* At first she didn't understand where the calls were coming from. Then she realized. That photograph of the first honor walk that the widow posted on Facebook: It got two million likes.

"It was as if the whole world was waiting for what we created," she said.

There are fifty donor procurement organizations in the United States; all fifty now host honor walks, along with countless countries around the world. Stories of honor walks are fixtures on television news; YouTube videos have garnered a quarter of a billion views. One viewer commented on the video of three-year-old Mars Bedell in Houston dressed in a Spider-Man cape and mask: "Instead of watching a three-year-old enjoy his first game at a ballpark . . . I end up watching a three-year-old . . . saving lives." She ended, "Way to go Hero."

Rituals thrive in moments when risks are highest and stakes are greatest; they offer glimmers of hope in the face of devastation. Forged in pain and conceived with love, an honor walk is a Hall of Fame modern ritual.

"I once handled a child who was killed in a tragic accident," Missy told me. "When I spoke to his family about donation, Mom was on board, Dad was not. But their son was eighteen and had made the choice to donate. Legally, it was his decision. Dad went along but was not real supportive.

"After the walk, I escorted the family to a little courtyard. The dad came up to me: 'I have to let you know that tomorrow I plan to change my license. I'm going to become an organ donor.'"

Missy wiped back tears. "I thought of my Dee-Dee. All I wanted that horrible day was for her to feel honored. I don't consider honor walks to be huge things, but I consider them to be small things with big power. We help people write endings to stories they never want to tell."

My mission in this book is to help all of us write better stories. With that goal in mind, I will try to answer four questions.

1: WHY DO WE NEED LIFE RITUALS?

Rituals, at heart, are means of attachment. Amir Levine, a neuroscientist at Columbia, once explained to me that each of us has a hierarchy of relationships, meaning if something bad happens, we have a ranking of people to call. In our early decades, the top rungs are usually our family. "The problem as you grow older is, how do you let somebody get close to you who's basically a total stranger? Nature came up with a trick: sex. Sexual attraction lets you get close to a new person in a physical way that you don't get close to your family."

Rituals perform the same trick. Sex is to couples as ritual is to groups—an accelerant to intimacy at first, then a tool to maintain intimacy over time. A downside with ritual is that it can be so effective at building connections that antisocial groups embrace it, too, from terrorists to gangs. "Human groupishness has many upsides," writes the Oxford anthropologist Harvey Whitehouse. "But these qualities typically extend only to the ingroup."

The challenge for humanity is to increase the use of rituals as rites of connection while decreasing their use as rites of division. To meet that challenge, I propose in this book that we focus on the four things that life rituals do best—*connect*, *correct*, *celebrate*, and *chronicle*. Life rituals connect the group, correct imbalances within the group, celebrate sacred moments in the group, and chronicle the story of the group.

2: WHEN DO WE NEED LIFE RITUALS?

Life rituals are designed to be solutions for the periodic moments of instability that unsettle any community. The earliest anthropologists, writing at the peak of the industrial age when factories embraced linear solutions like assembly lines and conveyor belts, insisted that these moments happen in a linear progression—childhood, adolescence, marriage, death. Cultures around the world normalized that life course and introduced preapproved celebrations to mark each milestone.

It was ritual by fiat.

The problem: Our lives no longer follow such preordained scripts. The primary takeaway I've gleaned from two thousand hours of life stories is that the notion that we follow a linear path of relationships, jobs, illnesses, and beliefs from adolescence to assisted living is dead. That fantasy of the linear life has been replaced by the reality of the nonlinear life in which each of us follows our own idiosyncratic fingerprint of life events. My data show that each of us goes through three dozen disruptors in our lives, brief spasms of change, and three to five lifequakes, forceful bursts of change that lead to upheaval and renewal. We spend twenty-five years—that's half our adulthoods—in transition.

The big four life rituals no longer meet the needs of these variable lives. If you never marry or have children, to cite just one common example, you will never experience half of the preapproved slate. Also, four life rituals may have been sufficient when the average lifespan was forty; now it's twice that. We have linear rituals but nonlinear lives. We have never-changing cures for ever-changing needs.

The solutions have become part of the problem.

This book introduces a new model. Instead of four linear life rituals, I believe it's more accurate to say that we go through five recurring life rituals, each of us in our own nonlinear way. I call these rituals *welcoming, becoming, loving, mourning*, and *renewing*. I've chosen these names because they're not restricted to age or circumstance. *Wedding* is an outdated term now that most people seal their loving relationships in nontraditional ways; the same with funerals now that we mourn not just the loss of a family but also jobs, homes, and pets.

Also, the idea that these rituals are fundamentally different from one another needs to be rethought. Every ritual contains elements of all the others; in effect, they're polyrituals. As we prepared to drop our daughters at college, for example, they were more emotional about the "end" of their childhood than the "start" of their young adulthood; I felt the same about fatherhood.

Rituals contain multitudes; they deserve names that capture their elasticity.

3: HOW DO YOU CREATE A LIFE RITUAL?

One advantage of old-fashioned life rituals is that the rules were clear. You belonged to a community; the elders handed you a script; you followed it. *Dearly beloved, you don't have to do a thing. Just repeat after me.* Today, that degree of compliance is gone—and unlikely to return. Hierarchical, institutional, patriarchal life rituals are deader than ever before.

The reasons behind this change are manifold: Women have claimed more leadership over events long controlled by men; the internet allows anyone to discover how things are done in other cultures; social media rewards spectacle and glam; make-your-own spirituality means that everyone wants their celebrations to be "unique." No one wants their grandmothers' formulaic weddings; gender-segregated showers; lonely, isolated mastectomies; or medicalized, meaning-free deaths. Bottom-up rituals are richer, deeper, and more personalized.

But they're also harder. *Do what you're told* means at least you're told what to do; *do it yourself* means you have to decide for yourself what you really want. I began to wonder: Is there a universal code of successful life rituals that anyone can follow to make them more meaningful, emotional, enduring? Is there a DNA of human connection?

I propose in these pages that such a blueprint involves five elements: *boundaries*, *stakes*, *compromise*, *empathy*, and *hope*. Successful life rituals create sacred space, demand skin in the game, promote collaboration, offer support, and leave everyone renewed.

4: CAN RITUAL SAVE US?

We live in a time when our maladies are growing but our remedies are shrinking. Faced with crises that demand unprecedented cooperation, our aptitude for cooperation is atrophying. We have a surfeit of selfishness and a deficit of groupishness; we lift up self-promoters and tear down groupkeepers. Our we-I axis is completely out of whack.

Having spurned our shared gods, weakened our shared trust, and undermined our shared language, will we turn our backs on ritual, one of the few tools we have left that has proven its ability to repair our shared humanity? "The abandonment of ritual can be devastating," writes the West African spiritual leader Malidoma Patrice Somé. "When the focus of everyday living displaces ritual in any given society, social decay begins to work from the inside out."

No rituals, no us.

A true community, Somé adds, begins in the hearts of its members. It's not a place of distraction; it's a place of restoration. It's not a world you escape from; it's a world you return to. Agreeing on a reimagined commitment to ritual, beginning in our backyards and rippling through a more relational world, may be the most critical ingredient to restoring our sense of togetherness and is surely the element that each of us has the most ability to control.

Two centuries ago, the German poet and novelist Novalis reflected, "Philosophy is really homesickness, an urge to be at home everywhere." Life rituals represent that urge today; they are our greatest means of converting homesickness into homecoming. They transform the unease of being in the world into the comfort of being at home.

As we face the possibility of a world without ritual, the question for each of us is this: Will we invest the time and effort to re-render our lonely world habitable? Will we restore life rituals to their time-honored place as containers of chaos, capsules of compassion, and creators of hope?

Will we let rituals lead us home?

1.

WELCOME WITH JOY

Circling St. Peter's Square

The front door of the Vatican is surprisingly hard to find. The Old City of Jerusalem, which is one third of a square mile, has seven entrances; Vatican City, which is half that size, has six. The one I was looking for is located just to the left of St. Peter's Basilica and just inside the two hundred eighty-four columns that make up Bernini's welcoming colonnade. Because the mother church of Catholicism is "almost like a womb," Bernini wrote, the elliptical porticoes were designed "to maternally open her arms to Catholics to confirm them in their beliefs."

But on this Sunday morning in late October, when the pope was hosting a contentious summit on women in the church and I had been invited to witness a novel approach to one of the more widely practiced life rituals in history, the entire complex seemed far less welcoming. I first had to walk through a temporary gate, then pass through security, then introduce myself to the Swiss Guard, then make my way to the parish office. The door was open, but the entrance was empty. For a few minutes I waited awkwardly.

Then someone called out my name. Instead of a prelate in cardinal-and-white finery, it was a burly man with a salt-and-pepper beard, a friar's black frock, and sandals. I reached out my hand, but he swatted it away and gave me a bear hug.

"Welcome!" Brother Agnello Stoia said. "Sorry to keep you waiting. Let's go for coffee. The baptism begins at noon."

After all that time I spent trying to get into the Vatican, Brother Agnello promptly led me out the back door and across the street to a café.

Exactly twenty-five years before this trip, I was strapped into the front seat of a car, speeding past tanks in war-torn eastern Turkey, careening around corkscrews in the Caucasus Mountains. Behind me, the Israeli archaeologist Avner Goren was punching numbers into a GPS. After several hours, he tapped on my shoulder. "Look!" Through a break in the peaks, thousands of feet higher than anything around it, was the snowcapped summit of a triangular mountain, like Mount Fuji, only taller.

"Mount Ararat!" Avner exclaimed.

It was my first glimpse of the highest spot in the Middle East, where Genesis says Noah's ark landed, and my first taste of a fundamental truth: Our most enduring cultural artifacts have a strong sense of place. Just as you can't understand the Bible without understanding its connection to holy land, you can't understand life rituals without understanding their connection to holy ground.

The first rule of life rituals is that they need sacred space. They are nonordinary acts that demand nonordinary settings. They literally *take place*: whether an altar, circle, pool, hill, ashram, temple, shrine, or wat. One place that has come to embody this lesson around the world is a day's drive from Mount Ararat; Avner and I visited during our journey.

Göbekli Tepe is Turkish for "potbelly hill." Located near the headwaters of the Tigris and Euphrates, at the intersection of Turkey, Syria, and Iraq, this dusty crossroads has seen more than its share of storied visitors, from Lawrence of Arabia to Alexander the Great to Abraham. But the most important visitors may be the unnamed ones who came twelve thousand years ago and built one of the earliest human settlements.

Startling excavations since the 1990s have revealed twenty circular enclosures of limestone megaliths with strong echoes of Stonehenge and striking similarities to the Vatican colonnade. Some pillars are carved with animal forms, including scorpions and lions; others are covered in humanoid forms, among them torsos and hands. The site has become known as the birthplace of ritual. A million tourists now visit every year.

Before we can understand the future of ritual, we must first understand its past. That effort begins with a simple point: that ritual *has* a past. Ritual itself has a history. While it may be tempting to assume that humans have always gathered together and thus always agreed on how to make meaning together, the truth is more complex—and more illuminating. The history of ritual shows that we're constantly changing our views of how we mark turning points in our lives. That history can be told in four places: Göbekli Tepe in Turkey, St. Peter's Basilica in the Vatican, the Château de Vincennes outside Paris, and the Little White Wedding Chapel in Las Vegas. Let's begin with the first.

When I began traveling around the Middle East in the 1990s, the history of civilization was told in a straightforward manner. Early humans wandered from place to place, until the agricultural revolution around 10,000 BCE, when they began to settle in one place. Cultivating agriculture gave humans free time, which in turn allowed them to tell stories, which in turn led them to build religions, which in turn inspired them to create rituals. This progression can be captured in a formula:

HUMANS → RELIGION → RITUAL

The discoveries at Göbekli Tepe almost single-handedly flipped that script, revealing that long before humans settled in one place and thousands of years before they formed organized religions, they were already practicing rituals. These fundamental human acts inspired stories, which in turn led to customs, traditions, liturgies, and laws, which in turn led to religions. The new formula looks more like this:

HUMANS → RITUAL → RELIGION

The big bang of this breakthrough occurred on December 18, 1994, when three amateur speleologists in the Ardèche valley of southern France noticed a faint draft coming from the blocked entrance of a cave. Soon, the park ranger Jean-Marie Chauvet, along with Éliette Brunel Deschamps and Christian Hillaire, breached the obstruction, spelunked twenty-six feet down, and found themselves in a pitch-black, one-hundred-thousand-square-foot chamber. Late on a chilly Sunday afternoon, in what is now called the End Chamber of Chauvet, the explorers discovered an astonishing sight: hundreds of depictions of thirteen different species—leopards, bears, horses—along with elaborate images of lions hunting bison and rhinoceroses butting horns. The trio also found a child's footprint, remains of ancient hearths, and smoke stains from human gatherings.

"They were here!" Deschamps cried, referring to our ancestors thirty-five thousand years ago.

The Chauvet discovery opened the floodgates. In the next four decades, more than three hundred fifty displays of cave art were unearthed around the world, a breathtaking string of Paleolithic art galleries. Time and again, these works show detailed evidence of ritual behavior.

The ceremonial Lion Man of Germany, from thirty-eight thousand years ago, combines the limbs of a human and the head of a lion. The Python Cave of Botswana, from seventy thousand years ago, features a twenty-foot carved snake with sparkling eyes, surrounded by thirteen spearheads and a secret chamber. The Norwegian archaeologist who led the discovery calls the finding a "loud archaeological signature" of collective ritual. A Sulawesi cave in Indonesia shows evidence of rituals involving red ocher, pierced shells, and engraved jewelry dating back one hundred sixty-four thousand years—that's forty times older than the pyramids. The La Chapelle-aux-Saints cave in central France has yielded evidence of Neanderthal burial three hundred thousand years ago, before the arrival of anatomically modern humans.

Göbekli Tepe weaves these tantalizing threads into a vivid tableau of late hunter-gatherer lives brimming with ritual. The site's earliest findings suggested that the structures highest on the potbelly hill were monumental gathering places where bands of wandering people would assemble to celebrate their hunt, bury their dead, and reaffirm their shared humanity. The site was not an ongoing settlement, stressed the archaeologist who led the excavation, Klaus Schmidt, "but a ritual site for surrounding communities."

Subsequent research has shown that some people did live on the hill, but the larger point still holds. The use of collective rituals to build group identity has roots much deeper than civilization itself. To be human is to seek out sacred spaces where you can escape the fragility of existential aloneness and create a vision of intentional togetherness; these sanctified domains domesticate the dangers that threaten your survival and honor the community with whom you forge meaning out of chaos. The underground sanctuaries and sacred relics that dot the harshest landscapes of our planet show that our oldest relatives did not just want to know *how* things were done, they also wanted to know *why*.

We are not just *Homo sapiens*; we are also *Homo ritualis*.

We may choose to reject any number of the practices of the civilizations that grew out of those early experiments of the human spirit. But to reject ritual is to reject the flint of that spirit, to throw the baby shower out with the bathwater. Ritual is the original fire in the belly of humanity; without it, we risk extinguishing the eternal flame that burns at the heart of being alive.

Brother Agnello looks like he stepped out of an Aesop fable—a shock of sepia in a neon-colored world. A crane in a muster of peacocks. As he led me through a promenade teeming with cafés, he was summoned for hugs and showered by the sound of his name shouted in greeting. He seemed to know everyone in Rome.

"I like to turn strangers into friends," he said.

Because the pope is the figurehead of Catholicism and St. Peter's is its mother church, you might think the holy father would be the head of its parish. You'd be wrong. The pope is the pastor of the nearby Basilica of St. John Lateran. The pastor of St. Peter's is appointed by the pontiff. As part of Pope Francis's effort to humanize the church, he chose Brother Agnello, a Franciscan and a Pompeii native who comes across as the happiest mayor of the busiest town. Ten million people a year visit the Vatican; Agnello would enjoy giving every one a hug.

"San Pietro is like a heart that receives blood from the periphery, oxygenates it, then sends it back into the body revived," he said.

But all the circulation masks a problem. The lifeblood of any spiritual institution is the life rituals of its members—for Catholics, those rituals include baptism, confirmation, weddings, and funerals. Yet nearly all of the 801 residents of the Vatican are in religious orders, meaning they're not allowed to be married and are forbidden from having children. Few families means few family celebrations.

Agnello set out to solve that problem. He flung open the doors; expanded the number of annual life rituals to two hundred baptisms and fifty marriages; added a new life ritual that locals were demanding, marriage renewals; and convened the first confirmation class of adolescents in one hundred fifty years. He is a shining example of what the smartest religious leaders I know are becoming: a ritual entrepreneur.

"Joy is the gift of life," Agnello said. "My goal is to share whatever joy I can in a world that can sometimes feel sad. But joy needs celebrations. If we can welcome people with joy, we can soften the jagged edges of humanity."

I asked him the most effective way to make people feel welcome.

"With sights and sounds and smells," he said. "When you visit on a Sunday morning like today, you are catapulted into the beauty of song, the aroma of incense, the splendor of light. Together they are open arms of celebration."

Such rituals are not easy, he cautioned. "Someone will always complain. *It's never been done like this! How dare you do that!*

"But people need to come together because they need serenity," he continued. "A warm pillow, a slice of tart, a roasted chestnut, a cup of tea. Celebrations are like living rooms for people who need to escape, however briefly, the weight of loneliness and indifference, and replace them with companionship and possibility."

I asked him which celebrations he most enjoys.

"I like to baptize," he said. "You have the opportunity to interact with families, to use the most beautiful spot in the basilica, and to welcome people into a life of grace."

"My sense is that rituals need flash, they need spectacle," I said. "How many wows do you need?"

"The wows are important," he said, "They catch your attention; they invite you in; they're like the miracles in the Bible. But the real miracles occur once you're in community—a parent and child, a parent and parent, a stranger and stranger. At the moment you're most in fear, you share that fear with another, and suddenly you're not alone. The wow is the hospitality of tending that fear together."

Brother Agnello grew quiet for the first time since we met. After a moment of reflection, he bowed his head, crossed himself, and stood up to leave.

"Come, you'll see."

Walking into St. Peter's Basilica can feel overwhelming—it's large enough to accommodate sixty thousand visitors and tall enough to fit the Statue of Liberty, Lincoln Memorial, and Michelangelo's *David* standing on top of one another. Ralph Waldo Emerson called the building "an ornament of the earth." Henry James crooned, "Few great works of art last longer" in the imagination. Even Mark Twain, who grumbled about its bulkiness, gushed that its dome offers a panorama "more illustrious in history than any other in Europe."

Yet it's the contentious story of building the basilica that earns it the second spot on our whistle-stop tour of the history of ritual. And no single day better captures that tension than April 30, 1586.

When we left our story in Göbekli Tepe, hunter-gatherers were just beginning to settle in communities and convert their yearning for ritual into patterned behavior. Over time, these settlements turned to narratives to explain their place in the world. From Mesopotamia to India, early cultures used creation stories, pageants, and art to introduce new levels of group cohesion. But these early stirrings of collective identity were isolated and decentralized. Rituals, from funerary rites to harvest festivals, grew in importance, but full-blown religion, from liturgy to laws, had yet to take hold.

That decentralization gave way to centralization during a remarkable period in the mid–first millennium BCE that the German philosopher Karl Jaspers termed the *Axial Age.* Between 500 and 300 BCE, Judaism emerged in the Mediterranean, Hinduism and Buddhism in India, Confucianism and Daoism in Asia, Hellenic philosophy in Europe. Jaspers suggested that this change represented a more cognitive approach to the world—"thinking about thinking." With leaders as diverse as Socrates, Buddha, Confucius, and Moses, "hitherto unconsciously accepted ideas, customs and conditions were subjected to examination, questioned and liquidated."

As significant as that intellectual shift was, it was overshadowed by an even greater shift. These new, universal religions launched a behavioral revolution in the form of new, universal codes of conduct covering everything from how to live to how to love, how to breed to how to bury. Ritual, which had been around for more than three hundred millennia, found itself by the first millennium CE as the centerpiece of daily life. Looked at in evolutionary terms, this once niche, adaptive human behavior had executed something of a coup over global human culture.

Ritual ruled the world.

And make no mistake, its influence *was* global. In China, Confucianism insisted that rituals be strictly followed. "Opposing ritual is to throw the world into darkness," wrote the third-century BCE philosopher Xunzi. Hindu texts from the same period stress the identical point: "The lord created humans with ritual," the *Bhagavad Gita* explains, "through ritual, they sustain it."

But no religion injected ritual more deeply into human life than Christianity. For centuries, the Hebrew Bible had driven home the idea that human families face volatility. God's first commandment to humans is "Be fruitful and multiply"; when Adam and Eve comply, their children end up in a murderous row. The first family of Genesis is racked by events surrounding the big four life rituals, including birthing problems (Abraham and Sarah, Isaac and Rebekah), coming-of-age problems (Jacob and Esau, Isaac and Ishmael), marriage problems (Sarah and Hagar, Leah and Rachel), and death problems (Abraham, Isaac, *and* Jacob).

The early church took this inheritance and turned it into a mandate to exercise strict ritual control over the most intimate moments of family life. Five of the seven sacraments cover life transitions. Such rule-heavy rituals are "necessary," Thomas Aquinas wrote, because they are "visible signs" of "invisible things." Ecclesiastical architecture made these mandates even more visible—babies are carried to baptisteries, brides are escorted to altars, corpses are rolled down naves. Even if you didn't grow up Catholic, if I asked you to picture a baby naming, a wedding, or a funeral, the one that would probably come to mind owes a deep debt to the theatrical innovations of the Roman Catholic Church.

This cultural imprint is why St. Peter's, the grandest of those constructions, plays such an outsize role in the history of ritual. Perhaps named for the vati, or soothsayers, who once told fortunes on this hill, the tiny plot on the west bank of the Tiber had been a ritual burial place for Romans, a ceremonial killing place for Christian converts, and the purported final resting place for the apostle Peter. The first basilica, begun by Constantine, stood for twelve hundred years. The pope who conceived its replacement was Julius II, the brutal warrior and lustful sinner (his nickname was "the Terrible"), who was Machiavelli's model for *The Prince*. From the day he laid the foundation stone in 1506, completion took 161 years, thirty popes, and the combined genius of Bramante, Michelangelo, Raphael, and Bernini.

Still, if we could pick one day to embody the basilica's significance for ritual, it would be the last Wednesday in April 1586. Pope Sixtus V, a parsimonious Franciscan with a sky-high imagination, announced a bold plan to relocate the red granite obelisk that had stood for sixteen centuries on Vatican Hill. Michelangelo had insisted it could never be done. To prove him wrong, Sixtus chose Domenico Fontana, a builder whose family had worked on St. Peter's for three generations. Over seven months, he assembled 907 men, 70 winches, and 145 horses, and miles of hemp rope.

On the appointed day, after the pope erected a gallows to warn anyone against making a sound, a trumpet blared and the removal began. But after twelve cranks of the winch, with Rome's only intact obelisk suspended in midair, the rope started to fray. At the risk of death, a voice cried out, "*Acqua alle funi!*" (water the ropes). Sixtus assented, the wetting restored the hemp's pliability, and the 327-ton obelisk floated to the ground. It was soon wheeled down the hill and erected before the basilica. St. Peter's had its needle in God's haystack.

That April day symbolizes the history of ritual for two reasons: First, it created a ritual. The man who dared issue the warning about the ropes was a sailor from Bordighera, a town on the Italian Riviera famed as the northernmost place in Europe that can grow palm trees. In gratitude, Sixtus V granted the community the right to provide Easter palms to St. Peter's . . . forever. Today, nearly 450 years later, more than two thousand Bordighera fronds are distributed on Palm Sunday to worshippers who assemble beneath the obelisk.

Second, the main reason Sixtus was so eager to relocate the obelisk is that he couldn't afford to finish the basilica. St. Peter's was spectacularly beautiful; it was also financially ruinous. To attract pilgrims, Sixtus promised that any visitor who prayed before the granite spire would be granted an indulgence.

Begun in the early church, indulgences are basically work-arounds for sin—perform an act of devotion, receive forgiveness. They're a way to jump the line to a better life or afterlife. As St. Peter's costs soared, popes began selling indulgences to make up the deficit, many to the most vulnerable. Outrage over this practice was a chief inspiration for Martin Luther. Thesis eighty-six of his famed Ninety-Five Theses asked, "Why does the pope, whose wealth is today greater than the wealth of the richest Crassus, build the basilica of St. Peter with the money of poor believers?"

In no time, the Protestant Reformation flowered, fueled in large measure by its wholesale attack on the ritual overkill of the Vatican. Most life rituals, reformers argued, including those covering adolescence, marriage, and death, were theologically unsound; most ceremonies, with their ostentatiousness, were sacrilegious. The church had become too enthralled with pageantry and too removed from scripture. As British historian Peter Burke wrote, "The Reformation was, among other things, a great debate, unparalleled in scale and intensity, about the meaning of ritual, its functions and its proper forms."

In Protestant churches, baptisms were marginalized, weddings were downplayed, divorces were legalized, funerals were streamlined. Having dominated the life cycle for longer than any institution ever had, the Catholic Church by the dawn of the modern era had lost its near monopoly over human behavior in the West. St. Peter's, the highest summit of Christendom, became the high-water mark of religion's control over ritual. Ever after, life rituals would become voluntary.

You need to take only two steps into St. Peter's to realize how much it venerates ritual. To the right is a mourning chapel, featuring one of the most poignant depictions of grief ever created, Michelange-

Figure 1: The baptistery chapel of St. Peter's Basilica in the Vatican.

lo's *Pietà*, a Carrara marble gut punch of a seated Mary cradling the limp body of her crucified son. To the left is a welcoming chapel, the baptistery, featuring an eight-foot painting of John baptizing Jesus and a purple marble basin adorned with gilded angels.

"My favorite place in the basilica!" Agnello proclaimed as he led me toward the baptistery.

Five couples were just arriving—men in black suits and patent leather loafers or unbuttoned shirts and fancy sneakers; women in white lace dresses, bright purple pantsuits, and shocking pink hair. Like any new parents, no less ones asked to swaddle their newborns in Victorian dress and carry them into the most hallowed church on earth, they looked uniformly dazed. The scrum of godparents, grandparents, and dozens of toddlers scurrying around like marbles on the marble floor didn't help.

My dear children, the Christian community welcomes you with great joy.

Baptism, at its core, is a ritual of welcoming. Like most life rituals, it was not invented out of whole cloth but adapted from preexisting traditions. Jews had long used ritual purification to welcome converts, laggards returning to the fold, or anyone going through a life transition. The Gospels include two accounts of Jesus being blessed with water.

Building on these accounts, Christians turned a relatively minor Jewish practice into a centerpiece of faith. Baptisms cleansed sins, purged wrongs, wiped slates clean. At first, converts were baptized until the end of life. But as the church grew stronger, attention shifted to children and their need for ritual training and eventually to babies and their need to be purified from "original sin." By the fourth century, baptism became less a personal choice and more a parental choice. Less joining, more welcoming.

Parents, you have asked to have your children baptized. It will be your duty to bring them up in God's commandments. Do you clearly understand what you are undertaking?

Agnello was not uttering these words; the service was being led by a seventy-five-year-old priest in a traditional white robe and stole. And the service was certainly traditional, nearly unaltered since the Middle Ages: the questioning of the parents, the liturgy of the Word, the prayer of the faithful. The climax was the blessing of the child, when

Figure 2: A baptism in St. Peter's Basilica overseen by Brother Agnello Stoia (right).

parents carry their babies to the altar, lay them backward to receive the water, and hear the Trinitarian blessing.

I baptize you in the name of the Father, and of the Son, and of the Holy Spirit.

But underneath this unchanging veneer, change was everywhere. As the priest conducted the service, Agnello pinballed around the room, chatting with parents, cooing at babies, polishing smudged candlesticks. It was as if he were saying, *Ignore all this stuffiness, God's house isn't any more perfect than your house.*

The parents, meanwhile, included interracial couples, intergenerational couples, international couples. The priests were Italian but the nuns were East Asian, Caribbean, African. The Vatican had just announced that transgender people could now be baptized as could the children of gay parents. The most unchanging life ritual was hardly immune from the winds of change.

And let us say, Amen.

Agnello, for his part, welcomed the fluidity. "My heart smiles on these days," he told me after hugging me goodbye. "But I also know what happens next. Today, your child is baptized in San Pietro; tomorrow, the parents come see me: *The event was so beautiful, but I'm sorry, we're not married.* Then they ask if I will host their wedding."

He smiled.

"That's how we welcome the children back home."

Following the service, I walked through the corridors to the Sistine Chapel. An old friend, the art historian Liz Lev, had offered to unravel a mystery I hadn't even known existed: why the majority of Michelangelo's paintings depict life transitions and what those images can teach us about life rituals.

The most famous ceiling in the world is a tutorial on how to welcome with joy.

Welcoming is not just the first life ritual; it's the first act in every life ritual. Since the one necessary ingredient of any celebration is that everyone feels invited, the one necessary step is to invite them in—open the door, ring the bell, extend the hand, unroll the carpet. The frame in this case creates the canvas. By allowing participants to feel protected, you allow them to take risks. In creating the space to be, you create the space to become.

Welcoming is partly physical. Games have fields, circuses have rings, plays have stages, trials have courtrooms. Rituals, like relationships, need boundaries: fire, water, candles, crystals, ropes, herbs, trees, walls. The threshold announces to everyone involved, *Outside we were that; inside we are this.* The separation encourages the transformation.

Welcoming is partly emotional. When disorder strikes, we become disordered. The ritual is designed to reorder us. To achieve that sense of rebalancing, we must feel safe, secure, comforted, protected. There's a reason so many ritual sites are likened to a "womb," "axis mundi," or "the navel of the universe." We feel like we're returning home.

But welcoming is also theatrical. The Nobel Prize winner Daniel Kahneman and the social psychologist Barbara Fredrickson identified what they called the *peak-end effect*, the idea that people judge an experience based on how they feel at the highest point and how they feel at the concluding point. But in life rituals, the opening point matters just as much. To be open to change, you must open with a symbol of change. You need what Aristotle called an *exordium*, a hook, a bang, an eye-catcher, an attention grabber.

A wow.

Loving rituals begin with wows: *all rise, all bow, all sing, all dance.* Traditional Irish weddings opened with a "race for the bottle," in which men rode horses to the groom's house and returned with a bottle of whiskey for the bride, who took a swig and handed it to the groom, who drank and passed it around the circle until the empty bottle returned to the bride, who smashed it against a rock.

Becoming rituals begin with wows: jumping over cattle, diving off cliffs, killing a lion, plunging your hands into gloves of bullet ants. The Ndembu in Zambia opened their circumcision ceremonies by having older women form a "tunnel of legs" that adolescent boys had to crawl through; medieval Jews kicked off a boy's education by handing him a tablet inscribed with Hebrew and smeared in honey, which he had to lick off.

Welcoming rituals begin with wows: Nepalese pierced noses, Yorubans cut faces, Mayans broke hips. English neighbors provided groaning cakes for mothers in labor (the name paid homage to the noises those mothers made), rocking cakes for fathers, and giant wheels of cheese, into which parents cut a hole to pass through their newborn child.

All of which may help explain why Michelangelo stood sixty feet in the air for four years to paint images of welcoming across the Sistine Chapel ceiling.

"The Sistine Chapel is a space where art is meant to evoke big questions," said Liz, a Pittsburgh native who's taught in Rome for thirty years and written four books on Christian imagery. "You have the creation of the world along the ceiling and the end of the world above the altar. They're a reminder that every person is at a beginning or an end—and unlike animals, we're supposed to find meaning in moments of change."

I asked her what percentage of the chapel's paintings depict life transitions.

"One hundred percent."

"Really?"

She ticked them off: the creation of light, the birth of Adam, the birth of Eve, the destruction of the world.

"Is that percentage unique to the chapel or common to the Renaissance?"

"It's common to Christian art in general. Everything is about moving toward God. The church tries to say that when you feel weakest, we offer you strength; when you're lost, we give you direction."

"What percentage of early Christian art is about such moments?"

"Seventy-five. Baptism is by far the most popular—Moses striking the rock, Daniel in the lion's den, Jonah in the whale. They're all symbolic immersions. The message is that in times of vulnerability, you can be born again."

"So the images themselves become stand-ins for rituals."

"Exactly. But they're also reminders: Your boat feels wobbly, your path is blocked, rituals get you back on track. But you need us to perform those rituals for you.

"The Vatican doesn't invent spectacle," Liz continued, "but it elevates spectacle like few places in history. When you come to a church to join a ritual, you feel a mixture of collective joy and new beginning. It's not just an individual who's reborn in a baptism; the entire community is reborn."

Welcoming plays such a critical role in life rituals that every one of the ritual designers I spoke with aims for an opening wow. Four in ten use boundaries (forming a circle, arranging rocks in the sand); three in ten use communal gestures (breathing, meditating); two in ten use physical objects (an altar, a candle). What these galvanizing acts have in common is creating a sense of "place outside of place," a crucible where the work of reconnection can begin.

Sarah Emerson grew up outside Boston in a large Catholic family. "I had a lot of relatives, so I went to a lot of funerals. I associate them with gladiolus and cold cuts." She also harbored a lot of resentment. "Like, why can't women be priests?"

So she became a priest. A Buddhist priest.

"My mom died while I was in college, and we lost our family home. I entered a state of disorientation." A boyfriend handed her a copy of *Zen Mind, Beginner's Mind*. "I don't know what this guy's talking about," he said, "but it's the same stuff you're always talking about." The book changed Sarah's life. She trained in Thailand, earned a master's degree in psychology, and at twenty-six joined the San Francisco Zen Center. She's never left monastic life.

"I find healing in the connectedness."

Sarah married a fellow priest, and they welcomed their first child. "We held an informal blessing when she was ten days old. The community was already gathered for the end of monastic season. I put my daughter in a sling, walked her around the circle, and she looked every person in the eye."

Sarah's second child, Sati, was born two weeks premature. "We were hopeful that she would live, but her lungs were not strong enough." Sati died the following day. "I was driven by this ritual instinct to clothe, nourish, and nurture my child," Sarah said. She sewed robes, burned offerings, said prayers. "The satisfaction I drew from those rituals is hard to describe."

By the time she adopted a son, Sarah knew she wanted a full-blown ritual.

"The primary thing ritual does is carve out space. That's what makes it different from a bunch of people standing around the lawn." Sarah set up an altar and summoned guests with a bell. "There's an oldness to bells, a sense of waking up that prepares you for what's to come." She invited everyone to bow, shared her intention, then unwound a red thread to weave everyone together.

"What I've learned from practicing ritual every day is that we crave the physical. Ritual reminds us that we can't celebrate alone any more than we can heal alone. We're made of relationship."

Manulani Aluli Meyer is the fifth daughter of a US serviceman stationed in Oahu and a "gorgeous Hawaiian princess" who was about to become a nun. "I always say my mother married my father on a rebound from God."

A ferocious athlete—"I'm five eight but could dunk a basketball"—Manu was raised Christian but at twenty-five, feeling stifled for being gay, moved to her family's homeland on the Big Island. She's remained ever since, except for five years in New Zealand earning a master's in applied Indigenous wisdom and three years at Harvard earning a doctorate in education. Today she teaches at the University of Hawaiʻi and is leading a revival of the traditional Hawaiian forgiveness ritual, hoʻoponopono.

The Hawaiian expression for "setting it right," hoʻoponopono is a centuries-old practice that brings harmony to families experiencing a rift. While mediation involves parties who don't really know one another, hoʻoponopono is specifically designed for people who are related. "The pain point is that they hate each other," Manu said. "The opportunity is that they want to get back into relationship."

In the 1990s, as part of a rejuvenation of Indigenous rituals across the Americas, the Native Hawaiian Bar Association officially recognized the practice. Manu has personally led hundreds of hoʻoponopono rituals, most in one of the knottiest family dynamics imaginable, where one person is in prison, often for doing harm to another family member.

"I've published a process that involves five conditions," she said, including choosing an impartial facilitator and agreeing to confidentiality. "But by far the most important condition is the first one: committing to a spirit of aloha; entering a state of love and affection. I use a practice called pikai, putting water in sea salt and sprinkling it around the room.

"We know that salt water heals," Manu continued, "so spreading it creates the intention of healing. You manifest your own readiness. You willingly agree to restate your aloha for one another."

"And how do you know if the ritual works?" I asked.

"Oh, you don't have to ask. You see it. We hug, we sob, we wear leis, we share food. Boy, do we share food. But it's not just *Yippee, yay! We wanted to kill each other an hour earlier and now we're kissing.* It's sincere, it's life-affirming, and it's radically transformational to forgive one another. And it all begins with affirming the essence of every individual, which is aloha."

Jeff Lieberman grew up as a science nerd in a family of Reform Jews in Miami. "When I learned about the burning bush when I was nine, I said to my teacher, 'That's not how oxidation works.'" He went on to earn two master's degrees from MIT, work as a kinetic sculptor, and host a television series on slow motion.

Then he had a lifequake.

"It started with a huge crash. I was suicidally depressed in high school and suddenly was back on the brink of tears. This time I decided to do something about it."

What he did was home in on the absence of life rituals for young adults.

"What if we had a rite of passage that instead of, like, wrestling with a bear, involved getting together with a group of peers and simmering in all the dimensions of adult reality."

With a friend he opened Sleepawake, a four-week, in-person retreat for young adults looking for "transformation, deep connection, and community." The program specializes in serving those facing mental health challenges. It's basically a boot camp for rebooting in the digital age.

"Our goal is to help campers express their vulnerability, regulate their nervous systems, and find safety. The reason you need a community is that the group replicates the group where you were programmed. Relationships caused the trauma; relationships must heal the trauma."

The single best way to begin that healing, he said, is to start right out of the gate.

"An insight I learned from a ritual designer in Africa is 'Don't wait for the wow. Do it right when people show up.' On the very first day, we create an empathy circle. I say, 'Step into the center if there was physical violence in your house.' Thirty percent step into the circle.

"The people on the outside think, *Whoa, a third of this community experienced violence?* The people on the inside think, *Whoa, two thirds of this community did not.* And holy moly, the tears on both sides start flowing. That's when I know the ritual is going to work. We achieve safety through shared vulnerability; we achieve community through saying what usually goes unsaid."

After my visit with Liz, I left the Sistine Chapel and happened onto a small desk, manned by a priest, with an invitation to chat. It reminded me of Lucy van Pelt's advice booth, THE DOCTOR IS IN.

I sat down.

Father Cyril was a thirty-six-year-old Nigerian whose birth name was Nnamdi and whose baptismal name was adopted from Saint Cyril of Alexandria. He had lived in the Vatican for seven years. I asked him why depictions of rituals were so prevalent.

"Rituals provide witness," he said. "To experience fear, to experience rejection, to experience frustration—these all make us feel isolated. What we learn from the Bible is that it's possible to pass through these uncomfortable times, but only if we have witnesses to our pain."

"But many people seem to be abandoning these rituals," I said.

"People may be turning away from rituals and turning toward their phones, but you can't abandon the values that created you. When we speak about fidelity, about honesty, about selflessness—these virtues didn't fall from the sky. They were forged from heartbreak and suffering. I don't believe society has disconnected from that legacy; we just appreciate it in different ways."

What message should we take from that heritage?

"It's like a child who carries an important name but fails to acknowledge his father. Whether you like it or not, your family name has shaped you. When you know where you came from, you walk with courage, you knock on every door with certainty, you step into every room with conviction. Our rituals are an inheritance that allows all of us to walk with more confidence into the future."

I said goodbye and set out through galleries lined with Renaissance tapestries and classical statues. Modern life, we often hear, has a God-shaped hole at its heart; ritual, I couldn't help but think, has a Vatican-shaped hole at its heart, one that will likely never be filled again with such a unified force.

But while the church may no longer enjoy the same hegemonic influence, there are still lessons to be learned from its eons in power: Use spectacle to draw people in, sow gladness in times of cheer, bear witness in times of suffering. One of the most memorable pieces of advice I received when my daughters were young was "Always be happy to see them." *Bright eyes, open arms, can't fail.* Someday they'll come to you when they're unhappy, and they'll need your welcome even more.

Now that my children are older, I've put this sentiment into words: *Our family is good on the good days,* I say; *we're better on the bad days.* Ritual is the same: It's good on the good days; it's better on the bad days. We need to practice ritual in the best of times, when we feel safe, secure, and loved, because we will need them in the worst of times, when we feel unsafe, unsecure, and unloved. It's on those latter days, after all, when we most need the reassurance of being welcomed back home, embraced with open arms, and reminded that we can lessen the pain, quiet the doubt, and soften the jagged edges of fear by tending the problem together.

2.

THE LOBOLA CONNECTION

What Happens Under the Mango Tree

The groom was late. The wedding caravan was delayed by a funeral cortege, and the dark green Toyota pickup with a cracked windshield, followed by a white Ford Ranger and several sedans, pulled up to the rickety gate on an unpaved road in Lillydale, a village in northeastern South Africa, at exactly thirty seconds after 10 a.m. That half a minute would prove critical.

A gaggle of elders climbed out of the vehicles; the men were wearing dark suits and serious expressions; the women black-and-white polka-dot skirts, white cotton dresses, and purple-and-orange headwraps. They had come for a party but also a business meeting: Today was the final showdown of a nearly two-decade-long negotiation between two families over a bridal contract.

The groom's family approached the gate lugging a pink suitcase; three black trash bags stuffed with duvets and clothing; two red crates filled with beer, Coca-Cola, and Fanta; and a three-liter box of Raindance natural sweet rosé. ("It's like sipping on a bouquet of rose petals!")

Then they waited.

And waited.

"We cannot greet them because they dishonored our family," one of the bride's aunties whispered. "A member of our family will come and sleep at the gate. If they tip her enough and she laughs, it means the family is welcome. If she does not laugh, they are not welcome."

The yard had been bustling for hours. The one-story, tan concrete-block house was surrounded by black monkey orange trees, apricots, sago palms, a blooming hibiscus, and an overgrown frangipani. Towering above them all was a marula tree, where at dawn the bride's family had gathered to pour home-brewed beer from the tree's nuts onto the earth to receive blessings from the ancestors.

A woman was sweeping the dirt in front of the house. "At night, a witch can ride around on her broom and cast spells," the auntie explained. "First thing in the morning, it's the daughter-in-law's job to sweep away anything the witch leaves behind. It's a ritual you have to do."

After keeping the visitors waiting in the stifling December heat for ten minutes, an elderly woman approached the gate, lay down on a straw mat, and rolled herself up inside an orange carpet. The groom's uncle offered her a 100-rand note, around $5. The woman poked her head out, examined the offering, then tossed it back. The uncle put down an additional 200 rand.

"The money is like a fine," the auntie explained. "It doesn't count toward the bride-price, which we've been haggling over for seventeen years."

This time the woman snatched the bills, threw off the carpet, and laughed. The groom's family cheered. The gate was flung open.

Now the real negotiations could begin.

From its opening scene of a communal wrestling match, nearly every page of Chinua Achebe's *Things Fall Apart* is infused with ritual. The 1958 Nigerian novel, which is widely considered a bellwether of African fiction and which *Britannica* listed as one of the twelve greatest books ever written, follows Okonkwo, a childhood wrestling star turned tribal elder, through rituals of planting, harvesting, warring, and peacemaking.

Perhaps the most vivid ritual occurs in chapter 8, when Okonkwo helps negotiate the bride-price of a friend's daughter, Akueke. Ambassadors from the two families gather; palm wine is drunk; nuts and alligator peppers are eaten. Then the bride's father hands over a bundle of thirty broomsticks, indicating that he expects thirty sacks of cowries for his daughter.

"We are at last getting somewhere," the suitor's father says. "Let us go out and whisper together."

The groom's party exits and returns having removed half the broomsticks.

"We had not thought to go below thirty," the bride's father says, but "marriage should be a play and not a fight."

He then adds ten broomsticks back to the bundle.

"In this way Akueke's bride-price was finally settled at twenty bags of cowries."

For as long as humans have been mating, bags of cowries, coins, jewels, shekels, beads, hides, and grains have been traded as a form of wealth transfer from the bride's family to the groom's, a practice known as dowry, or from the groom's family to the bride's, a practice known as bride-price. The Code of Hammurabi prescribes such transfers, the Torah details them, the *Iliad* describes them. Cultures from Polynesia to the Sahara practice the custom.

Looked at through the prism of the beloveds, this ritual has many disadvantages—it grants power to the elders, costs lots of resources, devalues individual choice. But looked at through the prism of the families, the practice has many advantages—it creates alliances, maintains cultural continuity, rewards investment in children. The single biggest reason bride-price survives in Africa and beyond is that it accomplishes the first of the four things life rituals do: They bring people together; they promote social cohesion.

They connect.

"Lobola keeps the family strong—and keeps the community strong," explained Mike Mabunda on the day before the wedding. Mike is a seventy-nine-year-old historian and a member of the elder council of the Tsonga tribe, a transnational community of eight million people spanning Mozambique, Zimbabwe, and South Africa.

A Pan-African word, *lobola* describes the elaborate, multiyear process by which families agree on how much wealth a groom's family must pay to the bride's in return for her coming to live with them. Cattle is the primary metric. A bride is worth six, eight, twelve, or more cows. A twice-divorced President Nelson Mandela paid sixty cows for his third wife, Graça Machel; Mandela's successor, Jacob Zuma, received one hundred cows from the king of Eswatini for the right to marry one of Zuma's daughters.

These days, a cow no longer means a cow; a "cow" is a unit of money, between 3,000 and 5,000 rand, or $175 to $275. Families must first agree on the value, then the means of paying that value—cash, clothing, housewares, food, drink, etc. Some cows are actually paid in cows. At Mike's second wedding, he had to import two plump cows from a nearby province.

The next question is *when* those cows are paid. "Even if you have the cows, you can't pay them right away," Mike said.

"Why not?"

"Because it's disrespectful. It suggests you're better than the other family."

The final matter is how to hand over the cows. Asking your uncles to make a cash-and-beer run is too risky; tipsy uncles have been known to skim a few bills off the top. But bank transfers are also forbidden, because they skirt face-to-face interactions. Mike told me about a negotiation in which a tech worker asked to send his cows via electronic transfer. The bride's family refused, the groom threatened to elope, and a compromise had to be struck: The bride's family would accept the cows by wire, but the groom's family had to buy them a sheep as an apology. Sometimes cows aren't even bovines.

These hiccups aside, lobola is still being dragged into the digital age. Determining a bride's value is considered so complicated that a developer in Johannesburg built a lobola calculator app. It asks height, weight, education level, childhood breakfast (cereals or porridge), preferred shoes (heels, sneakers, or sandals), sexually active (yes or no), number of children, and common activities (church, clubbing, work, driving, household chores, and loves soccer). The app's logo: a cartoon cow.

"Aren't you demeaning women by reducing their worth to such metrics?" a radio interviewer asked the twenty-four-year-old developer.

"Isn't that what we already do in our minds?"

Strictly for research purposes, I punched in the answers that described Linda at the time of our wedding. I lied and said she likes to drive, but told the truth that she doesn't enjoy household chores. The total came to $3,452, or seventeen cows. She was insulted, as much by my answers as by the price.

All of which raises the question: How does this ritual survive modern life?

A study of six hundred Black South African women by the sociologist Janet Shope found that women don't just tolerate lobola, they embrace it as a source of honor and power. "Without access to alternative sources of symbolic capital, women in South Africa's rural areas cling to *lobola* for the respect and dignity it confers and for the relational bonds of interdependence it cultivates among families." As one woman said, "*Lobola* is here to stay. If you don't pay *lobola* you don't respect your wife. But if you do pay *lobola* for your wife, you respect her and then you don't easily say 'go away.'"

Mike went further.

"Lobola survives because it's not about the price; it's about the ritual." He mentioned the mediation sessions he runs as a tribal elder. "In civil court, two parties walk in through separate doors and walk out through separate doors. In tribal court, two parties walk in through separate doors but walk out through the same door. We force them to reconcile; we insist that they hug.

"All families have conflict," Mike continued. "Lobola is about building trust and integrating families, so that when problems arise—over children, property, or money—the two families have become one family and have experience finding happiness together."

Once the groom's family passed through the gate, the negotiation reset. The yard had the frenetic atmosphere of a pregame tailgate party. To the left, a green-and-blue tent was being raised; to the rear, a dozen women were cooking in open cauldrons. The two families were divided into home and away. The groom's family was ushered into the modest living room and asked to wait without air-conditioning, water, or access to a bathroom. The bride's family returned to their place underneath a mango tree.

The matriarch, Patricia, sat directly in front of the tree trunk in a white plastic chair; she was wearing a black floral skirt and apricot-and-black shirt and clutching a leather ledger. "The first time the Mathonsi family visited," she explained, flipping through the pages, "was Sunday, October 16, seventeen years ago."

Jeffrey Mathonsi and Lillian Khoza met while working in Kruger

Figure 3: The Khoza family home in Lillydale, South Africa, on the morning of Lillian and Jeffrey's wedding.

National Park. Neither was married, though Lillian had a daughter from a previous relationship, whom she was raising with her parents in the home where we were gathered. After a few years of dating, Jeffrey and Lillian decided to marry. To begin the lobola, Jeffrey sent a delegation to visit the Khozas.

In that first meeting, the two families went back and forth for several hours before agreeing on a bride-price of four cows, or 13,000 rand, which at the time was around $2,000. The Mathonsis offered to pay 2,000 rand on the spot and added 300 rand in appreciation for the Khozas' hospitality. These details were carefully recorded in the ledger, along with the names of the witnesses and the following note:

> The Mathonsi family did not have enough money to pay the entire lobola and agreed to return later and stay for dinner. Balance: 11,300 rand.

The Mathonsi family did return later—*nine years later*—on Saturday, December 23. Lillian was still living with her parents officially. The Mathonsis brought a crate of cold drinks, a case of beer, one box of wine, one bottle of brandy, a pair of shoes for the father, another pair for the mother, a suit for the dad, two scarves, a hat, a blanket, and 10,000 rand.

One reason the family came with such bounty is that they also came with a request: They wanted permission to leave with Lillian so the couple could start a family. To sweeten their proposal, the groom's side offered to add 1,000 rand to the bride-price. The Khozas agreed, but the Mathonsis didn't have the cash, so the sum was added to the total:

Balance: 2,300 rand.

Six years later, on October 28, the Khozas received a letter: "Greetings in the name of Jesus." It informed the family that the Mathonsis would arrive today, December 30, at 10 a.m. to complete the negotiation and celebrate the wedding of Jeffrey and Lillian. A lot had happened in the intervening years. Jeffrey and Lillian had two children; Lillian had to stop working after she was attacked by a baboon and lost the use of her hands; also, her parents died.

Given that Lillian's mother and father had not lived to see their daughter's wedding, I asked Patricia, Lillian's aunt, if she regretted that the negotiation had taken so long.

"The wedding is not the most important part," she said. "The lobola is. My daughter is living with someone without having followed the ritual; she's what we call 'fat and sad.' She doesn't have the blessing of the ancestors, and she doesn't have my consent." Patricia stood up. "If we complete today's negotiation successfully, the marriage of Lillian and Jeffrey will be a success."

Then she led me inside.

At seven thirty in the morning on July 22, 1749, the Paris police commissioner along with the inspector of books burst into the second-floor apartment of thirty-five-year-old philosopher Denis Diderot. The writer's wife, Toinette, was dressing their daughter in the bedroom. The officials interrogated the editor in chief of the *Encyclopédie*, the first compendium of knowledge to express open suspicion of religion. "Skepticism is the first step toward truth," Diderot said.

The authorities hoped to unearth a trove of incriminating documents. Instead, all they found were twenty-one boxes related to the *Encyclopédie*. Still, the officials informed Diderot that he was the object of a writ of incarceration signed by Louis XV, and the writer was frog-marched downstairs, shoved into a coach, driven an hour west, and thrown into the tower dungeon of the Château de Vincennes, a former palace turned prison.

Though Diderot was released three months later after agreeing not to publish any more incendiary material, his legacy was set: Paris had its martyr; the Enlightenment had its bible. But it's the overlooked influence of the *Encyclopédie* on the study of human behavior that warrants the Château de Vincennes's place as a stop on our whirlwind history of ritual. While earlier compendiums had presented a religious version of truth, Diderot's project made religion subservient to science and opened the door to the idea that cultures outside the West could contribute to the understanding of a meaningful life.

Once that process began, ritual became a primary focus and chief beneficiary. Anyone who loves ritual today owes a debt to Diderot's iconoclasm.

Three breakthroughs over the next three centuries helped turn ritual into the phenomenon it has become. The first, in the nineteenth century, was the then-radical idea that ritual is a universal human act. Riding the coattails of the age of discovery, early anthropologists collected colorful accounts of exotic celebrations around the world. The 1800s was the era of the Brothers Grimm and Hans Christian Andersen, the birth of the museum and the world's fair. This curiosity-industrial complex helped boost secularism. It's no accident that just as religion began to retreat from the center of intellectual life in the West, interest in ritual as an irreligious alternative began to fill it.

At first most intellectuals condescended to ritual. Even the great anthropologists sneered that rituals in preindustrial societies were "primitive" and "irrational." Joseph Conrad, in *Heart of Darkness*, perfectly captures the mix of attraction and repulsion in his account of an "ugly, inhuman" ritual in the Congo: People "howled, and leaped, and spun, and made horrid faces; but what thrilled you was just the thought of their humanity—like yours—the thought of your remote kinship with this wild and passionate uproar."

The best example of how views of ritual evolved comes from Diderot's own invention. The first *Encyclopaedia Britannica*, in 1771, had a brief entry on ritual, calling it "divine services" in "a particular church, diocese, or the like." That description went unchanged for the next century and a half, until the encyclopedia's eleventh edition, in 1910, which quintupled the length. Ritual was no longer religious at all but a "routine behavior" that "hardly a known tribe" was without. In a warning observation that still resonates, the encyclopedia cautioned that ritual is "not absolutely rigid: it grows, alters and decays."

This transformation of ritual from something puerile and parochial to something glorious and global involved a conceptual leap. Two men are primarily responsible for that turnabout—and they hated each other.

One man was the father of social science, Émile Durkheim, who rose from three generations of rabbis in northern France to the pinnacle of European thought at the Sorbonne. Durkheim was disturbed by the breakdown of societal norms that led to alienation and disconnection. The best way to counteract that threat, he argued, was the embrace of rituals, which reinforce solidarity and reaffirm belonging by generating "collective effervescence." "Once individuals are gathered together" in ritual, he wrote, "a sort of electricity is generated from their closeness and quickly launches them to an extraordinary height of exaltation."

The other man was a "strangely shadowy figure," little known in history. Arnold van Gennep, the child of German and Dutch parents, grew up in France, became an ethnographer and folklorist, and eked out a living from writing. In 1909, he published *Les rites de passage*, which introduced the idea that "the life of an individual" is filled with "transitional periods" in which they move from "one phase to another." We mark these personal passages with rites of passage, Van Gennep argued, which contain three phases—separation, liminality, and integration.

The near-simultaneous appearance of these two seminal theories of ritual was thunderous: A field of inquiry that had not existed decades earlier suddenly became the talk of European salons. Given the two Parisians' shared interests, the world would surely have benefited from their cooperation.

Instead, the most powerful intellectual in Europe feared his upstart challenger. Durkheim blackballed Van Gennep, preventing him from getting an academic position, and all but guaranteeing that his ideas would disappear. Van Gennep struck back, dismissing Durkheim's writing as filled with "generalizations constructed on the flimsiest foundation," but the damage was done: The idea of rites of passage disappeared from public view for the next fifty years.

It was not until an American graduate student translated *The Rites of Passage* into English in 1960—and the University of Chicago published it—that the idea caught on. The phrase "rite of passage" went through its own rite of passage from forgotten afterthought to household name. That revival coincided with a boon to ritual: the sixties. The Age of Aquarius spawned an eruption of sit-ins, love-ins, freedom rides, bra burnings, flower power, Woodstock, Earth Day, Stonewall, the march on Washington. Google Books's Ngram Viewer shows the phrase *rite of passage* taking off in those years; even the word

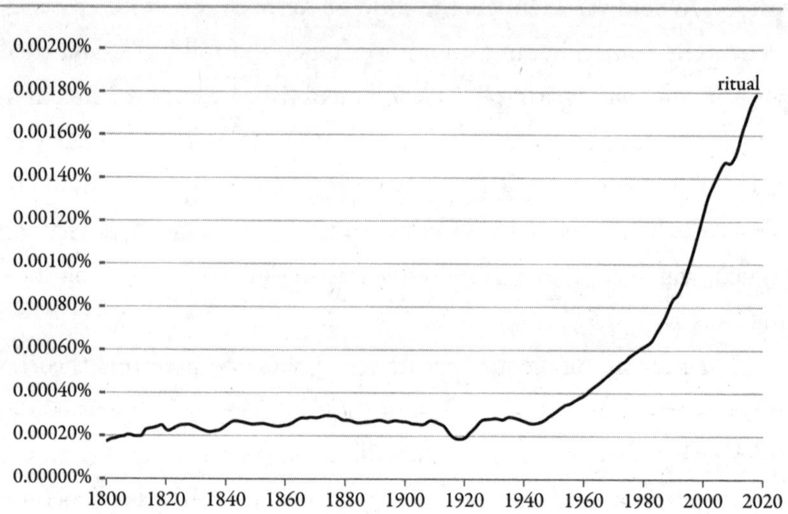

Credit: Google Books Ngram Viewer, https://books.google.com/ngrams.

ritual, which had been trending upward for decades, exploded like an Apollo rocket.

The charismatic Scottish anthropologist Victor Turner became the public face of this revival. Unlike "armchair anthropologists" Durkheim and Van Gennep, who never left home, Turner actually did field work in Africa, Europe, and North America. He returned convinced that ritual was "almost interchangeable" with theater in its ability to transform people feeling "betwixt and between" into ambassadors of togetherness. "As performance," Turner wrote, ritual "generates the power of communitas" that allows individuals to be "totally absorbed into a single synchronized, fluid" whole.

Coming at a time when more people were seeking alternative means of spiritual enlightenment, ritual by millennium's end had reached a new apex of influence—embraced by the religious and nonreligious, old and young. The field of ritual studies, as Diderot would have appreciated, grew into an academic powerhouse. Few could have predicted that the twenty-first century would see ritual spiraling into decline just as scientists made their biggest breakthrough yet—penetrating the human mind to discover how ritual transforms our individual brains into engines of cooperation.

The atmosphere inside the Khozas' living room was stern. Sixteen people filled a space designed for eight, spilling onto the arms and leaning on the backs of two brown love seats and two brown lounge chairs.

Jeffrey's family was on the right, led by his brother in what looked like a funeral director's dark suit and black tie. Lillian's family was on the left. Patricia positioned herself in front of the door, across from a bookshelf with a television set, photos of grandchildren, and a stuffed lion. In between was the considerable pile of goods the groom's family had brought. The whole setup screamed, *No one is getting out of here without a deal.*

What happened next echoed Durkheim's idea that rituals reinforce social order. Patricia rehearsed how the families had arrived at this point, going through each meeting and payment. The proceedings also reinforced Van Gennep's idea that rituals represent changes in status. When the groom's family laid out their gifts on the coffee table, the bride's aunties carefully unpacked the duvets, towels, clothes, shoes,

Figure 4: The final laying down of bills at the end of the lobola.

fabrics, and drinks. The women inspected them, then placed them into piles based on who would take them home. The sorting felt like the physical embodiment of a family being remade.

But for all the formality, the gathering also gave off the somewhat performative air of theater that Turner would have loved. The families went through the motions—the balance of 2,300 rand was paid—but the outcome seemed preordained. What happens if people disagree? I asked Jeffrey's brother William later. "If we knew we couldn't come to terms, we wouldn't start the lobola."

The one dissonant note came after all the pre-agreed transactions had been completed. Patricia looked at William and asked, "Is that all?" For the first time all morning, tensions rose. William looked at his relatives, bowed his head in resignation, then reached into his suit pocket and pulled out a wad of cash. He carefully stacked twelve 100-rand notes onto the table. One of the Khoza aunties swiftly scooped up the bills.

Everyone turned to Patricia.

She didn't flinch.

We weren't done yet.

William stared at her for a minute, then whispered something to *his* elder, the most distinguished member of the delegation and the only one wearing traditional African batik clothing. Poker-faced, he reached into his back pocket and handed William an envelope. William peered inside, took out 1,500 rand, and placed them on the table. He then looked up at Patricia and smiled coolly.

No one claimed this money. Patricia shifted in her chair, looked out the window toward the mango tree, and in a wistful expression that made me wonder if she was thinking about Lillian's mother, closed her eyes, made a half smile, then turned to the room and ululated.

Loo-loo-loo-loo-loo.

The sole woman on the groom's side soon joined her.

Lee-lee-lee-lee-lee.

Then the aunties on the bride's side chimed in.

La-la-la-la-la.

In what seemed like an instant, the bills were swiped up, the goods whisked away, the air-conditioning turned on, and fifteen brightly colored pots, pans, and bowls appeared, steaming with stewed okra, cornmeal mash, leafy greens, diced beets, white rice, fried chicken, and a kettle of beef stew from the cow that had been slaughtered that morning. The ritual had its feast. The lobola had its climax. Lillian and Jeffrey would be married that afternoon.

Scholars have long debated whether individuals or groups are more important to human survival. Are we fundamentally *I* people or *we* people? By the close of the twentieth century, the I's had won. As the evolutionary biologist David Sloan Wilson and two colleagues noted in a summary of this intellectual struggle, individualism had become "so widely accepted that group selection became a pariah concept, taught primarily as an example of how not to think."

Today that consensus has flipped. The supremacy of the individual has given way to a renewed respect for the group. "Ironically," Wilson and his colleagues wrote, "given group selection's previous pariah status, it is now the concept of groups as organisms that stands on a firm scientific foundation."

In the battle between *we* and *I*, *we* is winning.

This about-face came about because of one of the great discoveries of twenty-first-century biology: Living beings are wired to belong. Molecules join to form chromosomes, single-cell organisms join to form multicell organisms, multicell organisms join to form communities, and so on. "In a sense," writes the social psychologist Jonathan Haidt, "all life forms are now understood to be groups, or even groups of groups."

This change has altered how anthropologists do their work. Instead of isolating themselves in faraway tribes, they now band together with colleagues in neuroscience, data science, and AI to bring a wider skill set to the same inquiries. By replacing turf wars with peace pacts, writes Oxford's Harvey Whitehouse, social scientists better position themselves to harness the "formidable cohesive and cooperative capacities" of ritual to address global problems.

Rituals promote cooperation, these collaborations have found, by convincing people to do things that appear inexplicable—or even silly—simply for the purpose of belonging to the group. When Whitehouse and his team showed children instrumental tasks like drinking a glass of water accompanied by noninstrumental, seemingly irrelevant actions like waving a piece of cloth, the children tended to "overimitate" or "blanket copy" the unnecessary gestures. The reason: They believed their willingness to replicate the gestures would grant them admission into a coveted community.

When the behavior we're being asked to replicate is accompanied by verbal priming like "Our team always performs the task this way," we reproduce the behavior even more faithfully. When we are told that our disobedience will result in our ostracization, our fidelity grows even stronger. The bottom line: What Whitehouse calls our "ritual stance" shows that if we believe our actions will deepen our sense of belonging, we're willing to do almost anything.

Some of Whitehouse's students have taken these data-driven experiments to colorful extremes. Dimitris Xygalatas, a cognitive anthropologist from Greece, is among a wave of researchers who use wearable sensors, biochemical markers, and EEGs to analyze how our bodies react to rituals in real time. If the first generation of ritual scholars were armchair anthropologists and the second were field anthropologists, this new generation are biometric anthropologists.

Xygalatas's doctoral thesis was on firewalking, a ritual in which people walk across beds of coal carrying relatives on their backs. There are no shortcuts in firewalking, he found, no ointments or hidden pads, just slow traversing of coals measuring 1,250 degrees Fahrenheit that are inefficient at transferring heat. The biggest hurdle is the walker's emotions.

To understand how individuals manage such arousal, Xygalatas devised a study that his adviser called "the craziest research idea I've ever heard." Firewalkers at the annual solstice celebration in San Pedro Manrique, Spain, in which residents gather in front of packed bleachers at midnight on June 23 to tread across a twenty-three-foot carpet of embers, agreed to wear heart monitors.

"As soon as we saw the first analyses, we knew we had found something truly remarkable," Xygalatas writes. First, the heartbeats of firewalkers showed remarkable synchrony throughout the event, even though only one walked at a time. Second, the elevated heartbeats extended to spectators, whose feet weren't even held to the fire. Third, the more connected individuals were to each other—meaning they were family or close friends—the more their hearts beat in tandem. A pair of twins showed nearly identical heartbeats, even though one walked and one did not. By contrast, the heartbeats of unrelated spectators showed no correlation.

Xygalatas's conclusion: The ritual was not a personal phenomenon; "it was a fundamentally social phenomenon." It was not an individual event; it was a group event. As one walker told Xygalatas upon viewing a graph of her heartbeat, "I told you it was hard to express the feelings that I experience during this ritual. *This* is how I feel. Our hearts become one."

Unlike the lobola, the wedding started thirty minutes late and no one seemed to care. At half past three, about forty children lined up two by two in the yard. Dressed in black pants and white shirts, they clapped, stomped, and shimmied their way into the tent to an Afrobeat-disco hit. Then the host, DJ Colonel, introduced Jeffrey and his mother, who strolled down the white-cloth aisle to Ed Sheeran's "Perfect."

"Look at these two!" Colonel said. "So charmed!"

Jeffrey was in his forties, handsome, with a bald head and broad smile; he was wearing white sneakers, blue jeans, and a crisp white shirt decorated with a forest-green floral pattern on the cuffs and collar. Lobola negotiations are customarily followed by two ceremonies—a tribal wedding and a "white wedding." Like many couples, Jeffrey and Lillian combined the two for cost.

The setting reflected that blending. About sixty guests were seated at long tables with white tablecloths and forest-green runners and napkins. The altar where Jeffrey came to a stop had a white leather love

Figure 5: Jeffrey Mathonsi and Lillian Khoza at their wedding altar.

seat, a bottle of alcohol-free champagne, and a white fondant cake; it also had Zulu shields, Makenge baskets, and a homemade broom, the symbol of daughter-in-law duty.

"Ladies and gentlemen, please turn your eyes to the house!"

Colonel directed everyone to the front door, where Lillian appeared on the arm of her uncle. She was dressed in a flowing, forest-green gown with a taffeta skirt and fitted bodice embroidered with yellow, red, and blue flowers, the colors of the Tsonga tribe. Her hair was pulled back into a bun, and her face was reserved, even bashful, except for her vivid red lips. She approached the altar to the R&B ballad "Someone to Love Me Forever."

The ceremony began with a handwashing, followed by statements of support from the bride's and groom's families called "I Know Her" and "I Know Him." Then, a numbing twist, a solemnization and Word of God, delivered by Pastor Ad Mabunda, that was listed in the program as forty-five minutes but took longer. Halfway through, he used a passage from Genesis 2 to deliver a screed against same-sex marriage, which is legal in South Africa though still excluded from lobola. Months later, I met a tech worker in Nigeria who was having trouble finding a pastor for her wedding because no one would agree to her two rules: Don't speak too long and don't use my wedding to attack LGBTQ rights.

Rituals can be bubbly; they can also be soapboxes.

Those soapboxes, it turns out, extend to the bride and groom. Colonel indicated it was time to swap rings. Jeffrey took the microphone, thanked the families for completing lobola, honored his late in-laws for "giving birth to my beautiful wife," and praised God for leading them to this moment. "We're like the Israelites leaving Egypt. Today, we are in the promised land."

He then slipped a ring on her finger.

But his presentation didn't stop there. He removed a watch from his pocket and waved it at the crowd. Mike Mabunda had prepared me that Tsonga wedding toasts are not just blessings; they're also admonitions. "They're warnings of rules you have to follow." Most of those rules, notes the folklorist Rosaleen Nhlekisana, come in the form of songs directed at the bride, including one counseling her to "sweep, sweep, sweep":

> Mother-in-law is a bully, a bully of a woman
> Sweep girl, do not eat in a dirty place

Jeffrey delivered a similar warning. "This watch is set to nine, because every day I must have breakfast at nine a.m. I must have lunch at one p.m. Then I must have dinner at five. So you must always look at this watch."

Then he buckled the timepiece on her wrist to cheers of approval from the crowd.

How on earth would Lillian respond?

After claiming the microphone, she, too, thanked her family, his family, and God. "It's difficult to believe that this day has come. I would like to tell everyone how much I love you, Jeffrey, that I will look after you, and that we have already proven that we can overcome challenges." She then placed a ring on his finger.

But she also showed that she was a Tsonga bride and understood the rules of the ritual.

"You may not be the man for everyone, Jeffrey, but you are my special man. This ring is a warning as you walk around that other women shouldn't snatch you from me. And as for this gift"—she tapped her wrist—"I will make sure that you have your three meals . . . and a fourth meal at night."

The guests erupted in hoots and howls. Having been warned by her husband to stay in her place, Lillian quickly asserted her place as the wife completely in charge.

The time had come for the most Western ritual of all, the cutting of the cake.

I asked all the ritual designers I interviewed how they cultivate connection—not in an abstract way but a technical way. What steps do they take? What tricks do they use? Their answers were surprisingly simple: If you want to make people feel connected, make them feel included; if you want them to feel included, well, include them.

Emily Blake grew up in Springfield, Massachusetts, determined to be a rabbi or a doctor. "I wanted to work with women, so I became an ob-gyn." In school, she learned to perform circumcision. One day, a Black male friend approached her: "Do you know that there's a qualitative difference between Black and white circumcisions? Ours don't look as good. Can you help?"

For the next twenty years, Emily became the go-to foreskin snipper in every hospital where she worked. "It was a social justice issue," she said. One day she realized she could combine her two childhood interests and become a certified mohel. "Females have performed brises for thousands of years," she pointed out. "In Exodus, Moses's wife, Zipporah, circumcises their son."

But Emily quickly learned that, unlike hospital circumcisions, brises can be stressful—one parent might fear that the baby will be in pain; another might find the custom uncivilized; a grandparent might hate the sight of blood. Emily's solution: Give everybody a role. "Somebody gets the honor of carrying the baby, somebody gets the honor of sitting with the baby, somebody gets the honor of holding the baby."

Then she gives short remarks.

"In 90 percent of cases, the baby sleeps through the procedure. I say, 'The reason the baby isn't crying is because you're here to comfort him—and you'll be here to comfort him when he grows up so that he never experiences pain alone.' Suddenly everyone who was feeling queasy now feels a connection. The definition of a perfect bris is when the baby doesn't cry a peep but everyone else is moved to tears."

Micah Bucey was a preacher's son from Ohio who vowed never to become a preacher; today he's the senior minister at Judson Memorial Church in Greenwich Village, a storied Baptist parish beloved by New York City creatives. "I'm not the kind of priest who's going to tell you what to do; we're a priesthood of all believers. I give the same speech before every ritual: 'This is not a scripted event for your entertainment. This is audience participation—and your participation is necessary to make it a success.'"

At funerals, he asks everyone to think of a story of the deceased. At baby namings, he puts votives in an empty bowl and asks each guest to utter a wish for the baby as they pour water into the vessel until the candles are floating. At weddings, he passes the rings around the room during the vows so that each person touches them and they're still warm when the bride and groom slip them on.

"I would like to believe that anyone who leaves a celebration I'm involved in doesn't feel like they've witnessed something for somebody else; they feel like they've helped create something that allows everyone to feel a little more connected."

Ed Sheeran made an encore for the final act of Lillian and Jeffrey's wedding. The cake was about a foot tall, covered in white fondant, and wrapped in the same embroidered forest-green floral fabric that the bride and groom both wore. On top was a spray of white plastic flowers and two glittery gold entwined hearts interlaced with *Mr.* and *Mrs.*

Darling, you look perfect tonight.

Lillian removed the flowers, plucked the gold hearts, and with Jeffrey's assistance cut through the top. Instantly the entire fondant shell unfolded and plopped on the table. Undeterred, Lillian rotated what was left of the cake and took another slice, then another, and another. At this point, the entire dessert opened like a sea anemone into four equal crescents, each with six decomposing layers of yellow and chocolate, interspersed with vanilla icing.

My first thought was that the climax of the wedding was a complete disaster. The scene reminded me of my own wedding, where the cake factory burned down the week before our event and we had to make do with a shadow of Linda's vision.

But I was wrong.

Unfazed, Lillian pushed the first quadrant of cake onto a serving platter, carried the platter into the audience, and made a beeline to where the groom's lobola delegation was sitting. Lillian stopped in front of William, her new brother-in-law, and in a gesture of deference right out of a Tsonga wedding toast, extended the platter. William grinned and lifted his arms. But instead of taking the platter, as I expected, he plunged his hands into the middle of the cake and lifted a hearty serving to his mouth. One-by-one, everyone at the table did the same. The audience cheered. Lillian, for the first time all day, smiled.

What I thought had been the tragic collapse of well-coiffed imported tradition was the prelude to a triumphant local rite of connection. And it was a reminder of what those studies of children and firewalkers showed, and what my conversations with Mike Mabunda and Patricia Khoza revealed: that the purpose of this gesture was not to let them eat cake but to help them become family. Lillian understood better than anyone that what transpired that evening under the tent paled in comparison to what had happened that morning under the mango tree. She and Jeffrey may have been married by law and united by rings, but they were wed by lobola.

3.

THE TAYLOR SWIFT DIVORCE PARTY

How to Create a Ritual, Volume 1

Ritual entered its Taylor Swift era in 2019. That's the year Olivia Dreizen Howell got divorced and took inspiration from the queen of celebrating your breakups.

Olivia was born with a broken heart. "I had a congenital heart defect at birth and open-heart surgery when I was eight months old." She was also born into a broken home. "My grandparents on both sides were divorced before I was born; my parents got divorced when I was ten. I've had a hard time celebrating anything in my life because I never knew who to invite."

Surrounded by shattered relationships, Olivia was drawn to piecing things back together. "I'm very much the family historian," she said. She studied classics in college, which led her to become a Latin teacher near her hometown on Long Island, which led her to settle down, get married, and have two sons.

"I really wanted to be married young. I wanted to be a good wife and raise kids with my husband. I was educated about divorce, right?"

Her dream did not come true. At thirty-four, with a husband who traveled all the time and two young boys at home, and having quit teaching to start a mommy blog and open a social media marketing company, Olivia got divorced.

"I knew right away that I was not the same person I was when I got married, but I had no idea how to become the person I wanted to be."

On the day her husband moved out, Olivia laid out all of her remaining belongings in the living room and invited her sister over to go through them. "Everything was from our wedding registry—the sheets we slept in, the towels we bathed in. We put everything in the car and donated it. I came home and thought, *Oh my God. My husband took half my stuff; I just gave the other half away. I need a toothbrush holder that doesn't have an empty slot so that every time I walk into the bathroom I don't think, 'Wow, my marriage ended.' I need new cereal bowls. I hate his fucking big forks. Wouldn't this be a good time for a registry?*"

Olivia paused.

"And that's when this whole other story took off."

In the early hours of June 1, 1891, the Illinois Central steam engine passenger train, drenched in soot and belching smoke, pulled into Sioux Falls, South Dakota, under dark skies and pouring rain. A well-dressed woman, attended by her maid, private secretary, and dog, Tweedles, disembarked into the periwinkle depot, stepped into a horse-drawn carriage, and rode a few blocks to the legendary Cataract Hotel.

Baroness Margaret Laura Astor de Stuers, known as Maggie, was a thirty-seven-year-old descendant of John Jacob Astor, the fur trader, real estate mogul, and figurehead of Manhattan society. A member of the preeminent socialites of New York, the baroness earned her title by marrying Dutch diplomat Baron Alphonse Lambert de Stuers in an 1875 wedding whose "elegance and importance deserve to rank foremost of the many that have occurred."

The couple returned to Europe and had three children, though the independent-minded baroness increasingly found her husband cruel and demeaning, and resented his seizing control of her $80,000-a-year inheritance and million-dollar real estate portfolio; at one point he tried to institutionalize her for mental instability. Though many women of her era would have been trapped, the heiress had the means to flee, which is why in the seventeenth year of her unhappy marriage, she joined hundreds of her Gilded Age peers in making the arduous, fifteen-hundred-mile journey to this dusty outpost in the American West for the one thing that East Coast money still could not buy.

A divorce.

For as long as there have been marriages, there have been ways to end marriages. Like most life rituals, marriage was long controlled by religions, and those male-dominated institutions invariably gave greater authority to husbands than to wives. In the early days of the United States, beleaguered spouses had to petition state legislatures to end their unions. Even as courts assumed control of breakups through the nineteenth century, laws still varied by state. The rise of legal divorce gave women more power but also spurred an arms race among newer states to attract wealthy divorce seekers to their startup economies. Each decade gave birth to a different "migratory divorce" haven where deep-pocketed women could more easily secure their freedom: Ohio and Indiana in the 1850s, Illinois in the 1860s, Iowa in the 1870s.

Fed by this surge in divorce tourism, the number of divorces exploded, doubling between the 1860s and 1880s, then nearly tripling in the next twenty years. While the overall divorce rate remained low—less than 1 percent of marriages—the rate of growth alarmed many traditionalists. "Is Marriage a Failure?" one newspaper asked. In 1891, a Cornell University professor made the outlandish prediction that by 1980 more marriages would end by divorce than by death. "As it turned out," Stephanie Coontz writes in *Marriage, a History*, "he was off by only ten years!"

South Dakota, coveting its share of this growing pie, enshrined the country's most lenient divorce laws when it joined the Union in 1889. While divorce was customarily permitted only in cases of adultery or desertion, South Dakota added cruelty, alcoholism, and incompatibility. It also shrank the required residency to just ninety days. Women (and some men) flocked across the plains, turning "going to Sioux Falls" into a euphemism for seeking marital emancipation. The sorority of unmerry wives included a Vanderbilt heiress, the daughter-in-law of the Republican nominee for president, and the sister-in-law of John Wilkes Booth.

Sensing pay dirt, East Coast gossip columnists followed, staking out the lobby of the Cataract Hotel seeking scoops and surreptitious snapshots. The divorce rate in South Dakota surged 7,000 percent in the decade following statehood, the highest pace of growth in the country, earning the fortieth state the nickname "the Divorce Colony."

Maggie Astor, having spent her entire life in the spotlight, played the paparazzi like a Stradivarius. She booked a suite of four rooms on the top floor, ordered new furniture, a bigger bath, and a piano. She gave a hand-picked reporter a strategic quote: "I made up my mind to leave my husband to save myself." And on the evening of Thursday, September 3, ninety-four days after taking up residency and late enough to miss the deadline for the morning papers back east, Baroness Margaret de Stuers, with the counsel of her lawyer, W. H. "Cap" Stoddard, and her private secretary, William Elliott, filed for divorce.

Only by that time, the press had sniffed out that Mr. Elliott was not exactly her secretary.

Olivia Dreizen Howell opened Fresh Starts Registry in August 2021. The "world's first divorce registry" offered curated collections of basics for every room—kitchen, bedroom, kid's room, home office—as well as a few for non-rooms—the "vacay bundle," "move-in bundle," "first-time-dog-owner bundle." Nearly fifty collections were listed for sale on the Fresh Starts Amazon storefront, at prices ranging from $99 to $500, or clients could assemble their own personalized lists.

"We don't call items in our registry 'gifts,'" Olivia said. "We call them 'support.' They are physical manifestations of the support you can give somebody."

Naming was only the first problem she faced. Her next problem: Clients were too ashamed to ask for help, so Olivia posted examples of divorce announcements (*We are dissolving our marriage but not our respect for each other*) and three possible scripts to email friends:

> AS YOU KNOW I'VE BEEN GOING THROUGH SOME BIG CHANGES, AND YOU HAVE BEEN SO WONDERFULLY SUPPORTIVE. YOU WERE ASKING HOW YOU CAN HELP, SO I PUT TOGETHER A LIST OF SOME THINGS I REALLY NEED THAT WILL MAKE ME FEEL SUPPORTED, LOVED AND RALLIED AROUND.

The site also listed sixty different categories of professional service providers: *Stop your Google-overwhelm and browse the expert guide to search for your new hype-team.* The alphabetical list of examples includes accountability coaches, astrologers, body confidence coaches, breathwork facilitators, divorce doulas, healers, lawyers, mediators, menopause coaches, mortgage lenders, reinvention coaches, sex coaches, trauma coaches, and virtual assistants. The biggest single category: therapists.

"We are the first place that does this work with a forward-thinking mindset," Olivia said. "We are not about being bitter or dissing your ex. We are about changing the narrative around divorce so there is no shame or moral judgment. There is only, *This is just another life transition that we will get through with the help of those around us.*"

The press lapped up the story. Olivia and her sister, Genevieve, who joined the company following her own failed engagement, were featured in *The New York Times*, *The Washington Post*, *The Wall Street Journal*, *New York* magazine, and on *Today*. The *New York Post* headline captured the spirit of the coverage: "Divorce Registries Help People 'Getting the S—t Kicked out of Them.'"

It turns out a lot of people fit that description. Fresh Starts Registry soon garnered seventy thousand monthly visitors, which, considering that there are around seven hundred thousand divorces a year in the United States, is remarkable market penetration.

"I'm actually very pro-marriage," Olivia said. "And I'm very pro-love. I'm like a Pisces–romantic comedy girl at heart. But I'm also pro *It's okay to leave.* I'm pro *Divorce is not a bad thing.* I'm pro *Finding your joy in life and remembering that you were not born to wear a wedding ring.* You can be upset that your marriage didn't work and fucking happy that your marriage is over."

But for all the early success that Fresh Starts enjoyed, Olivia had the nagging sense that something was missing. She needed a way to move beyond all the practical problems that divorced people face—the hiring of lawyers and replacing of toothbrush holders—to address their underlying malaise and untapped happiness. She needed a recipe to help them turn their moment of vulnerability into an occasion for celebration.

She needed a ritual.

If Baroness de Stuers had any delusions that in getting a million-dollar divorce on the banks of the Big Sioux River she could avoid the rabid glare of a growing global press, she was quickly disabused. Staggering forces lined up against her.

The first was Bishop William Hobart Hare, a mutton-chopped Philadelphia transplant and Episcopal heavyweight who was known as the Apostle of the West. "There is no man in Dakota who will not take off his hat to Bishop Hare," locals swooned. Prominent Easterners poured money into his efforts to aid the Sioux and educate girls, including the baroness's uncle John Jacob Astor, who donated $25,000. Hare, a savvy fundraiser, would normally have been thrilled that someone as deep-pocketed as Maggie Astor started frequenting his pews in Sioux Falls.

Only he detested divorce—a trend he called "lamentable," "lax," and a stain on "human conscience." As Hare wrote to his daughter-in-law Rebecca that July upon returning home from a mission to Japan to find the besmirched baroness the talk of the town, "The scandalous divorce mill which is running at Sioux Falls, with revelations of the silliness and wickedness of men and women, has made my return home a very gloomy one. I despise people who trifle with marriage relations so intensely that the *moral* nausea produces nausea of the *stomach*."

He vowed to use his considerable influence to force the state to overturn its permissive divorce laws.

The second force lined up against Astor was her own family. The fear of being tarnished by divorce was still so strong that when the trial of the baron and baroness finally got underway in January 1892, two of Maggie's brothers, Arthur and Harry, submitted testimony against her. "As to the baron's treatment of my sister," her younger brother Arthur swore in an affidavit, "I should say that he never treated his wife in a cruel or inhuman way. He was intentionally kind and considerate."

But by far the biggest attack on the baroness came from her husband, who directly accused her of adultery. "For the sake of the good name borne by me and my children," the baron fumed in a seventy-page statement read aloud in court, he tried to ignore the rumors of his wife's infidelity, but once he was compelled to investigate the matter by her filing, he found conclusive evidence that she was living in "an open state of adulterous intercourse." The smoking gun: a registration at the Caledonian Hotel in London the prior February under the name "Mr. and Mrs. William Elliott."

Onlookers in the courtroom gasped. Mr. Elliott was sitting alongside them.

In many ways the story of the De Stuerses would be a small, tawdry sidebar. What makes it relevant to the history of ritual, especially in the fraught moment we're in today, is that it brings into focus the complex interplay that makes forfeiting old rituals and embracing new ones so tricky to pull off.

Ever since the dawn of civilization, the most powerful groups in society—tribes, clans, religions, nations—have tried to control human mating. Modernity unleashed varied threats to that control, from increased economic opportunity for women to decreased moral authority of religion. One underappreciated factor in the rise of divorce was longevity. As people lived longer, forcing them to stay in unhappy marriages became harder. In 1700, the median age of death in England was thirty-two; a century later it was forty-four; a century after that it was fifty-eight. As a result, the average length of marriage doubled from around seventeen years in premodern Europe to thirty-five years in 1900. Figuring out how to end marriages without ripping apart society went from an irrelevancy to an essential task.

That challenge pitted some of society's most entrenched elements—lawmakers, clerics, patriarchs—against some of its fastest growing and most clamorous for change—youth, nonbelievers, women. In the winter of 1892, that clash pitted Baron de Stuers, Bishop Hale, and the House of Astor against Baroness Maggie Astor de Stuers, who just before 9:30 a.m. on the second Monday of February climbed to the second floor of the Minnehaha County Courthouse in Sioux Falls, stepped into the elevated, waist-high witness dock, and quietly took her seat.

Olivia Dreizen Howell also faced pushback for her divorce. "Even my own grandmother looked at me and said, 'What happened in your marriage?' I was like, 'You were divorced twice. Why are you asking?'" Olivia's own lawyer questioned her decision to treat signing her divorce papers as a festive event. "My dad and sister came; we took photos. 'I've never seen anyone do that before,' the lawyer said."

But Olivia viewed the occasion as liberation. That night she hosted a party and gave every guest a playlist of breakup songs called *Olivia's Virtual Divorce Dance Party*. The rundown included "I Will Survive" by Gloria Gaynor, "Don't Stop Me Now" by Queen, "You Oughta Know" by Alanis Morissette, "Light of a Clear Blue Morning" by Dolly Parton, and "Bridge over Troubled Water" by Simon and Garfunkel.

Putting together that celebratory gathering helped her realize that everyone should be encouraged to do the same. Olivia made a blog post on Fresh Starts Registry: "10 Reasons to Celebrate with a Divorce Party," with entries on embracing liberation, sparking joy, honoring closure, and cultivating gratitude. Then she released her coup de grace, Shake It Off: Hosting a Taylor Swift Themed Divorce Party. "Taylor Swift's music resonates with themes of resilience, self-discovery, and empowerment," she wrote, "making it the perfect inspiration for a celebration of newfound independence." The planner included "Shake It Off" cocktail mixers, "Blank Space" cupcakes, and "Love Story" cake pops. "Raise a toast with 'Red' sangria," and curate an empowering playlist with "We Are Never Ever Getting Back Together," "Mean," and "22." The post drew so much traffic that Olivia created additional prototypes for Beyoncé and Kelly Clarkson, along with a guide to designing your "own symbol of self-love: the divorce ring."

Olivia's timing was perfect. Breakup albums have long been a staple of pop culture (Joni Mitchell's *Blue*, Fleetwood Mac's *Rumours*), as have breakup books (*Heartburn*; *Eat, Pray, Love*), and breakup films (*The Graduate*, *Legally Blonde*). But by the 2020s, what had been an occasional side dish became a 24/7 feast, fed in large measure by the biggest pop star in the world building a multibillion-dollar brand on the back of her oft-broken heart.

Podcasts swelled with names like *Divorced and Happy*, *Divorced Girl Smiling*, *Divorce Goddess*. Pinterest brimmed with "Best Divorce Party Games!," "Breakup Bingo," "He Was a Dick" napkins, "We Never Liked Him Anyway" streamers, and "Your Vagina Deserves Better" banners. Etsy overflowed with "Smells like life without a narcissist" candles, "With every ounce of my being, I HOPE HIS DICK FALLS OFF" note cards, "Adios Loser" cake toppers, "HOT EX-WIFE #DivorcedAF" halter tops, "I do. I did. I'm done." T-shirts, and "Thank U Next" rose gold foil balloons.

I asked Olivia what explains this outpouring.

"Women got online," she said. "Millennials were born; we grew up, logged into AOL chat rooms and later Facebook groups, and started talking to one another about what was happening behind closed doors.

Suddenly we gained insight into stuff that had always gone on but that no one had spoken about publicly.

"That's exactly what happened to me," she continued. "I started posting things like, 'My husband's doing this' or 'Is it normal that my husband's doing that?' Other women responded, 'No, it's not normal!' or 'My husband's doing the same thing!' Then women our mothers' age chimed in: 'Actually, my marriage has never been that good.' We began bonding and connecting, working through our shame and self-loathing, until we turned our vulnerability into empowerment and self-love."

Then those women did something even more emblematic: They converted their passion into profit.

"Women have always done this kind of work," Olivia said. "Yentas, doulas, wedding planners, corpse washers. We've always helped people through life changes. We just weren't paid for it.

"The difference today," she continued, "is that we've realized that not only can we charge for this work, we can also change the world along the way. People like to call me a divorce vigilante, but I'm not here to celebrate your broken heart, I'm here to celebrate your following your heart. Every new ending can be a new beginning in disguise."

Led by her lawyer, Cap Stoddard, Baroness de Stuers carefully described her husband's malice to the court. "He was very unkind to me. He would scold me before people. He said I was 'a savage American' and a 'baby'." She told of public humiliations, physical assaults, and an incident in which he beat her in public with a parasol. "You might frighten your Dutch women that way, but you can't thus scare an American."

The cross-examination was equally intense. "When did you come to Sioux Falls?" the baron's lawyer, Joseph Lawrence Glober, asked.

"Who came with you?" Glober accused the baroness of disinterest toward her children, then he pounced on her travel companion for the last year and a half. "Who is William Elliott, and what is your relationship with him?"

Judge Frank Aikens quickly interjected. "This case closes on June 13, 1890," he declared, referring to the date when the baroness fled her marriage. Glover threw one last haymaker: "Isn't it true that if you get a divorce, you intend to marry Mr. Elliott?" But the judge cut him off.

Sitting in the witness stands, Maggie Astor laughed.

One month later, on March 5, Judge Aikens issued his decision: an absolute divorce. Unlike many of her peers, who threw over-the-top, black-tie divorce celebrations in the Cataract Hotel, featuring French champagne and Russian caviar, Maggie Astor was more discreet.

Two days after she was declared a free woman, the ex-baroness once more climbed to the second floor of the Minnehaha County Courthouse, submitted an application to the clerk of the courts, attested to being "single and unmarried," and received a license to wed the man who stood by her side; not William Elliott, as he had pretended to be, but William Elliott Morris Zborowski, a New Jersey–born heir, equestrian, and race car driver, as well as a self-proclaimed Polish count.

Countess Maggie Zborowski didn't need to throw a divorce party in Sioux City; she threw a wedding party instead.

As for the other figures involved, Bishop Hare was a short-term loser. He complained to Rebecca, "One of the Astor family, after cultivating our church in Sioux Falls and playing the role of an injured woman, has turned a disgusting somersault" by instantly marrying her secretary, "one Elliott Zborowski, or some name of that kind!" Hare promptly canceled an order for $1,000 stained glass windows that the baroness had paid for.

But Hare was a medium-term winner. In response to his anti-divorce campaign, South Dakota lengthened its residency requirement to six months in 1893, then to one year in 1908, effectively ending the divorce colony just as divorce was becoming more widely accepted across the country.

The count and countess followed the inverse path. They were short-term winners, shuttling among European capitals. They had a son, Martin, who died in infancy, then another boy, Louis. But Elliott was killed racing a Mercedes in 1903 at forty-five, when Louis was eight, and the countess died eight years later. Sixteen-year-old Louis inherited his mother's money, £11 million, or $1.5 billion today, along with his father's love of racing. He, too, was killed racing, in his case in the Italian Grand Prix at twenty-nine. Newspapers called it the Zborowski curse, as did Bishop Hare.

Louis Zborowski's greatest legacy, however, was building a series of "flying cars" that he called Chitty Bang Bangs. Those quixotic inventions inspired the children's novel *Chitty Chitty Bang Bang*, by James Bond creator Ian Fleming, which in turn inspired the film starring Dick Van Dyke. Producers built six winged cars for filming, one of which was bought by Michael Jackson, another by *The Lord of the Rings* director Peter Jackson, and another by a BBC radio host, who used it to shuttle guests to weddings and other celebrations.

One of those guests was Camilla Parker Bowles, the onetime mistress of Prince Charles. That unlikely coincidence means that the most famous divorce of the nineteenth century was connected to the most famous divorce of the twentieth century by one degree of, well, separation.

After the Church of England finally permitted divorced members to remarry in 2002, the Prince of Wales married the Duchess of Cornwall in a wedding that included the admonition printed on invitations: *There Will Be No Wedding List.* The future king and queen would not be using a divorce registry, a wedding registry, or any registry whatsoever. When pressed for a reason, Buckingham Palace explained that when Prince Charles married Lady Diana in the "wedding of the century," they received more than six thousand unwanted gifts, all of which had to be given away or burned, including two of the items that inspired Olivia Dreizen Howell to start Fresh Starts Registry, matching his-and-hers toothbrushes.

"There was happiness because of you," as Taylor Swift sang in one of her breakup anthems, "there'll be happiness after you." Today there are rituals for both.

4.

SKIN IN THE GAME

Coming of Age in Bali

Few things sharpen the mind more than a sharp object plunging directly toward your face. For Gita Bima, a sixteen-year-old Balinese girl lying on an elevated bed in a white lace shirt, a yellow sarong, and a shimmering, sun-shaped crown decorated with dangling gold coins and a single red rose, that sharp object was a six-inch steel chisel headed straight toward her smile.

Only, at the moment, she was hardly smiling.

The sun had just crested on a humid summer afternoon in the village of Banjar on the northern coast of Bali, the jewel in an archipelago of 17,504 islands that make up Indonesia, the fourth most populous country in the world. The Land of a Thousand Temples is also a global hub for ritual. Bali is a "theatre state," wrote the legendary American anthropologist Clifford Geertz, governed by rituals more than by force. The Balinese do not specialize in tyranny, conquest, or effective administration, he added, but in the sensuous panoply of spectacle, "a lexicon of carvings, flowers, dances, melodies, gestures, chants, ornaments, temples, postures, and masks."

Those rituals cover almost every minute of daily life, with ceremonies for sunrise, midday, and sunset; honoring ancestors, gods, and nature; starting your car, riding your bicycle, and taking a walk; getting pregnant, going into labor, and giving birth; the first time your baby touches the ground (105 days), the first time your baby hears their name (210 days), and the first time your baby gets a haircut (365 days).

But no ritual is more treasured—or more feared—than matatah, the millennium-old custom of manually grinding down an adolescent's front teeth to rebalance their character, curb their impulses, and ease their transition into adulthood. All of which helps explain why Gita, upon catching sight of the glint of steel slicing downward toward her mouth, widened her eyes to the size of her crown, gripped the trembling hands of her mother, and let out a plaintive yelp.

Then she heard the clang of the hammer as it drove the blade into her incisor.

Black Elk, the famed Oglala Lakota medicine man, was galloping across the Great Plains in 1868 at age five, when he was visited by two spirits: *Behold, a sacred voice is calling you.* Those spirits returned when the boy was nine, now taller and able to shoot prairie chickens and rabbits.

Hurry! Come! Your grandfathers are calling you.

Black Elk follows the spirits into "a great white plain with snow hills and mountains," where he is surrounded by twelve black horses with "necklaces of bison hoofs," twelve white horses with "manes flowing like a blizzard," twelve sorrel horses with "necklaces of elk's teeth," and twelve buckskins with "horns above their heads." A rainbow directs the boy to a tepee, where his grandfathers are having a council. Black Elk receives a wooden cup, a bow and arrow, and a red stick, along with a message: *On earth a nation you shall make live.*

The grandfathers dispatch the boy on a mission. He leads the forty horses toward the "daybreak star," across a "fearful road," beyond "hills and valleys and creeks and rivers," until the entourage arrives at a sacred spot, where Black Elk thrusts the red stick into the earth and declares the land the home of his people. Thunder claps, rainbows flare, a day of happiness breaks out.

"He has triumphed!" the grandfathers cheer.

"I never felt nearer to the earth," the boy declares.

But Black Elk, who would grow up to fight alongside his cousin Crazy Horse at the Battle of Little Bighorn and survive the massacre at Wounded Knee, also doubts his destiny. "When the singing stopped, I was lonely," he confesses. "I walked very fast, because I was homesick."

This account from the landmark memoir *Black Elk Speaks* is considered a classic of the second genre of life ritual, often called "coming-of-age," "initiation," or "puberty." In classical anthropology, these rituals were the archetype for all rituals. Van Gennep devotes more time in *Rites of Passage* to "social puberty" rites than any other, and these rituals are responsible for his model of separation, liminality, and integration. The appeal for scholars is obvious: Some of the most memorable life rituals ever cataloged commemorate the transition to adulthood.

The Wiradjuri in Australia would send masked men to seize pubescent boys, cover them in branches, deprive them of sleep, and force them to drink water through a reed; the Zulu in South Africa would isolate marriage-age girls, have them slaughter a cow, wear fat from its guts, and then perform a ceremonial spear dance; the Gisu in Uganda would smear boys with agents of transformation, including yeast and chyme, the half-digested contents of animals' stomachs. Some of the most well-known contemporary life rituals are connected to puberty, from confirmations to quinceañeras, bar mitzvahs to vision quests.

For better or worse, a century and a half after scholars first elevated the idea of life rituals, celebrations of adolescence retain their grip as *what life rituals should look like.*

But this romanticization has problems. For starters, "coming-of-age" rituals for teenagers aren't all that common. In the 1960s, a rigorous cross-cultural analysis by the American anthropologist Yehudi Cohen found that only 28 percent of traditional societies held life rituals for adolescent males, and 10 percent for females. Subsequent studies have shown similar or smaller percentages.

Even more problematic, what these life rituals do commemorate—periods of awakening, evolving, emerging—happen not just in adolescence but across our lifespans. Black Elk was nine when he was sent on his mission, twelve when he fought at Little Bighorn, twenty-six when he became a worldwide celebrity. I was ten when I discovered my love of storytelling, twenty-three when I quit my job to chase my dream of becoming a writer, forty when I got my ultimate job, being a dad. Linda was twenty-eight when she became an entrepreneur, thirty-six when she became a mother, forty-eight when she split with her co-founder and became the leader she was destined to be. All these experiences were signature milestones of the real purpose of the second life ritual.

Becoming.

Becoming rituals mark defining moments of personal transformation, when we become new versions of ourselves and begin to relate to the communities around us in more complex and meaningful ways. And they happen at any age—not just teen age. Take a second and plot out the major turning points of your life—sure, any number might have occurred between twelve and twenty, a time of enormous change; but a far greater number happened before or after. Rituals of becoming have become a never-ending need.

Ronald Grimes, the editor of the Oxford Ritual Studies series, argues that we should recognize the personal growth rituals taking place all around us under different names: promotion, conversion, orientation, transition. The explosion of modern rituals has only increased this number, with celebrations for starting a company, going vegan, getting sober, taking a gap year, onboarding, intention setting, progress pinning. Given that everyone from employers to brands has adopted the language of personal growth these days—*Where are you on your fitness journey? Your career journey? Your spiritual journey?*—it seems safe to say that we may actually go through *more* becoming rituals today than our preindustrial ancestors.

This turnabout demands that rather than whine about the loss of some mythical adolescent rite of passage, a complaint that goes back decades, the time has come to turn the page on the hackneyed idea that every celebration of personal transformation needs to involve months in the wilderness, having your body mutilated and your psyche traumatized, all while the rest of the community sips coconut water and nibbles roasted goat. Instead, we should be asking a different question: What can we learn from successful becoming rituals across time and space that might help us improve becoming rituals of today?

The answer to that question is one of the more surprising things I learned and the second rule of contemporary life rituals: They have stakes. There's a direct correlation between how much time, effort, and emotional resources we invest in life rituals and how much growth, insight, and meaning we extract. Each of us must assume some risk, take the leap, put something on the line.

We must have skin in the game.

Matatah also begins with skincare. It was just after nine on Sunday morning when I arrived in the village of Banjar, a hamlet tucked into the rolling hills and terraced rice fields overlooking the Bali Sea, for the daylong tooth-filing ritual. A makeshift beauty salon had been set up outside the village temple, where a half dozen stylists were brushing on makeup, clipping on earrings, and tucking in tiaras. A sign on the wall read SUKA DUKA.

"It means 'happy-sad,'" explained Gita, who was texting her boyfriend while a stylist applied passion-rose lipstick. "Whether we're happy or unhappy, the only way to get through this is together."

I asked how she was feeling.

"Maybe a little nervous."

Then she turned back to her phone.

The Temple of Inner Strength occupies a crowded acre in the heart of Banjar. While 87 percent of Indonesia's nearly three hundred million people are Muslim, in Bali those figures are reversed: 87 percent of the island's five million people are Balinese Hindus. A distinct branch of the Indo-Asian faith, Balinese Hinduism gives more weight to local deities and traditions. The central goal is creating harmony—among humans and nature, humans and gods, humans and one another.

The temple was guarded by two ten-foot-tall bamboo goddesses adorned with white masks, sundial headdresses, marigolds, and orchids. Inside was a city unto itself, with performance spaces, living quarters, and food stalls. At the center was a warren of moss-covered pagodas, teak gates, and lava sculptures, topped with golden umbrellas and draped in colorful silks like Christo and Jeanne-Claude used to wrap monuments around the world. The scene felt like a cross between a cemetery and a bazaar, vibrating with Bali's signature rainbow of papaya orange, dragon fruit pink, and mango yellow.

Just before ten, the initiands gathered in the central corridor. They were thirty-one in all, slightly more females than males, struggling to form a line while checking their makeup and snapping selfies. The entire cohort was dressed so ornately that they could have been cardinals entering the Sistine Chapel for a conclave.

But one thing surprised me: They weren't all young. About a third were adolescents like Gita, but a third were young adults, and a third were men and women in their sixties and seventies. By tradition, tooth filing is for adolescents, but like much of ritual today, the reality is more fluid.

Named after the Balinese word for *chisel*, matatah is the ceremonial act of shaving down and smoothing over an individual's twelve front teeth: six on the top, six on the bottom. The ritual has three functions: tempering a person's bestial qualities, since the fang-like canines are considered animalistic; warding off the "six enemies"—lust, greed, anger, intoxication, confusion, and jealousy; and lessening a person's unattractiveness. Matatah is one of the few life rituals, writes the Indonesian anthropologist Fred Eiseman, that "every Balinese Hindu absolutely must have performed to insure an orderly transition of his or her spirit from birth to death and later reincarnation."

Still, the expertise required to perform the ceremony and the expense demanded to put on the celebration mean that most families cannot afford to host a tooth filing. As a result, families band together or piggyback on wealthier clans. Bali's other life rituals follow a similar playbook. The "stupendous" weddings, cremations, and tooth filings, writes Geertz, are not the means to political ends but the ends themselves. "Power serves pomp," not the other way around.

Today was a perfect example. A gong tolled, and the ceremony began. A voice chanted over the raspy PA system as the initiands strolled in single file to the end of the corridor and laid small baskets of saffron rice, banana leaves, and diced meat on a straw mat. An elderly priest in a white tunic waved a chalice of incense. Smoke filled the courtyard, making the morning light streaming through the thatched roof appear like rays of revelation you might see on the cover of a holy book.

O Divine Essence, we call upon your presence to purify this place. May you accept our offerings with grace.

After the spiritual cleansing, the initiands and scores of well-

Figure 6: Initiands pray before having their teeth filed in Banjar, Bali.

wishers walked the few steps to an open-sided pavilion festooned with golden curtains. Two dozen boys in white T-shirts and black headbands serenaded the crowd with a gamelan of hand drums, bowls, and wooden metallophones. A priest made his way along the supplicants, washing their hands, ladling out sips of water, and pressing grains of moist rice onto their foreheads and into their hair. Each participant was given a coin to place under their pillow during the filing.

O Almighty Spirit, may these coins bring forth blessings of prosperity, peace, and harmony.

Another gong sounded. The initiands rose and stepped in unison toward the row of platform beds. Instantly, their smiles disappeared.

Day Schildkret had two becoming rituals in his adolescence—one left no impact; the other changed his life. The difference, he said: One was a matter of life and death.

As a boy growing up on Long Island, Day didn't care about religion but loved running outside in the rain to return displaced earthworms to their holes, which he decorated with berries and petals. His bar mitzvah was bland and forgettable. "It was supposed to end my childhood, but there was no real risk. What's the threat of failure: You forget a word?"

Seven years later Day was living in Jerusalem, studying theater, when he was almost killed in a bus bombing. "I was supposed to be heading to school, but decided to sleep in. Terrorists blew up my bus stop. If I had gone to class, I would have been dead."

He decided it was a sign to face his deepest shame.

"I was directing a musical at the time, and the lead actor and I took a walk to an outdoor amphitheater where Albert Einstein used to give lectures. I knew my friend had recently come out of the closet. I all but forced him to ask about my sexuality."

Day considers what happened next to be his defining life ritual.

"Almost dying forced me to confront the issue that had almost killed me. Coming out of the closet doesn't carry the same severity today, but to me the threat of death was real."

Day returned to New York and became a theater artist. When his father died a decade later at the same time as a relationship ended, Day knew what he needed to do: return to ritual. He started going to the park every day, collecting sticks, stones, pine cones, and berries, and arranging them into devotional artworks that he called morning altars. After posting photos of these works on social media, he heard from people around the world who felt inspired to do the same. Day soon became something new in the long history of ritual: a ritual influencer, with a hundred thousand followers, two books, and a yearlong certification process in ritual design.

"What connects losing a loved one to having a baby to just being alive is that we fear change," Day said. "We suffer from a brokenness that is really a kind of grief or loss. What I learned in Jerusalem—and later making impermanent art every morning—is that ritual is about rearranging the dead parts of our lives into beautiful creations. It's about finding wonder in the face of death."

The idea that a meaningful life ritual requires momentous, even existential stakes at first struck me as a bridge too far. While I appreciate the inherent gravity of having a child or losing a loved one, sometimes a wedding is just a wedding, right? But the deeper I plunged into this world, the more I changed my mind.

Research going back half a century shows that how much people suffer for an experience correlates with how much they value that experience. Scholars call this tendency the "ritual learning process." As Ronald Grimes puts it, "Ritual knowledge is rendered unforgettable only if it makes serious demands on individuals and communities."

Going through shared stress creates shared meaning.

Becoming rituals for adolescents are renowned for creating extreme physical stress—exposing, fighting, flogging, burning. Becoming rituals for adults also generate extreme physical stress—scarring, branding, fasting, purging. Other life rituals, too, are steeped in the language of physicality, from pushing to catching, hitching to crossing, lifting to laboring.

Oxford University's Harvey Whitehouse argues that the "extreme dysphoria" of life rituals—intense, unpleasant, anxiety-producing experiences—is central to their success. He and a colleague identified 645 rituals in seventy-four cultures. While everyday rituals scored lower on metrics of pain, fear, and agitation, periodic rituals like those used to mark life transitions scored higher. "Dysphoria is more important than euphoria" in generating feelings of community, they note. More pain for the individual means more gain for the group.

What would explain this positive impact of otherwise negative emotions?

Stakes contribute to memories. Life rituals brim with extremes—

bright lights, blaring music, goose bumps, tears. All these amped-up stimuli send increasingly urgent messages to our brains to amp up memory creation, in the process etching the experiences more deeply into our consciousness.

Stakes also contribute to attachment. Elliot Aronson of Stanford University tested the proposition that the more challenging the ritual the more people appreciate it. In an iconic study, he invited three sets of women to join a discussion group about sex. Members of the first set had to pass an "embarrassment test" in which they read aloud highly explicit material; members of the second read only mildly sexual content; members of the third had no initiation. The group conversation that followed was specifically designed to be "one of the most worthless and uninteresting discussions imaginable." Still, those in the first set loved it! Subjects who underwent a severe initiation perceived participating in the group "as being significantly more attractive than did those who underwent a mild initiation or no initiation."

The more you invest in a group, the more you value the group.

Finally, stakes contribute to communal pride. When our daughters were approaching their bat mitzvah, I originally wanted to opt out of a conventional ceremony, which, as Day found, often leads to bland, forgettable experiences. "Let's do something more original," I said. "Visit their grandparents' birthplaces! Read Torah in the desert!" Linda quickly shut down my idea. Our girls were on the shy side, she pointed out; for them, standing in front of their community, chanting Torah in Hebrew, and offering their own interpretations of Abraham going forth to the promised land would be a demanding but rewarding ordeal.

Though we didn't know it at the time, Linda was giving voice to a rich vein of research on the benefits of public declarations of belonging. Through a process known as costly signaling, participants use effortful rituals to communicate their commitment to the larger group. While some of the "costs" of rituals are financial, like food and drink, others are physical, like removing a finger or getting a tattoo; still more are emotional, like making yourself vulnerable or performing in public. Merely asserting your commitment to the group is "cheap and can easily be faked," writes Xygalatas, the firewalking expert, "but engaging in costly rituals is expensive and hard to fake."

The more sacrifices a life ritual demands, the more rewards in group attachment it delivers.

Two women and one man were the first to climb onto the beds; they were the most senior of the group, and the ritual would proceed from oldest to youngest. The three beds were just under three feet tall, with cushioned orange tops, orange-and-gold bed skirts, and orange pillows. The left side of each bed had a privacy screen made from multicolored sarongs.

At the head of each bed stood a sangging, the specialist who would conduct the ceremony. Dressed in priestly white, with headcloths knotted in front and namaste pendants, these holy men wore blue surgical masks and rings on every finger with bulging pieces of onyx, jade, or amethyst. Each sangging was flanked by a small table holding a brass bowl filled with water, a hammer, a chisel, and four files. There was no sterilization.

A stately woman climbed onto the middle bed, prayed, tucked her coin underneath the pillow, then lay on her back with her arms crossed corpse-like over her chest. At least twenty women scrummed around her, washing her feet, wrapping her in prayer shawls, tucking and fussing with her finery as if trussing a holiday fowl. The musicians resumed their clanging; the chanters began a liturgy.

The sangging took out a small cylinder of sugarcane and wedged it between the woman's top and bottom teeth, both to keep her mouth

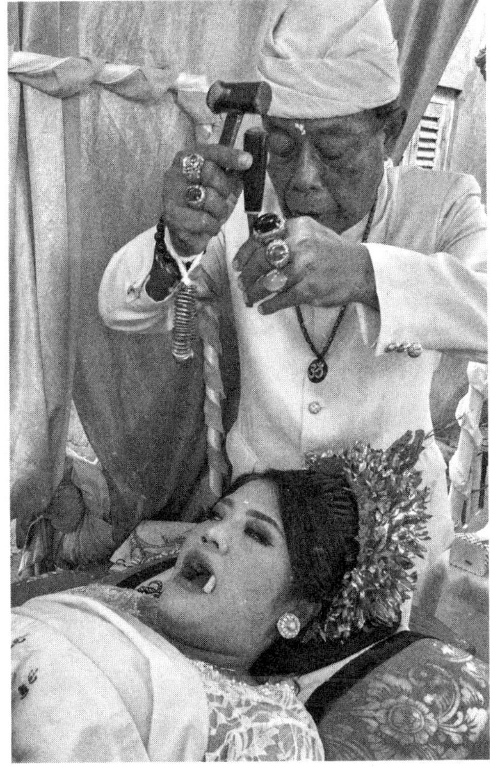

Figure 7: A sangging raises a file over the mouth of a woman, who has a cylinder of sugar cane between her teeth.

open and provide a sweet distraction. He lifted the hammer and chisel heavenward, placed the blade against her right canine, then smartly rapped the handle. The grating of iron on enamel sounded like fingernails on a chalkboard. The woman winced but remained stoic. He then proceeded methodically across her six top teeth, followed by her six lowers. When he turned to replace the instrument, the ladies pulled the woman into a seated position, gave her a cup of water, which she sipped through a straw, swished, and spat into a decapitated coconut. Then they laid her back down.

The four files came next. The first was designed to grind down the sharp edges of greed and lust. Unlike the chisel, which involved a vertical chipping away, the filing involved a horizontal scraping and scuffing. The sangging raked his arms back and forth aggressively. With each successive file—for anger and intoxication; confusion; then jealousy—the handiwork became more refined. After each filing, the ladies would lift the woman to swirl and discharge. In the final step, the sangging used his black onyx ring to polish off the bottoms of each tooth, thereby restoring harmony to the mouth and balance to the soul.

In almost every way imaginable, the matatah seemed like a quintessentially Balinese ritual—the joyful if jarring cycle of scrape, sand, rinse, and spit; the luminous theatricality of gongs, garlands, prayer beads, and parasols. But what I thought was the most Balinese feature of all—the fixation on teeth—turns out not to be unique at all.

Rituals of dental modification go back to the early Bronze Age and were popular in the ancient world among Egyptians, Etruscans, and Aztecs; in Africa among Ethiopians, Tanzanians, and Angolans; and in Asia among Malaysians, Filipinos, and Vietnamese. Popular practices include inlaying, lacquering, staining; and lip plates, tongue piercings, and palate implants. Part of this preoccupation with orality is appearance, part is health. A study of ritual practice among early Mayans by a team from the National Polytechnic Institute in Mexico found that the act of inlaying gems into artificially drilled cavities increased hygiene and reduced disease.

But as Freud would have appreciated, part of this obsession with orality reflects the larger cultural obsession with controlling the body. Like eyes, ears, and genitalia, teeth exist at the intersection of survival, beauty, and sex. And lest you think Western society has outgrown this infatuation, a partial list of contemporary becoming rituals that exploit the same terrain includes summoning a tooth fairy to exchange currency for baby teeth; clamping stainless steel bars around the adult teeth of adolescents at exactly the moment they're most self-conscious about their appearance; gemming teeth of grown-ups with diamonds, opals, mother-of-pearl, aquamarine, cubic zirconia, even specks of meteorite that provide "out-of-this-world appeal." Teeth-whitening bridal showers "will keep you and your bridesmaids glowing from the inside out."

All of this ritualized dental enhancement is not without controversy, of course. Grills, a type of tooth jewelry that grew out of Southern hip-hop and is used to convey higher social status (Justin Bieber wore a $25,000 lavender-diamond-encrusted grill to his wedding), are considered so culturally specific that practitioners have scolded outsiders for appropriation, even though their own marketing highlights four-thousand-year-old Bronze Age skulls with similar decorations, a custom they had no problem appropriating.

What swirls around comes around.

And swirling is exactly what the filing pavilion felt like. With the work complete, the woman was again pulled upright, given water, and for the first time handed a small mirror. Peering into her mouth, she seemed unsure how to react. Like Black Elk, she was proud but also a bit homesick, perhaps. Was the rattling of her brain commensurate with the alteration of her mouth?

After gritting her teeth, scrunching her lips to either side, then running her tongue over her bite, she finally burst into a smile. The attending ladies smiled, too, large, toothy, extravagant smiles that seemed less about the moment and more about the grander momentousness of the occasion—a small, imperceptible win for upholding tradition and fending off the growing threat of forgetting where you came from.

Tooth filing, I sensed, is less about shaving off enamel and more about staving off erasure.

The most successful ritual designers understand the importance of stakes. They don't just identify the risks; they underscore them, elevate them, make them central to the enterprise. Sure, they traffic in bright, shiny objects, but they force everyone to confront the low, simmering boil.

Sometimes the stakes of the ritual are physical. Joe Karetak was born three hundred miles south of the Arctic Circle in a largely uninhabited stretch of ice called Polar Bear Alley. "We lived in Eskimo Point, a hamlet on the western edge of Hudson Bay," he said. When Joe was ten, his father, a constable in the Royal Canadian Mounted Police, was teaching him how to hunt. "One day we were in a canvas canoe with a twenty-horsepower engine. 'Anytime you see a seal, shoot,' my father said. A seal came up pretty far away. My father revved the engine and headed that way; I aimed for its head . . . and shot."

By the time they arrived, the spot had iced over, and the seal was gone.

"I think I got him," Joe said.

"Nah, you were too far," his father replied.

"Would the seal float?"

"Yeah, they're fat this time of year."

"Would it look like that hump of ice?"

Joe and his father pulled the carcass into the boat, then drove home silently.

"Three hundred people lived in Eskimo Point at that time. I was so excited to eat the seal and be the hero. But Father cut it up and shared it with everyone else. I didn't get a bite. The lesson of the ritual was humility."

Joe went on to work in commercial fishing and to watch his culture erode. But in 1989, as part of the same wave of recognition of Indigenous culture that elevated ho'oponopono in Hawaii, Eskimo Point was renamed Arviat, the "place of the bowhead whale"; the region was rebranded Inuit territory of Nunavut; and Joe was hired to design a survival ritual for young people.

"The first thing I teach is respect for nature—you can die out here fast. You must never be cross with the weather, because it might get cross with you."

The second thing is noticing. "You have to scan the surroundings every five minutes, because animals with four legs are usually faster than we are. You can't outrun danger; you have to outsmart it."

The last thing is, know your snow. "To build an igloo, you need snow that's not too hard but not too soft. The base is the most important part. It must be secure but also angled just right." And when the igloo is complete, he said, and you make tea, roast caribou, and crawl inside, you feel like a new person.

"I tell young hunters, 'If you can build an igloo, you can get married. Because you've learned the lesson of survival: Nature doesn't belong to you; it belongs to everyone.'"

For other rituals, the stakes are emotional. Colorado native Ben Martin was a middle-aged middle manager in Middle America when he had an experience that forced him to take a stand. Ben was born into a fundamentalist family in Aurora; he had a full-immersion baptism at ten and led a Christian theater troupe in high school.

Ben married young, had three children, and now has eighteen grandchildren. Two of his children—one a teacher, the other a parent—were at Columbine High School during the shooting. Ben is a poet at heart, but to pay the bills, he became a corporate science writer and eventually a VP of marketing at a tech company. Nearing seventy, he heard an interview on NPR about a death café by a woman who described herself as a "celebrant."

"The minute I heard that term I knew, *That's what I'm going to do the rest of my life.*" Ben became an ordained interfaith minister and in his first seven years performed three hundred life celebrations. He developed an unexpected expertise in shadow rituals—suicide, stillbirth, and overdose. "The most important antidote to tragedy is authenticity," he said.

But the experience that tested him the most was the one closest to home.

"I have a granddaughter—I'm sorry, a grand*child*—who ditched their female name for a gender-neutral name. They asked if I could help their family understand, and though I was a little ambivalent myself, I offered to host a ritual."

Ben's grandchild was a big fan of magpies. "That's their spirit animal. I had them draw a giant pair of wings and gave everybody feathers and art supplies. I invited guests to write out a message—*I love you*, *Have courage*, that sort of thing. Everyone pasted their feathers on the magpie wings, which my grandchild hung in their room."

Ben's takeaway: "For a ritual to have meaning, you have to spear the salamander. As a celebrant, my job is not to resolve anything for my guests; it's to trigger something in my guests that will allow them to transform themselves. Whoever you might have been when you walked in, I want something alchemical to happen to you during the ritual so that you walk out someone else."

For still more rituals the stakes are so all-encompassing that they challenge an entire family.

Alisa Tongg was born in Maui into a family with Hawaiian, Cherokee, and Pentecostal roots. When her peers in church camp were speaking in tongues, Alisa felt left out. "You have the spirit of discernment," her pastor said. "Everyone else is faking it."

Alisa attended a Christian college in Washington state, earned a master's degree in higher education, and became a college career counselor. In her forties, as a divorced single mom in the Pocono Mountains, she heeded the advice she often gave her students: Follow your heart. After attending the listless funeral of her mother, Alisa became a life celebrant, creating rituals for addicts to reconnect with their families and for big siblings to adjust to new babies. She helped her daughter and friends make orchid leis for beloved teachers at graduation. She thought she had seen it all.

Then she got a call from her friend Tisha.

"In our junior year in college, Tisha took a pregnancy test in the dormitory bathroom. It was positive." Facing expulsion from their Christian school, Tisha took a semester off, delivered a healthy boy, Josiah, and found a loving couple to adopt him. At the last minute, the boy's father appeared at the hospital and announced he would raise the child himself in Montana. Tisha held her son for a few minutes, then said a heartbreaking goodbye. She sent Josiah gifts for his birthday and ornaments for Christmas but was forbidden from seeing him. She got married and had two more sons.

Twenty years later, Tisha logged onto Facebook one day and saw a friend request from a handsome young man she didn't know. "His eyes were mine," she told Alisa. The next day they Skyped; the next month they met. "I have twenty years of love to catch you up on," Tisha told him.

As Tisha set about reconnecting with her son, Alisa set about creating a ritual to heal canyons of family wounds. The following year, Josiah, Tisha, and her extended family gathered in the Olympic National Forest. There was no avoiding the painful stakes; the ritual was about the stakes.

"I want to start with a little science lesson," Alisa said. The heart is made up of cardiac cells that synchronize with their neighbors, she explained. If you separate those cells in a lab, they fall out of sync; if you reunite them, they sync up again. "When Tisha and Josiah were first reunited, they embraced for five minutes, and their hearts realigned. 'You don't ever have to let go.' Tisha said. 'I don't plan to,' Josiah responded."

Tisha's family has a motto, "Grip fast," which means that you show up for one another. They also have a family tartan featuring navy blue, hunter green, and white. At Alisa's request, Tisha removed the tartan blanket she'd been wearing and passed it around the circle, until her father, Grandpa Bob, draped it over the shoulders of his firstborn grandson.

In talking to adoptees, Alisa learned that the most painful question that haunts them is, *Why didn't you love me?* Alisa invited Tisha to give her answer.

"As we look toward the future together, I want to thank you for finding me, for forgiving me, and for giving me the privilege to be a mother to you again," Tisha said. "Whether you were aware of it or not, you have always been an important part of me and this family, and you've always been loved.

"I can't promise you that life will always be easy," she continued, "but I can promise that you have my loyalty, gratitude, and unconditional love. I will grip fast to this sacred connection between us—today, tomorrow, and forever."

I asked Alisa what she learned from the experience.

"That stories have many heroes. Josiah was a hero for being brave enough to search for his mother. Tisha was a hero for confronting her shame and guilt. Josiah's father was a hero for raising their son. Tisha's family were heroes for viewing the situation with compassion.

"On that drizzly day in the woods," Alisa said, "we created a space that honored everyone's vulnerability; acknowledged the messy, complicated situation before us; and allowed everyone to imagine a slightly less messy, slightly less complicated, maybe even beautiful future together."

Gita was in the final cohort to be filed. Several hours had passed since the first initiands had climbed onto the beds. Some guests had drifted away, started eating, or gathered with relatives to snap photos. There is epiphany in life rituals but also monotony.

Figure 8: The older participants went first in the tooth filing, followed by the younger ones.

Gita was as frightened as anyone I'd seen, which was surprising considering that she'd watched so many others get through the experience, though perhaps less surprising in that she had so much less life experience. Tooth filing is clearly painful, but it's not childbirth. Still, like those before her, Gita's yelps soon gave way to smiles. Those files don't just smooth out jagged teeth, they also calm nerves.

Afterward, I found her sitting with some friends.

"I was warned not to smile to avoid being cursed," she said. "I was so worried about doing the wrong thing that I forget all the right things that were happening. At least now I can marry!"

Next to her was a slightly older participant, Desak, who had bright eyes and a bounce in his step. He had returned home from university on the island of Sumatra, two thousand miles away, where he was studying business. I asked why he felt the need to come.

"You don't have to choose between the future or the past," he said. "You can have a job in the city and still honor your ancestors at home. Today has more to do with being true to my family than being true to myself."

Just then one of the older men joined our conversation. His reason for having his teeth filed: "Now I can die in peace."

I can marry now.

I can come home now.

I can die now.

The heart of the matatah is in the eye of the beholder.

And that may be the greatest lesson of all. Life rituals are collective events that have personal interpretations; they increase our awareness of ourselves while broadening our appreciation of others; they find us in moments of self-obsession and help us become part of the whole.

When Clifford Geertz and his wife, Hildred, arrived in Bali in 1958 to study the illegal practice of cockfighting, they were "malarial," "diffident," and treated as "intruders." The next week, they attended their first underground ritual, which was broken up by police swinging "their guns around like gangsters." Like everyone else, the Geertzes fled and ducked into a home, where their unknown hostess, "who had apparently been through this sort of thing before, whipped out a table, a tablecloth, three chairs, and three cups of tea, and we all, without any explicit communication whatsoever, sat down." When the police stormed in, their hosts lied that the Americans had been interviewing them all along as part of their mission to inform the world about Bali.

"The next morning the village was a completely different world for us," Geertz wrote.

Cockfights, Geertz discovered, are not just cockfights. They are parables in which cocks (the double entendre works in Balinese as in

English) become stand-ins for powerful men. The same is true for all rituals, Geertz writes in "Deep Play: Notes on the Balinese Cockfight," a seminal work in anthropology. They are metaphoric gatherings, set "apart from the ordinary course of life," infused with "an aura of enlarged importance," and steeped in "the thrill of risk," that offer essential insights into how a community interprets itself.

"Man is an animal suspended in webs of significance he himself has spun."

Three generations later, as the threads of meaning that bind us seem more tenuous than ever, the importance of spinning those webs of significance feels more urgent than ever. As the initiands of the Banjar tooth filing attested: We cannot become ourselves without first becoming larger than ourselves.

Which is exactly what happened all those years earlier when my daughters stood side by side in a Brooklyn synagogue and chanted the story of Abraham, a man who in leaving his family behind gave rise to the greatest family that ever lived. A hero becoming. Sitting in the front row, having been admonished by the rabbi not to grimace or judge but just smile and kvell, I was struck by the outward manifestation of my girls' inward growth. At one point, as they together sang of seeking the future, they reached down and silently clasped each other's hands.

I didn't need to be instructed how to react to this gesture. Linda had been right: The girls grasped instinctually the stakes before them. They would go forth on separate paths; they would reunite down the road. They had no choice but to let go; they had no alternative but to hold on.

They had skin in the game.

5.

HOUSE OF CORRECTION

The Grieving & Weaving Circle of Green-Wood Cemetery

"Thank you for crossing over to the dark side of death."

Gabrielle Gatto is never happier than when she's talking about dying, or funerals, or coffins, or grief drinks. This particular passion, while setting her apart from every other thirty-one-year-old single woman she knows, means that on this Tuesday evening, standing in front of the mauve velvet pews and illuminated glass altar wall of the modern chapel of Green-Wood Cemetery in Brooklyn, wearing a black pantsuit that would make Morticia Addams proud, oversize black Carol Channing eyeglasses, and a necklace made of thirty-two miniature silver skulls, she's in her happy place.

"We're here to create an open, safe, playful space to discuss grief and loss of any kind," Gabrielle says. "We also have snacks to make it easier. We have olive oil, because my Italian Catholic family always poured olive oil at funerals. We have rosemary syrup, because mourners from ancient Greece to medieval Britain used it for remembrance. And we have grief seltzers that you can make with lavender—just ask our volunteers Ross and Lisa for help."

Covering 478 acres, Green-Wood Cemetery was founded in 1838 as a trailblazer in the rural cemetery movement, which set aside landscaped spaces outside of cities where guests could gather, picnic, and celebrate life not just mourn the dead. With 570,000 permanent residents, the burial grounds, an important inspiration for Central Park, house luminaries like Leonard Bernstein, Boss Tweed, Jean-Michel Basquiat, Currier *and* Ives, the namesakes of Tiffany and FAO Schwarz, and MGM's original Wizard of Oz.

"It is the ambition of the New Yorker," wrote *The New York Times* in 1866, "to live upon Fifth Avenue, to take his airings in the [Central] Park, and to sleep with his fathers in Green-Wood."

In recent years Green-Wood has become America's hipster graveyard and a vanguard of the death positive movement, the grassroots campaign to make being six feet under the grass—or, in the case of cremation, sprinkled on the daisies—less taboo. Led by Gabrielle, the cemetery's head of programming, New York's "Village of the Dead" now hosts more than three hundred events a year, including birding, crafting, an annual Victorian circus, walking tours like "Crime and Catastrophe" and "Gay Gothic," and world premiere operas in the catacombs.

"I'm thrilled to share that after the incredible outpouring of support, we've decided to make Grieving & Weaving a regular monthly event."

The three dozen crafters in the purple pews oohed, yayed, and raised their Solo cups of Chardonnay. The mostly female guests ranged in age from grannies to Gen Z, their hair color from white to pink, though they all cradled similar NPR-style tote bags stuffed with tangled skeins of yarn and candy-colored needles. This session would be my first in a year of attendance.

"I always try to find a way to make at least one Green-Wood connection," Gabrielle said. "Today I read about a two-hundred-twenty-five-year-old family-run company in the UK that makes wool caskets. It's called Rest in Fleece. We, too, offer 'green goodbyes'! But the true Green-Wood thread is that they make the uniforms of the royal guard at Buckingham Palace and the felt lining of Steinway pianos. Wellllllllll, who has a big 'ol granite mausoleum here?"

"The Steinways!" the weavers cheered.

"One final word. Mother's Day is coming up. There's a lot of joy around this celebration, but also a lot of grief. We all carry tension around our biological mothers, our chosen mothers, our maternal figures. I just want to open up honestly and say that we're here to share stories from our painful past and our hopeful futures, validating whatever feelings you have, because sometimes our mothers can be our greatest source of love and sometimes our greatest source of regret.

"Now, let's go create! Share! Grieve!"

My father's funeral is the last one I thought would have been interrupted by conflict. An old-fashioned civic booster from Savannah, Georgia, with an easy smile and warm laugh, my father was the kind of person who stopped strangers in the street to offer directions and was stopped by strangers in airports because he looked like someone who would be fun to talk to.

Nearing eighty and beset by Parkinson's, my father became depressed and tried to take his own life. The experience sent my family into a tailspin. Through the near-mythic self-sacrifice of my mother, my father was able to stabilize his depleted serotonin and live for another eight years. During that time, I emailed him weekly questions about his life, and he completed a sixty-five-thousand-word memoir just weeks before he died.

"I want to be celebrated," he often said, "not mourned."

But two days later, in a funeral planning call with the rabbi, I found myself in the middle of a standoff between my mother and sister. My mother announced that she did not want to observe the Jewish custom of having mourners shovel dirt on the coffin. "I find it barbaric," she said. She preferred tossing long-stemmed roses. My sister found the idea of roses too Hallmark and preferred shoveling dirt. "For me, it's the most important part of service." To my surprise, neither backed down. Temperatures escalated.

"Um, I think we need to discuss this as a family," I said to the rabbi.

One can be forgiven for finding the conversation around ritual sometimes a little too rah-rah. Rituals are magic! Rituals are miracles! They're fairy tales and pixie dust, rose buds and rosé. The truth is often darker. Rituals spawn squabbles, storm offs, setbacks, and showdowns. They reveal fissures, fractures, fault lines, and feuds. They engender fights over money and battles over power, clashes over religion and disputes over seating arrangements. They're conflict factories.

Which is why the second most valuable thing that rituals do is force families to address those underlying conflicts. They challenge us to rethink, regroup, and reframe.

They correct.

Conflict is the backbone of biology and the foundation of evolution. "Wherever cooperation exists," writes the English evolutionary biologist Nichola Raihani, "we know that there is the potential for conflict." The cells that make up our bodies "squabble and bicker," as do the genes that make up those cells, and the atoms that make up those genes. "For cooperation to prevail, and for the integrity of the whole to be preserved," she continues, "these inner conflicts must be reduced or resolved."

Given that our smallest biological parts generate discord, who can be surprised that our biggest biological extravaganzas do, too. Life rituals are occasions when we're called on publicly to *do* family, to *perform* family. This public pressure to present cohesion heightens the private pressure to achieve cohesion. We want things to go smoothly—no jealousy over who's in the limelight, no quarreling over the estate—yet things invariably go unsmoothly. Life rituals "can seem perfectly magical," writes Grimes, the Canadian professor of ritual studies, "but only if you keep your eyes and ears trained on what transpires center stage. Backstage, there often seethes a morass of spiritual stress and social conflict."

Mourning rituals are among the worst offenders. Family members who may not see one another all that often—and may not have solved problems together in decades—are suddenly thrust into resolving some of the thorniest challenges human beings face. As Thomas Lynch, the mortician we heard from earlier, writes of the greater role that families must now play in deciding which of the many rites around death they wish to observe, undertaking has evolved in a generation from "something done with the dead, to something done for the living, to something done by the living."

Make-your-own funeral has given rise to solve-your-own conflicts.

Which is why so many funeral homes have pages on their websites like "How to Manage Funeral Feuds," "When Death Brings Out the Worst," and "Family Conflict at the Funeral? Follow These Five Steps." And why there's a surge of death whisperers like Gabrielle, a certified thanatologist, a death doula, a graduate of the Going with Grace training program, and a proud creator of the brand Grim Reaper Gossip.

"I'm a perspective provider," Gabrielle said, "because when death comes up, everyone loses perspective."

Gabrielle Rose-Reggie Gatto was a "miracle" only child born on Long Island to older parents, "a plumber and a living saint." From her earliest days, death was calling. "My first memory of being alive on planet Earth is looking up at a casket. I was three and a half, at a wake in Brooklyn, and I remember the feeling in the room was deep love."

Funerals were a centerpiece of Gabrielle's working-class Italian family full of firefighters and cops. "From a very young age, I remember thinking, *OK, somebody dies. You're gonna get a new black dress and a new pair of stockings. You'll send flowers and make food. Four hundred people will show up, and you'll hear 'a time to mourn, a time to dance' from Ecclesiastes.*

"I can't tell you how many times I've seen someone like my Aunt Rosie dive into the casket and cry on top of the body."

Gabrielle embraced the darkness. She held a "sour sixteen" instead of a sweet one; she attended college in America's headquarters of creepiness, New Orleans, where once again death called. "I took a class called Living with Dying Studies because you got to watch *Six Feet Under* in its entirety. I had just discovered that I'm neurodivergent, which explained why I viewed everything as patterns and shapes. I saw my life winding all over the place with a giant *X* at the end—death."

Gabrielle eventually returned to New York, where once again death called. "I went to a film screening at a cemetery. I was doing this millennial crying thing that my life was going nowhere, when a notification popped up on my phone: an opening in programming at Green-Wood Cemetery."

She started on March 4, 2020; the following week the entire country shut down from COVID. The entire country, that is, except cemeteries.

"Once again, death called," Gabrielle said. "I mean literally called. Every single phone rang off the hook. I said to my new colleagues, 'Throw me the binder!' On hyperspeed, I had to learn that it's not really six feet under, it's nine, seven, or five. I had to learn the difference between burying cremains in a niche or the ground. On my first day, I took one hundred eleven calls."

And she found her calling.

The pandemic was a watershed in the history of death, Gabrielle said. People flocked to cemeteries—to eat pizza, get haircuts, take walks—exceeding the wildest dreams of the rural cemetery movement. People crowded into Zoom rooms to attend death cafés that Gabrielle and others organized. People stared mortality in the face and found meaning staring them back.

But it was when Gabrielle tried to apply what she learned in the cemetery to her parents that she learned the niche she was truly destined to fill. "My parents were already in their seventies, but when I said that we needed to talk about their impending deaths, they completely shut down. A death doula gave me a piece of advice: 'You've got to make it a family activity.'"

Gabrielle telephoned her parents. "I'm coming over on Friday night. We're gonna have some hard, messed-up conversations. We'll probably feel really vulnerable. We're not going to attempt all 'Sixty-Four Questions to Answer Before You Die'; just three—your advance directives, your funerals, your wills. Afterwards, we'll order Chili's, drink wine, and rewatch *The Godfather*.

"There's a crazy statistic," Gabrielle went on. "Eighty percent of people think that if they talk to someone about dying, the person will die right away. What I realized is, if you have the conversation while watching a movie, baking cookies, or knitting, you'll make everything a little safer. You say, 'We're going to face this head on, it's going to suck, there's going to be conflict, but we can make this a little less emotional and a lot more effective if we put ritual around it.'"

And that's when the light bulb went off.

The Grieving & Weaving Circle does not actually involve a circle. Guests scatter in pews, huddle in front of the glass altar wall with the pressed leaf design, or assemble at the snack table. It doesn't involve weaving, as most people knit, darn, crochet, quilt, or embroider. And it doesn't especially involve grieving, as some members talk about loss while working and others talk about patterns and yarn.

"Ever since my mother died, I've always hated Mother's Day," Mary Pat Klein shared with the group. A professional crafter and coleader of the circle, Mary Pat has made knitwear for *Good Housekeeping*, *Today*, and *Frozen* on Broadway. Each month, she offered advice at the outset (*Never hang your sweaters!*) and tips throughout (*Don't use cotton yarn, it loses shape!*).

"A lot of us learned to craft from our mothers or grandmothers," she continued. "When we were cleaning out the attic after my father died, I found these gifts from my grandmother. I must have been eight when she knitted my cousins and me twenty-one outfits for our Barbies, including evening gowns, coats, and a peignoir set. I'm sad that I don't have more."

Once the weavers settled into their routines, I hopped from group to group, before ending up in a conversation with Anika, an arts educator and mom, and Sarah, a retiree who had been married at Green-Wood. Anika, who was knitting a green NICU cap for a nonprofit, said that she was drawn to the circle because her mother had just been diagnosed with cancer.

"It's not curable, and she's only in her sixties. Plus, she lives in the Bay Area, so it feels nice to work on a project in community, while also remembering times when I helped with her quilts. I can intellectualize what's happening, but there's something about the tactile, meditative quality of knitting that allows you to move through the sadness."

"What happens if you feel upset or angry?" I asked.

"Oh, that's happened to me," Sarah said. She was knitting a red scarf for a teddy bear she'd made for her great-nephew. "I was crafting something for my husband. It started out as an act of love, then I got really pissed off at him. I knitted about a third of the project before realizing, *Oh, there are holes everywhere!* I had to rip the whole thing up. It's like when you cook when you're angry, the food is not as good."

"Is that a thing?" I said.

"Oh, yes," Sarah said. "A couple of years ago, my husband tried to make me tacos from scratch for my birthday. We were having a lot of conflict at the time. At one point, I screamed, 'I don't want your hate tacos!'"

"You can't hate cook any more than you can hate knit," Anika said.

Between NICU caps and chemo blankets, breakup mittens and mourning scarves, I asked if it was a coincidence that most people in the circle seemed to be making gifts for people in transitions.

"Knitwear is very comforting," Sarah said. "My maternal grandma was an absolute badass. She worked in an auto factory, was a chain-smoker, and when she got a cancer, she knitted the most hideous army-green, mustard-yellow, and cream afghan. She gave it to me shortly before she died. Whenever I'm feeling vulnerable, I snuggle up under that afghan and think, *Good lord, how did she think these were good colors?*"

"For me," Anika added, "I get the pleasure of using these beautiful materials to make something for a family, knowing that it will keep their baby warm while the parents are going through a scary time. I don't need to know the family any more than I need to know the people in this room. There's something about talking to strangers that's liberating. The crafting creates a permission structure to talk about painful topics."

"I agree," Sarah said. "I come from a family that was stoic and never talked about difficult issues. When I was young, I was told that my grandmother 'went away.' It wasn't until after my grandmother died that my mother found papers that she had been sent to a mental institution. Something about being in a group like this makes you feel supported even if you don't talk about why you need support."

"It sounds like you don't just pass down love through knitting," I said. "You also pass down trauma."

"I think you may be right," Anika said. "But places like this allow us to heal from that trauma. There's so much diversity in the world these days; we don't have shared traditions, so we never experience togetherness. It makes sense that we're trying to create new rituals like this to give ourselves permission to be human together."

Sometimes, when I visited the Grieving & Weaving Circle, I wondered if the Great Ritual Thinkers of the Past™ would consider it a ritual. It didn't sparkle with collective effervescence. It had no separation, liminality, and integration. It lacked performativity. Also, it failed the spectacle test—there was no dancing, singing, chanting, drumming, or toasting. By most metrics, including many of my own, it should not be viewed as ritual.

And yet, the more I returned, the more I questioned my assumptions. The circle met my foundational definition of a ritual—it was a doing; it was shared; it was unnecessary. And it fulfilled my highest aspiration—it was a communal act that made people feel at home. It was absolutely a cure for homesickness. But perhaps the most persuasive way that this gathering captured both the historic legacy of rituals and the promise of what they might become is how it harnessed the power of community to spread meaning and connectedness in times of isolation and fear.

Science, it turns out, agrees: Groups excel at self-healing.

In 1976, the then little-known Oxford professor Richard Dawkins published the pop-science sensation *The Selfish Gene*, which championed the idea that evolution occurs through the relentless drive of "selfish genes" to pass on their attributes regardless of the impact on the group. As often happens, the rest of us over-fixated on the topline, the idea of selfishness, while overlooking an important corrective.

Writing at the same time as Dawkins, the American ecologist Egbert Leigh demonstrated that while selfish genes are part of every community, they are held in check by a "parliament" of unselfish genes. Because these prosocial genes are far more numerous than selfish genes, when they detect a threat from their rivals, they form a "united front" to block "the cabal of the few" from overtaking the well-being of the many.

Life rituals are among our most effective tools for empowering the parliament of good. They achieve that goal by being proxy wars for deeper struggles. Fighting over canapés and cake decorations is a lot healthier than fighting over blood and treasure. The standoff between my mother and sister had little to do with roses and dirt and everything to do with simmering anxieties over religious observance, worries about how others might perceive us, and looming battles over who would fill the vacuum left by the loss of our family patriarch.

The South African anthropologist Max Gluckman calls these episodes "dramatizations," miniature skirmishes of contained aggression that reduce the risks of runaway aggression. Many traditional cultures have rituals *specifically designed* for this purpose. The Inuit host drumming duels in igloos in which individuals who feel wronged can challenge their opponents to a public competition involving jokes and song. The Ndembu of Zambia isolate infertile couples to a grove where they are put through a series of wrenching challenges to restore conjugal "success."

Modern cultures have our own, more domesticated versions of such rituals, from AA to Compassionate Friends, couples retreats to group therapy. Scholars have amassed impressive research that sharing your experiences in curated environments can be remarkably healing.

Women who join cancer support groups live a year and a half longer than those who don't; cancer cells are less aggressive and metastasize less rapidly in people who are less lonely. A 2019 meta-analysis of twelve randomized studies found "robust" positive benefits of going through stressful life experiences with the help of others.

"The overall message of this extensive body of expert research is hearteningly simple," writes the Stanford psychologist Geoffrey Cohen. Shifting your mindset from "I am alone" to "I belong" improves health. The best way to achieve that end, he writes: "subtle, brief, psychologically 'wise' interventions."

Rituals are increasingly understood to be among the most effective of those interventions. A cohort of young scholars has found that group therapy that *specifically incorporates ritual* has profound benefits. Kathryn Berg of Loyola University Chicago has shown that the use of collective rituals in clinical intervention, including meditation, wilderness survival, and art therapy, helped Black women recover effectively from incest, eating disorders, and homelessness. Similar patterns have been found among South Asian women who were victims of intimate partner violence.

Karen Neuman Allen of Indiana University Bloomington and a colleague studied domestic violence survivors in three states who joined a therapeutic group called Rites of Passage. The women burned sage at the start of every session, recited blessings at the end, and wore T-shirts with animal totems (*Free as an eagle but powerful enough to prey on any threat*). In one ritual, women who had fled their abusers abruptly and lost their belongings took new photographs with their families to create a "scrapbook for her future." In another, women climbed to the top of a bridge, declared their healing, and tossed a vial of water symbolizing their freedom into the river. While these rituals "do not 'cure' women," Allen writes, "they do position women to clearly see what comes next on their healing trajectory."

They also serve as a reminder: The handmaiden of shame is silence. For as long as humans have been alive, we have used collective, ceremonial experiences to help endure the most painful anguish imaginable. Today, just as we have broadened the range of once-shameful afflictions we're willing to discuss in public, we are also broadening the definition of ritual to include more inventive ways of counteracting those afflictions. We can reduce hardship with harmony; we can balm grieving with weaving.

The parliament of unselfish genes may be the most effective parliament on earth.

I met Joanne in the July meeting. She was one of the older members, with layered hair that was more salt than pepper and a sweet if somewhat sad demeanor. She joined the circle to get better at knitting. "I've gone to yarn stores a few times to ask for advice, but they're very snobby."

Joanne was born in Brooklyn into a family she described as total white bread. "I'm 100 percent Irish and English; my family came to this country in the 1700s, but in steerage class."

Joanne was knitting a heather-green and gold sweater for a child. I asked who the child was. She went silent for a second but kept her hands moving. It was almost as if she were thinking with her fingers. Then she turned, smiled wistfully, and told me a story.

"The year was 1963. I had just graduated from Catholic high school. Something was happening with my body, but I was too naive to know what it was. But my lovely mother knew. She took me to a home for unwed mothers."

"Wait, so you gave your child away?" I said.

"No, they took her away."

For as long as anyone could remember, Joanne explained, when girls in her neighborhood became pregnant, they would "go away" for a while, have their baby, then return and pass off their child as their sibling. "I know many people who think their grandmothers are their mothers and their mothers are their sisters."

After World War II, she continued, "families got smaller, people started moving around more, and there was not the same culture of community. Yet the shame was still real." So the church opened so-called maternity homes. By the 1960s, more than two hundred institutions for unwed mothers were operating in forty-four states; between 1945 and 1973, 1.5 million pregnant girls were sent to these homes to surrender their children in secret.

"They call it the 'Baby Scoop Era,'" Joanne said. "And that's exactly what happened to me. I gave birth to my daughter, and they immediately scooped her up and took her away."

"Did you consent?"

"I did not. Six weeks later I had to return to sign the papers. They let me hold my daughter for an hour, which seemed like an eternity. I cried the whole time."

I asked Joanne if she was allowed to mourn.

"I had a picture from the day my daughter was born, October third. Every year on her birthday, I took it out, looked at her, and wondered about her life."

Joanne was married for a few months in her early twenties—"Mostly to get the hell out of my mother's house"—and had a son in her thirties. But she never achieved the family of her dreams and never went searching for her daughter. "You never know if you're going to fuck up somebody's life. Maybe she didn't know she was adopted; maybe her parents would freak out. It was not my place to look for her."

But all that time—nearly sixty years—her daughter was looking for her.

"One day I got a letter." *Dear Joanne, My name is Christine Leora.*

"I fell on the floor. I just started crying and crying. It had been so long—and so longed for."

I don't know if you're my mother, but here's how I found you.

One of Joanne's cousins was on ancestry.com, when she was notified of a relative. The two strangers connected but couldn't find the connection. "My daughter didn't originally want to say she was adopted, but my cousin was like a detective."

If you want to, I would very much like to get in touch with you.

Mother and daughter made a date to meet at the Museum of Fine Arts in Boston.

Joanne is just one of millions in what was a global epidemic of forced adoptions, from Europe to the Pacific. In Ireland alone, between 1765 and 1996, as many as fifty thousand women were not just sent to homes for "fallen women" to give birth but *compelled to remain there* to repent for their sins, performing forced labor in what are now called Magdalene laundries. An unmarked grave behind one such asylum contained the bodies of fifty-five women.

A devastating feature of the Baby Scoop Era is that families rarely spoke of the matter. There were no baptisms, no send-off ceremonies, no mourning rites for girls locked away. Coerced adoptions came with no life rituals. But by the time these stories began pouring into public view in recent decades, things had changed.

Sure enough, in country after country, people turned to ritual to mourn these crimes against humanity. Archbishops issued mea culpas; churches held vigils. The prime minister of Australia hosted an apology ceremony in the Great Hall of Parliament: "Today this parliament, on behalf of the Australian people, takes responsibility and apologises for the policies and practices that forced the separation of mothers from their babies, which created a lifelong legacy of pain and suffering."

This embrace of public healing was part of the larger movement of communal responsibility taking that began with the Truth and Reconciliation Commission on apartheid in South Africa and grew to include treatment of Indigenous people, enslaved people, and molested people, a groundbreaking mix of civic ritual with life ritual that created a new model of collective renewal. South Korea appointed a Truth and Reconciliation Commission on adoption, which apologized for exporting two hundred thousand children "like luggage" for profit.

Joanne's reunion was more modest but no less emotional. "I walked in, and I couldn't believe my eyes. We were practically wearing the same outfit. Her life was my life—I grew up in Brooklyn, she grew up in Queens; my father was a cop, her adoptive father was a firefighter; we both went to Catholic schools. Also, she's a doctor."

"Congratulations. Your daughter, the doctor!"

Joanne and her daughter started seeing each other regularly; they travel abroad; they celebrate Mother's Day. And that sweater Joanne was knitting? It's for her granddaughter.

As for her own mother, they also shared a reconciliation.

"When she was dying in the hospital, she apologized." Joanne said. "She told me, 'I made a big mistake.' I remember asking, before I gave birth, 'Mom, is it going to hurt?' She said, 'People die from this.'

"I didn't die from it, though I almost died from the aftermath. I only wish my mother could have known her granddaughter; she's a very special lady. But in my own way, I do think I've forgiven my mother. After all, I gave my daughter her name.

"Leora."

I asked all the ritual designers I interviewed two questions about conflict. The first: Do life rituals make conflicts among participants better or worse? Ninety-seven percent said better—a finding as close to unanimity as I've ever received. The second: Is the conflict resolved before, during, or after the ritual? Fifty percent said during, 44 percent said before, 3 percent said after. These numbers are a reminder that the halo effects of life rituals extend far beyond their borders.

As important as the sacred circle is, half the benefits occur outside it.

Jen Boyes-Manseau grew up in Vancouver, British Columbia, in a family of Unitarians who loved the outdoors. "My religion was the natural world." Jen spent decades designing immersive experiences for museums and national parks, until friends started asking her to do the same for them—"blessing ways" before the birth of a child, "home blessings" for moving out of or into a new home, "crowning ceremonies" for women entering a new phase of life. Finally she read the room and became a certified life celebrant.

"What I learned from my Unitarian upbringing is that the key to a successful life celebration is crafting language that points to something but doesn't insist on anything; it's inclusive, offering everyone their own interpretation, whatever that means to you."

In practice, this strategy corrects for conflict not by avoiding it but by allowing people to have their own individual experience within the larger group. At her mother-in-law's funeral, rife with tension among an unwed child, a black sheep, and a child in a same-sex marriage, Jen created a concentric candle lighting where each generation lit flames in a spiral. "I've never seen anything like this," the funeral director said. "I must give thanks to the family."

Jen faced her toughest challenge with the funeral of a woman who died by suicide.

"She had been troubled for most of her life and left a long trail of broken relationships. I was visited by her husband and father; her mother refused to come." The family requested a memorial service at a dog park, the one place where the deceased found happiness.

"The setup was a nightmare," Jen said. "The traffic was horrendous;

the family hired a film crew who were being intrusive. The husband set up a folding lunchroom table that was too big. He spread out a plastic tablecloth decorated with dogs, dumped out a pile of miniature toy unicorns, then plopped down a bejeweled, wooden treasure box containing her ashes."

Jen went to work. She arranged the unicorns in a phalanx, gathered everyone in a circle, then led a service that honored the wishes of the family. When the husband handed out unicorn stickers at the end, she invited everyone to stick theirs to the box and share a memory.

"The last person to go was the mother. What could have been a nightmare was a moment of deep healing."

Wendy Haynes, the most distinguished ritual designer in Australia, was born into a Church of England family in Great Britain that moved Down Under when she was seven. Pregnant at twenty, Wendy and her husband moved into a home outside Canberra. "I was planning on a hospital birth, but the previous owners had forgotten to leave a forwarding address, and I kept receiving newsletters about home birth. It was an act of providence."

Wendy gave birth to three naturally born children in the coming years, helped only by her mother, her sister, her husband, and a midwife. She joined the home-birth association, taught classes, ran seminars. It was the start of her "celebrant years," four decades leading thousands of births, baby namings, weddings, and funerals; writing eight books; and becoming a voice on ritual respected around the world.

I asked Wendy what percentage of her time is spent not in joyful communion with families but in resolving conflicts. "Twenty-five percent," she said. "Weddings are worse than births; funerals are worse than weddings."

What techniques has she found most effective in correcting those tensions?

"I would say two. First is for me to be really aware of my own presence. I'm not someone who likes conflict, even though I deal with it all the time. Viktor Frankl said, 'Between stimulus and response there is space.' In that space we get to choose how to respond. I like to acknowledge how tricky the situation is. I might say, 'This is a difficult moment.' But I don't run from the conflict; pointing it out calms everybody down."

Second is to make sure everyone is heard. "I had a situation recently where an estranged son returned home for his father's funeral. The father had recently reconnected with the son, but the son had never met the second wife."

The father's will said that he wanted a particular prayer read at his funeral. "We've got to have it," the son said. But his second wife insisted that he had not been religious for years and preferred a secular reading. "I refuse to allow the prayer," she said.

"We were in a family meeting with twenty-five people," Wendy recalled. "I could feel my heartbeat rising. I turned to the son. 'It sounds like you really want to honor your dad's wishes, and this prayer is about being compassionate.' I turned to the wife. 'It sounds like you want to honor his wishes, too, and this credo is really about kindness. What if I combined the two into one reading?'

"There was a pause," Wendy said. "Both parties felt completely heard. And when I sent the combined prayer later that night, both were 100 percent happy."

The moral of the story: The work of the ritual begins when the talk of the ritual begins.

"I always tell families," Wendy said, "the first meeting is as much a ceremony as the ceremony itself."

The Grieving & Weaving holiday party was a DIY fiesta, with lactose-free eggnog, hand-braided wreaths, and vegan sprinkle brownies. Mary Pat brought in hats, scarves, and yarn for a raffle. A member made a two-foot-round geodesic dome out of gingerbread filled with miniature people standing around a hearth; it quickly got dubbed the gingerbread crematorium. Some guys from the real crematorium came in to help smash it with a wine bottle so everyone could eat a triangle.

Gabrielle told the story of Charles Christmas, a nineteenth-century British banker who lived on the same Brooklyn street as I do and is buried in the "Christmas crypt" at Green-Wood. Five hundred people had attended the circle this year, she noted, allowing her to secure funding for the following year. She'd also heard from a hospital in Connecticut that wanted to open its own group.

"Grieving & Weaving is going national!" someone shouted.

I noticed a millennial couple that I hadn't seen before. Sebastian had unkempt brown hair and a beard and wore a long-sleeve black T-shirt from an organic farm; Ro had a purple buzz cut and was wearing dangling geode earrings and a tie-dyed hoodie.

"We live in the neighborhood and have been wanting to come to Green-Wood for a while," Sebastian said. "We both like creating things."

"Also, the world feels very disappointing these days," Ro added. "Coming to a place like this helps. Grieving is a reminder that we're not alone."

I asked if she was mourning someone in particular.

"Actually, I had an experience recently of creating a ritual for my community to help me grieve. My dog, Orson, died in a terrible accident; he drowned in a pit that some plumbers dug behind my building. It was pretty traumatic because I saw the whole thing and couldn't help him."

Ro, who is a therapist, went to see a grief chaplain, who recommended that she host a ritual. Twenty friends and neighbors gathered in her apartment, brought noisemakers and jingle bells, along with blown-up pictures of themselves with Orson.

"We lit candles, burned rosemary, and made music, then we said Kaddish and sang 'Hallelujah.'" Ro had been unable to touch Orson's bed, so guests placed his cremains on the mattress, along with his leash, and carried the makeshift memorial into the backyard, where Ro had planted marigolds, pansies, and cilantro. "I picked flowers and herbs that looked like him. He was gray with blue eyes and black spots. Some people spoke to him directly."

They sprinkled his ashes in the garden.

Mary Pat came over and examined Ro's knitting. "I think you need to rip out what you're working on. It's too tight."

"Oh. Okay. Cool," Ro said.

"I guess we're accepting the impermanence," Sebastian joked.

I asked Ro what she learned from Orson's ceremony.

"I'm very ritual forward," she said. "But I don't like tradition. I don't want to get married, for example. Maybe because I'm healing from sexual violence, but I'm skeptical of anything associated with replication.

"What felt important about the experience was personalizing it, creating something specific that I could invite people into. Abraham Joshua Heschel described the Sabbath as a palace in time. This felt like a palace outside of time. A moment of godliness, where past, present, and future were all rolled into one. Maybe that's a good definition of what ritual is."

"And what do you feel in that moment?" I asked.

"The opposite of aloneness."

I stepped to the back of the chapel. The smell of elderberry wine and the click-clack of needles filled the room. In 1989, the American sociologist Ray Oldenburg coined the expression *the third place*, referring to public locations that are neither home, the "first" place, nor work, the "second." These environments, among them parks, libraries, coffeehouses, and gyms, are neutral ground where conversations happen, connections occur, and camaraderie deepens.

My experience at Green-Wood Cemetery made me consider that there are also third circles, spaces that are neither secular nor religious, where the work of contemporary spirituality, meaning making, and ritual thrive. Some of these third circles are in nature—groves, cliffs, beaches, mountaintops; some are urban—storefronts, backyards, barbershops, parks; others are already in the business of human life but get repurposed for spontaneous gatherings—hospitals, crematoria, courthouses, even amusement parks.

Disney regularly has to shut down its Star Wars and It's a Small World rides because families choose these beloved destinations to scatter their loved ones' ashes, jamming up the mechanics, freaking out children, and forcing the company to call in a HEPA team. Cast members even have a secret name for such incidents: "Code Grandma."

Dark humor aside, what's happening in these third circles is no less than the remaking of long-standing norms around how we share space and how we make meaning in communal environments. The mountains of flowers, teddy bears, and cards laid at the gates of Buckingham Palace following the death of Princess Diana in 1997, for example, are often cited as jump-starting the spontaneous shrines that now dot every highway curve and downtown street corner where tragedy occurs. These tributes feel even more universal considering how reminiscent they are of the cairns and cave paintings of our prehistoric ancestors.

Still, contemporary rituals like honor walks, adoption reunions, and hoʻoponopono prison gatherings, held in improvised third circles, serve a profoundly contemporary function, too. They are neutral, nondenominational arenas where the dramatizations of contemporary domestic strife are adjudicated and where the proliferation of microconflicts that afflict intergenerational and intercultural families are mediated.

"I think what we do best here is informality," Gabrielle reflected as we glanced around the room. "We create the container where you find similarities in your stories and kinship in your vulnerabilities.

"But having informal spaces like this one opens you up to more formal ones later." She continued, "The goal is to plant seeds in this room that turn into flowers elsewhere. Grief is not linear, neither is healing."

Perhaps the greatest gift of third circles, I was discovering, is that they extend the work of life rituals to the ad hoc gatherings and informal healings that begin long before the main event and continue long after. The lobola of Lillian and Jeffrey did not supplant the wedding ritual; it extended it for seventeen years. The Grieving & Weaving Circle did not replace mourning rituals; it allowed grievers to rework and reweave their emotions months, years, even decades later.

A similar displaced grieving, I now realized, is what happened with my father's funeral, with its out-of-nowhere conflict over long-stemmed red roses versus Georgia red clay. After we got off the phone with the rabbi, I middle-childed my way through my own version of what I now think of as the ritual designer's creed: I asked my mom what she was really thinking; I asked my sister what she was really saying. Our impromptu third circle created a third way: We ordered three dozen yellow roses that could be laid on the casket; we assembled packets of white sand from my father's beloved Tybee Island that could be sprinkled in the grave. And we gave everyone a choice.

From flora and terra he came; to flora and terra he returned.

The ritual had unearthed the problem; the ritual corrected it.

6.

JUMPING THE BROOM

How to Create a Ritual, Volume 2

As a child, Danita Rountree Green loved church but hated ritual; as an adult, she revived a ritual that would reshape church.

Danita was born into a devout family in Richmond, Virginia; her father was a Baptist minister, her mother an usher. "I loved the ceremonies but questioned the rituals, especially baptism. I grew up in the sixties; my family didn't swim because Black people in the South were not allowed in public pools. But at eight I was expected to be baptized in a pool." Her father left her mother when Danita was five, deepening her distrust of religion.

Danita always had a rebel streak. "When I was thirteen, my mother took me to the beauty parlor to get my hair straightened. It was a rite of passage for all Black girls. But I announced to everyone in the salon, 'I'm not sitting in that chair. I like my hair natural!'"

In college, Danita was drawn to community building. "I'm of the generation that was cultivated to integrate. The University of Virginia was the first place I met African American mentors who encouraged us to think bigger, act bolder." Her thesis was on interracial couples in the rural South who invented alternative wedding ceremonies because they were not allowed to marry.

After graduating, Danita taught school, married a freelance photographer, and began managing his business. "He wanted to be an artist but had to do weddings to pay the bills. He would set up a large-format camera and spend hours crafting the perfect pose for the bride and groom. Meanwhile, the wedding party was left sitting around, growing antsy."

Danita realized she had the perfect recipe for a failed business.

"So I started talking to the family about relationships. I'd say, 'You are the community that's going to help this couple pull through. It doesn't matter whether you think they're a good match or not. What matters is whether you commit right now to contribute to their success.'"

And families would oblige. "They'd say, 'I like the groom, but I wish he knew how to play golf or had a more stable job,' or 'I love that that the bride makes my brother so happy, but she's going to need some parenting skills or a new hairdresser after they move.'"

Danita pounced. "OK, so will you agree to take him golfing or help him find more stable work? Is there anyone here who has some parenting skills or a good hairdresser you're willing to pass on to this young woman? My message was, 'Will you promise to drop all this bullshit about *you wish they'd married someone else* and actually do something to help the marriage they're in?'"

I asked Danita where she got the moxie to run these sessions.

"I'm a teacher by nature," she said. "I'm not afraid of confrontation. And the feelings were already there. I was just giving people the opportunity to voice them.

"Still, I think I got the idea from those interracial couples. The world is changing; you can't expect conventional rituals to have much impact anymore. My parents were the golden couple. They failed because no one was there to help them, while those couples who had everything stacked against them managed to make it work. We need to rethink weddings to ensure that everyone in attendance sees themselves as part of making the marriage work."

All of which helps explain why a few years later, holed up in bed after a near-fatal car accident, Danita had an idea to create a ritual that would, well, sweep out the new and sweep in the old.

I was eleven the year Kunta Kinte came to town.

Savannah, Georgia, is a place of legendary charm. Laid out in 1733 on a grid of two dozen squares, America's "first planned city" is lined with redbrick mansions and stucco churches, steeped in magnolias, azaleas, and Spanish moss. Savannah's beauty is so renowned that General William Sherman did not torch the city at the end of his march to the sea in 1864 but presented it to Abraham Lincoln as a Christmas present.

That preservation proved key when Hollywood discovered Savannah a century later, making it the romantic backdrop for hundreds of movies including *Cape Fear* starring Gregory Peck and Robert Mitchum, the latter of whom was briefly jailed for wandering drunken in those streets; *The Legend of Bagger Vance*; and Oscar winners *Forrest Gump* and *Glory*.

But by far the most famous production ever filmed in Savannah is *Roots*, the 1977 landmark miniseries of Alex Haley's fictionalized saga of his family. The story traces the life and lineage of Kunta Kinte, a teenage boy stolen from Gambia in 1750 while returning from his "manhood ritual" and sold into slavery in North America. The book spent forty-six weeks on the *New York Times* bestseller list, including twenty-two at number one, and won the Pulitzer Prize.

The capture of Kunta, played by LeVar Burton, was filmed not far from my childhood home. His arduous journey on the Middle Passage was also shot in Savannah, though the extras who were paid thirty dollars a day to be smeared in oatmeal and shackled in a hull were so traumatized that two thirds did not return the second day of shooting. For the auction in which Kunta Kinte was sold to his enslaver, producers blanketed Oglethorpe Square, a block from my father's office, with dirt and covered the parking meters with oleanders. We skipped school to watch the filming.

But it was a scene in episode two in which Kunta marries Bell, played by Madge Sinclair, who would later voice Simba's mother in *The Lion King*, that occupies a footnote in the history of ritual. Bell makes her fiancé spend an entire day practicing a betrothal rite he finds "ridiculous for such a solemn occasion."

Jumping the broom.

"Kunta and Bell jumped high over the broomstick together," Haley writes. "She had warned that a marriage would meet the very worst kind of bad luck if the feet of either person should touch the broomstick, and whoever did it would be the first to die." When the couple lands safely, "all the observers applauded and cheered."

As I witnessed at the lobola in South Africa, brooms have long played a colorful role in ritual. Folklore going back to the ancient world celebrates brooms as both domestic necessities and ominous accessories. Greek philosopher Pythagoras warned his followers "not to eat in a chair, not to sit under a vine, and not to step over a broom." The Christian world built on this legacy, highlighting the phallic qualities of brooms and linking them to coitus and witchy power.

The earliest recorded examples of jumping the broom as a matrimonial rite appeared in the British Isles in the sixteenth century among working-class whites. The ritual served couples on the margins, unbound by church customs and unserved by law. A 1598 account relates how a "bryde and brydegroome, not handyely fyndeing a Parson, and being in grievous haste to be wed" did "jumpe from one syde of ye Broome-stycke over to ye other syde" becoming "lawfulle Man and Wyffe." Dickens includes a broomstick wedding in *Great Expectations.*

From those white Anglo roots, jumping the broom jumped the Atlantic and entered the lives of enslaved Africans. The first known documentation in the United States describes a North Carolina couple in 1814 who "saluted each other as bride and groom, jumped over the broomstick in the kitchen, and were pronounced married." Tyler Parry, a historian of the African diaspora, speculates that "given that enslaved people and poor whites fraternized in underground networks," Black families adopted the custom. Leaping over broomsticks, often while balancing candles or glasses of water on their heads, joined a slate of renegade rituals for couples with no legal rights, including kissing a horseshoe and Indigenous blanket ceremonies. Parry's review of forty-one volumes of slave narratives found that 28 percent of weddings involved jumping the broom.

Just as quickly as this ritual rose up, however, it faded. Once emancipated, the formerly enslaved sought legal validation for their marriages, in part because Black spouses could be refused inheritance and Black veterans denied pensions if "they married by jumping over a Broomstick." Also, freed people no longer wanted to validate the rites of their captivity. By the early 1900s, jumping the broom had been relegated to the dustbin of history.

It took one of the biggest events in television history to dust it off again.

Roots premiered on ABC on January 23, 1977. Over the next eight nights, one hundred forty million Americans watched—85 percent of all homes with televisions—the largest viewership of any series before or since. One of those viewers was fourteen-year-old Danita

Rountree Green. After the second episode, she wrote in her journal: "*Roots* was on again last night and I can't get anything done. Kunta and Bell got married and jumped the broom just like those old folks used to talk about."

"I'm a *Roots* baby," Danita explained. "I would often think about how it would feel to be ripped from one continent and planted in another—the hopelessness, having to disavow everything you left behind then set about building something new. Plus, people who came from different tribes in Africa were forced to live together. How do you create community out of that?"

Those questions simmered in Danita's mind for nearly twenty years, through teaching, leading weddings, and raising a son. "Then I got into a horrific car accident, had major burns on my legs, and was rushed to the hospital. I was supposed to have a skin graft but instead had one of those Marcus Welby moments. The doctor walks in and says, 'You can't do the surgery, you're pregnant!'"

Danita spent the next seven months lying flat on her back with her legs elevated. "I couldn't take morphine because of the baby. I can't entirely explain why, but somehow my mind drifted back to *Roots* and that broom jumping. It must be that I was thinking about building a family. I've been a writer of some sort forever—journals, poetry, songs that are awful. So I wrote a book!"

Broom Jumping: A Celebration of Love is a sixty-eight-page love story to a forgotten life ritual. Danita reviews the symbolism: "The pole represents your spiritual home; the straw represents your ancestors; the binding represents the forces that are working to hold us together."

She offers tips for the bride and groom: "Hold the handle together, sweep in a circle, lay the broom on the ground. Then, jump over it together."

She throws in some levity: "We're going to see who the boss really is—the bride can't jump and yank the groom across. But if you do things together, there really is no boss."

She gives tips to the audiences: "Guests have to extend their hands forward and wiggle their fingers to send good energy to the couple."

And she offers this promise to the bride and groom: "If you follow these rules, you'll be exuberantly happy. Just as you can't count the straws in your broom, you can't count the souls who are rooting for your success."

Danita printed a few hundred copies of the book at Kinko's, sent out a press release, and waited for the orders to flood in.

None came.

"Months passed. Nothing. But I knew a lady who worked in the mailroom at the *Richmond Times-Dispatch* who really wanted to become a reporter. She called me up. 'Ms. Nita, I read about your broom ceremony. Can I come take a picture and write an article?'"

The article appeared in the paper. Soon, the AP picked it up, *USA Today* ran it, *The Wall Street Journal* published it. Once again, Danita sat back, confident she knew exactly who would be the first to call.

She was wrong.

At Queen Victoria's funeral on February 2, 1901, Her Majesty's coffin was making its way through Windsor Castle, mounted on a carriage drawn by the Royal Horse Artillery, when the horses became spooked by the ceremonial gun salute, bolted, and nearly toppled the deceased monarch. The queen's grandson-in-law, Prince Louis, barked, "Give the honour to the naval guard!" One hundred thirty-eight bluejackets promptly unhooked the horses and pulled the carriage the rest of the way. Ever since, the Royal Navy has performed these honors at state funerals, including for Winston Churchill and Prince Louis's granddaughter-in-law, Queen Elizabeth II.

Out of chaos, a ritual was born.

Of all the myths surrounding life rituals, perhaps the most enduring—and the most misleading—is that for every occasion there is a *pure ritual* out there, a holy grail, a lost ark, inside of which is the original recipe, which everyone can just follow. There is no such truth.

Instead, there is a deeper truth: Every life ritual is invented, reinvented, improvised, plagiarized, forged in crisis, modified in real time. We saw this process unfold with baptism, a pagan rite that became a Jewish rite that became a Catholic rite that became a Protestant rite, each slightly different. It's equally true of breaking the glass at weddings, a folk custom that medieval rabbis tried—and failed—to squelch, so they co-opted it, turning it into a symbol of the fragility of being Jewish, which later generations turned into a symbol for finding strength in shattered times, which contemporary couples turned into a branding opportunity to mold the broken pieces into candlesticks, photo frames, car mezuzahs, or "custom snowglobe wedding breaking glass keepsakes," available on judaica.com for $497.65, a savings of 9 percent.

This tale of evolution holds one more truth: The biggest breakthroughs in how we make collective meaning tend to come in periods of larger social change. The British historian David Cannadine has shown that the queen's funeral horse episode was part of the larger "invention of tradition" in Victorian Britain, a time of rapid industrialization, national rivalries, and the remaking of the family. Scottish kilts and English tea were "invented" in the late 1800s, as were imperial parades and milestone jubilees. The signature *Pomp and Circumstance* march was composed days after Victoria's death and was performed at her successor's coronation.

The "enhanced and ritualized public face of the British monarchy," Cannadine writes, "was but one example of a more general proliferation of new or revived ceremonial." Within families, silver spoons became popular baby gifts, lockets popular courtship tokens, black clothes popular mourning attire. This eruption of invention was not limited to Britain. In America, the baby shower, wedding shower, photo album, obituary, embalming, and séance all became standard, as did Memorial Day, Valentine's Day, Thanksgiving, and the Fourth of July. The net result of this mass rush to ritual was to create a calendar of communal gatherings and shared celebrations that reinforced the fragile creation of national identity.

E pluribus ritualis.

And it wasn't just mainstream culture that blossomed with ritual; counterculture did, too. In *Singing the Master*, Roger Abrahams, a folklorist at the University of Pennsylvania, chronicles the emergence of African American culture during this period. Abrahams focuses on corn-shucking ceremonies, elaborate, multiday festivals held every fall, in which white masters played host to enslaved Africans in exuberant displays of singing and dancing. Like Balinese cockfighting and other pageants of resistance, the "obligatory play and performance," Abrahams writes, inverted existing power structures, temporarily leveling the field of lonely, isolated owners and captive, "homesick" workers, allowing them to briefly find common ground and an "opportunity for cultural invention."

And what a legacy of invention they left behind.

"Slave holidays left traces on American life that went far beyond the corn-shucking," Abrahams writes, including minstrel shows, blackface, fiddle-and-banjo ensembles, vaudeville, Mardis Gras, mummers, *Amos 'n' Andy*, the Grand Ole Opry, *Ed Sullivan*, and *Hee Haw*. "The black skiffle and jug bands of the early twentieth century were descendants of minstrel music, and (just to show how far the historical string can run), the Beatles began their career as an English skiffle band." *Breakdancing* entered American vernacular from the "breaking down" at the end of Black dances, which in turn came from cutting the ears off the stalks, or *breaking down the corn*. What once was a ritual of the oppressed became a ritual of the world at the 2024 Paris Olympics.

Danita had a clear idea of what her self-published book would unleash.

"I was waiting for all these Black people to flood my mailbox. But the first couple that contacted me was two men who wanted to get married in Florida. At the time, I didn't even know how I felt about such weddings. My first thought was, *Hell, no! That's not why I created this ceremony*. Then I slept over it, and my second thought was, *Hell, yes! Broom jumping has always been for the marginalized or oppressed. Who am I to say no to these people?*"

For weeks, every single order she received came from a couple facing a different barrier to love. "There were couples from different religious backgrounds or ethnic groups. A Muslim and a Christian, a Hindu and a Jew. I heard from people with disabilities or whose parents didn't approve of their partners. It was probably two months before I heard from a Black couple."

Black families did embrace jumping the broom. By the early 2000s, writes Michael Eric Dyson, an acclaimed historian of the African American experience, young Black people turned to Afrocentrism in an attempt "to celebrate the spirit of ingenuity and survival in the face of suffering." "Heritage weddings" became a prominent feature in that effort, "heritage brooms" a prominent feature in those weddings. Purveyors offered "custom brooms and favors, broom bouquets and DIY broom kits"; couples demanded "a broom that looks like the slave brooms of history but is ornate enough to be considered a keepsake." Artisanal broom sets cost as much as $200.

Bell's dream had become the belle of the ball.

Yet as Danita's experience foretold, Black Americans weren't the only ones to adopt the idea. Jumping the broom became a signature feature of LGBTQ weddings, Indigenous weddings, cross-cultural weddings. *Noah's Arc: Jumping the Broom*, a film about the wedding of two Black men, was released in theaters; *Jumping the Broom*, a play about same-sex marriage, premiered in San Francisco. Articles ran in *Oprah*, *Brides*, *The Knot*, and *The New York Times*. There were even signs that jumping the broom might be jumping the shark, with online posts like "Jumping the Broom: Slave Ritual Meets Couture" and "Jumping the Broom: An Anarchist Perspective on Marriage."

For Danita, however, who has gone on to lead thousands of broom-jumping ceremonies, the popularity of the ritual she first fell in love with as a girl reflects a deeper turn to meaning.

"The broom is a symbol of home," she said. "When I perform celebrations, I try to get not just the couple involved but the entire family. I have the audience count, 'Three . . . two . . . one . . .' Then the couple has to decide, 'Are we going to jump on *one* or jump on *jump*?'

"I don't care how they figure it out," she continued. "The point is they're taking time, we can see them discussing it, and we're joking with the cousin standing next to us or the college roommate behind us, neither of whom we've ever met. We're laughing. We're bonding. We're creating what I've been trying to create since I first started doing weddings all those years ago: community."

And in that moment before they leap, Danita observed, no one particularly cares where jumping the broom came from. "It's long since transcended its murky origins." People care about what the custom means today.

"You know that son I was carrying at the time of my accident?" Danita said. "He grew up to become a professional dancer. He's deaf, and he's . . ."

Her voice trailed off for a second, and I couldn't hear her.

"He's what?" I asked.

"He's gay."

"Of course he is," I said. "That's how the universe works."

"Exactly. And today he performs more jumping-the-broom ceremonies than I do. He does them for deaf couples, for gay couples. He's like me in that he doesn't suffer religion. But he's deeply attracted to spirituality and deeper meaning. And he taught me that in African dance, jumping over anything, even another dancer, is a metaphor for transition.

"That's why jumping the broom endures. It's a way of honoring tradition but also celebrating starting over. It's a visual, embodied metaphor that stays with you for a lifetime. I know couples who still have their brooms. I married these two ministers; they tell me when they have a disagreement, they pull their broom off the wall."

"Why?"

"So they can remember why they used it in the first place—all the work that goes into keeping a marriage together, a family together, community together.

"Then they jump it again."

7.

THE FOUR SOMETHINGS

All Your Dreams Fulfilled

The day I discovered the four somethings is the day I attended six weddings in Las Vegas.

The first wedding was an elopement.

Just before nine on a chilly December morning, a black town car rolls into the gravel parking area at the head of Ash Spring Trail in Red Rock Canyon. Nevada's first national conservation area comprises two hundred thousand acres of oxidized sandstone cliffs in the Mojave Desert, filled with rhubarb, mesquite, and fishhook nipple cactuses; jackrabbits, coyotes, and endangered desert tortoises; along with the occasional tarantula and scorpion, all just fifteen miles from the Las Vegas Strip. In other words, a perfect spot to tie the knot.

Yay! Congrats on planning your elopement! You're in great hands with Cactus Collective Weddings. We know these deserts like the backs of our hands, and we're going to make sure you have the most unique, stress-free, gorgeous wedding day.

The first person to emerge is Remington, a six-foot spitting image of his name, with unwashed Wranglers, tan boots, a blue-checked blazer and white western shirt, topped off by a brand-new, off-white rabbit fur cowboy hat. He also has a goatee, a blond mullet, and a bashful smile.

"We met on Tinder at Texas Tech," Remington says. "Then we took a class together." Today the recent grads live in Colorado and work at the world's largest supplier of livestock feed.

Jana appears next. She, too, is tall and is wearing a white minidress with a sweetheart neckline, covered from neck to toe with see-through lace. She has straight black hair, white sneakers, and an expression that says she would rather be wearing sweatpants and listening to Luke Combs.

"I don't like being the center of attention," Jana says. "We were having these fights about which family members to invite. Finally, I said, 'We're already going to the rodeo National Finals in Vegas. Let's just get married!'"

Your wedding day packing list: marriage license, lip gloss, vows, water, sunscreen, walking shoes, tissues (for your tears of joy!).

Angie Kelly is the last to arrive. An upbeat Michigander with a blonde updo, Angie is the maestro behind Peachy Keen Unions, "modern-day marriage officiants" with a staff of fifteen who perform a thousand weddings a year. "Quickly, before we go up to Ash Spring, I want to review your keepsake certificate. Julie, on our team, will be your witness, which means she'll get invited to all the birthdays of your kids." Everyone chuckles. "Groom, do you have the rings?"

Remington produces his-and-hers boxes. Hers is from a jeweler in Oklahoma that specializes in rings that "can be paired with a dress or blue jeans and cowboy boots"; his is from a wildlife design company in Texas that inlays bands with naturally shed antlers.

"Jana, do you have your bouquet and change of shoes?"

She raises them in the air.

"And just to confirm: You're expecting zero guests?"

They nod.

"All right, the wind is picking it up, the sagebrush is tumbling, it's beginning to feel a lot like Lubbock. Let's go elope!"

The December 16, 1967, issue of *The Saturday Evening Post* featured a profile of Jackie Kennedy's sister, an interview with Ho Chi Minh, and a column by the ruthless bard of Americana, Joan Didion, titled "Marrying Absurd." The article opens with understatement: "To be married in Las Vegas, Clark County, Nevada, a bride must swear that she is eighteen or has parental permission and a bridegroom that he is twenty-one or has parental permission."

It ends with condescension. A "bored waiter" pours out "a few swallows of pink champagne ('on the house') for everyone except the bride," who's underage, pregnant, but still blubbers that her shotgun wedding "was just as nice as I hoped and dreamed it would be."

In between when the article ran and the essay appeared the following year in Didion's breakout book, *Slouching Towards Bethlehem*, however, the author changed her tune. Instead of sneering at starry-eyed Vegas sweethearts, she pays grudging respect to Sin City for becoming the worldwide headquarters of the most flamboyant and polarizing life ritual of all.

Loving.

"Las Vegas seems to offer something other than 'convenience,'" Didion observes in a sentence added for the book. "It is merchandizing 'niceness,' the facsimile of proper ritual, to children who do not know how else to find it, how to make the arrangements, how to do it 'right.'"

That triumph of "niceness" and "rightness" earns Las Vegas in general, and the Little White Wedding Chapel in particular, a stop in our around-the-world-in-eighty-centuries tour of the history of ritual. In this case, what happens in Vegas has not stayed in Vegas.

Loving rituals have always been stalked by strife. "There is no occasion for a feast that is as conspicuous and much discussed as a wedding," Plutarch wrote. A persistent source of that strife is that most celebrations of lovemaking rarely involved love. In ancient Greece, weddings were sad, sober affairs in which the bride was abducted by older men, veiled, and locked in her conjugal chamber; in ancient India, falling in love before marriage was considered offensive and antisocial; in ancient China, the word for *love* was never applied to husband and wife. Even as late as the Renaissance, Montaigne is said to have quipped that any man who was in love with his wife was "a man so dull that no one else could love him."

Instead, weddings were less about lovemaking and more about dealmaking—exchanging capital, forming alliances, securing labor, breeding assets. The pomp was designed to mask the circumstance. Sure, some couples developed affection for each other, but their main purpose was to serve the needs of the larger group. Marriage converted strangers into relatives and neighbors into networks. With a system that worked so efficiently, what external outside force could possibly be strong enough to overturn it?

Eternal bliss.

While romantic love had percolated underneath mating for millennia—often for relationships outside of wedlock—it didn't upend marriage until the modern era. Some date the origin to 1549, the year Thomas Cranmer, the archbishop of Canterbury who had presided over Henry VIII's serial weddings, compiled the Book of Common Prayer. Its marriage rite was the first to include the word *love* ("love, cherish, and obey") and introduced the lingua franca of contemporary nuptials: *Dearly beloved . . . we are gathered together to join this man and woman in holy matrimony . . . to have and to hold, from this day forward, for richer or poorer, in sickness or health . . . till death do us part.*

Given how these phrases have echoed not just through the English-speaking world, but through colonialism to every continent and through Hollywood to every couple, it seems safe to say that they constitute the most influential script in the history of ritual.

The most influential wedding in history was Henry VIII's thirteenth successor.

By the nineteenth century, marriage in the West had become less about creating a "house," as in a family lineage and social network, and more about creating a "home," as in a private domicile or nuclear family. The decision of twenty-year-old Queen Victoria to break from tradition in her wedding to her first cousin Albert and walk down the aisle of Chapel Royal in 1840 to musical accompaniment, dressed in pure white satin instead of the traditional silver-and-white brocade silk, orange blossoms in her hair, an eighteen-foot train, and twelve bridesmaids in white by her side, "invented" the modern template. The first wedding of a reigning English queen in three hundred years and the last of a sitting English monarch popularized the white wedding cake (hers was a three-hundred-pound, three-tiered fruitcake topped with a faux marble bride and groom), the romantic honeymoon (hers was at Windsor Castle), even the wedding photograph (hers was staged fourteen years later).

Coming at the dawn of mass media (her funeral was among the first to be captured on film), Victoria is the OG ritual influencer.

Ironically, given her role in shaping the middle-class fairy tale, her great-great-great-grandson probably did more than any single person to kill it. In the decades after 1840, what Victoria invented, capitalism exploited. An entire ecosystem built up around engagements (parties! registries!), births (showers! rattles!), deaths (caskets! flowers!). Rites of passage became the hunting ground for large swaths of the modern economy: the ritual-industrial complex.

The crowning jewel of that complex was the brainchild of Frances Gerety, a copy editor at the Philadelphia ad agency N. W. Ayer & Son, who in 1947 was tasked with writing a catchphrase for De Beers. The rare woman in a man's world, Gerety was exhausted and out of ideas when she prayed one night before bed, *Dear God, send me a line*, then scribbled something on a piece of paper. When she awoke the next morning and looked at the paper, it read "A diamond is forever." Fifty years later, *Ad Age* named it the slogan of the century. Women wanted their men to spend money on "a washing machine or a new car, anything but an engagement ring," said Gerety, who never married. She persuaded them to spend "three months' salary" on an invented ritual.

In retrospect, it was only a matter of time before the fairy-tale-wedding bubble burst. July 29, 1981, is as good a date as any to call the top of the market. The global spectacle of Charles and Diana's loveless vows is the ultimate example of irrational exuberance: $50,000 dress! Ten thousand pearls! Twenty-five-foot train! Five-tier cake (with twenty-seven backups in case of accidents)! And most important: seven hundred fifty million viewers worldwide.

Within a decade the couple was separated—exactly the same time that big weddings, small weddings, and weddings of any kind began their sharp retreat as a cultural mandate.

One of the greatest satisfactions in life is meeting the person that awakens the love.

Angie was standing in a dirt clearing, framed by a backdrop of sage and cactus, reading a script that she'd worked on with the couple. Jana was to her left; Remington to her right. Jana had changed into heels and was holding an oversize bouquet of Thanksgiving-colored flowers.

The person that expands your thinking, helps you feel alive, creates magic in routines. Sharing activities like sitting on the couch with popcorn, candy, and a good movie. Enjoying a bond so singular that your relationship represents the most authentic level of commitment you've known.

The story of how Las Vegas became the wedding capital of the world begins not long after Sioux Falls stopped being the divorce capital of the world. In 1931, Nevada legalized gambling, reduced residency requirements for divorce to six weeks, and relaxed marriage laws to make it the easiest state in the nation in which to take the plunge. With no blood test or waiting period, the desert getaway became the outlet of choice for "Vegas vows," "neon nuptials," "Sin City specials," and all manner of last-minute hitch-and-runs.

Fed by GIs heading to and from war, the number of annual weddings tripled during World War II, ballooned in the fifties after the *London Daily Herald* deemed Vegas the "Marriage Capital of the World," and then took off during Vietnam. The annual tally reached 125,000 around Y2K.

Ever since, the number of weddings has steadily dropped, settling around 50 percent of its peak. The size of weddings has also plummeted. McKenzi Taylor, the founder of Cactus Collective, told me on our hike up Ash Spring Trail that when she started her business in 2016, 80 percent of weddings had more than fifty guests while 20 percent had fewer, a category known as microweddings; a decade later that percentage had flipped.

"Millennials changed everything. They get married later, which means they're more independent. They want to pay for their own weddings, write their own vows, invite their own friends. They tell their parents, 'Butt out!'"

Gen Z is going even further, she said, with even more personalization, branded swag, and behind-the-scenes footage designed to pop on social media "for you" pages. To meet this demand, Cactus Collective offers three packages—Ocotillo, Agave, Saguaro—with hundreds of customizations for day of the week, venue, officiant, bouquet and boutonniere, eco-friendly decorations, magazine-quality art photos, acoustic guitarist or professional violinist, hand-painted watercolor or acrylic painting, and a "request your song" processional or recessional. The company performs up to ten weddings a week.

Today, the two of you are receiving a precious gift. That gift is a loving person to share an alliance with. The best marriages nurture each other as individuals while allowing for mutual growth.

Jana and Remington chose the simplest package, with an approved mention of God, a passage from the book of Ruth, no music, and a doughnut-and-champagne cart to follow.

Let's take a moment and place your rings in the palms of your hands. Feel the weight of that ring, its loving energy. Worn on the side of the body closest to your heart, these rings will be an outward, visible reminder of the promises you make today.

Remington went first. "Jana, with this ring, I give you my promise to honor you, to share my love with you, to walk with you through joy and sorrow, sickness and health, from this day forward."

He started sobbing.

Jana followed but didn't cry. Later, when I asked what they learned about each other during the ceremony, she answered, "That he's more emotional than I am!"

Now, Remington and Jana, squeeze those hands in front of you. We have two best friends on their wedding day. Prior to this moment, you have held many different roles and titles, none as important as the one you leave here with today. By the authority vested in me, I proudly pronounce you husband and wife. Remington, you may kiss your bride!

Angie Kelly likes the hardest weddings—they remind her of her own wedding and her upbringing.

Angie grew up in a large Polish family in Michigan that never felt like family. Her military father deployed to England when she was five, and never returned; her aunt and uncle moved in to help. "My uncle basically raised me—he's the one who took me to daddy-daughter dances, taught me about basketball and how to clean a fish tank. But my family never accepted him because he's Black."

Eager to escape, Angie became a flight attendant and FAA analyst, before settling in Vegas "because I knew I could find a boyfriend here." The boyfriend she got was in a band; had a shaved head, piercings, and tattoos; and was the exact opposite of the Midwest nice that Angie, who looks like a Dallas Cowboys cheerleader, detested.

She interviewed eight wedding officiants before picking one. "At our first meeting, I prodded my fiancé: 'You need to wear a button-up shirt, sit up straight, and answer his questions. He has to approve our wedding!' 'Angie, he's not approving anything,' her fiancé said. 'Marry me for who I am or don't marry me.'"

In the end, Angie got the wedding she wanted—traditional, conformist, and nice—and she hated it.

"My husband was right. I was mortified, embarrassed, and humiliated at the altar thinking, *I tried so hard to prevent this.*"

Six weeks later she became an officiant.

"I remember thinking, *Why are there no couples in* Brides *magazine who look like us? Where are the tattoos? The bikers? The biracial couples?* I became a marriage officiant to represent the underrepresented."

And she quickly discovered that the most important moment in any loving ritual is the one that she had screwed up: the negotiation, the deliberation, the mediation.

The peace plan.

The morning after Linda and I got engaged on a "mystery trip" I planned to Puerto Rico, she surprised me by announcing that even though her family is from Boston, she wanted to get married in Savannah. "It's historic," she said. "It's beautiful." The synagogue my family belongs to is the third oldest in the country. Also, she was convinced that the out-of-the-way location would deter her legion of distant cousins from making the trip. Instead, the opposite happened!

Even more notable was that her decision set off a series of great powers–style negotiations. The wedding would be in Savannah, but her parents would still "host." The ceremony would be at my synagogue, but her rabbi would still "officiate." The reception would be at an old horse stable but refashioned in the style of a Moroccan princess. That last request would prove challenging. When Linda described to Savannah's top caterer her vision of tables filled with colorful fabrics, flickering lanterns, and family-style platters of breads, olives, and hummus, his response was, "What's hummus?"

For months on my round-the-world travels, I tried to identify common traits that unite people who care about life rituals. Surely, those of us who are groupkeepers share certain qualities: *We are dreamers, we are seekers, we are huggers.* In the end, I scrapped the list after concluding that people who care about life rituals today share one overriding quality: *We are mediators.* We like tradition but don't mind bucking tradition. We have strong opinions but like building coalitions. We realize that with no sect that unites us and no script we agree on, everybody involved in a life ritual faces a choice: Be a troublemaker or be a peacemaker.

Being a peacemaker means being good at finding a happy medium. At the risk of sounding unromantic, life rituals are about compromise rehearsal. Resolve tensions around the wedding, or find those tensions even more entrenched by the time you're deciding how to raise children or whose job takes priority. Resolve tensions around the funeral, or find those tensions even more hardened when it comes time to divvy up the jewelry or sell the house.

The unsung reason to hold a life ritual is to practice resolving conflicts around the ritual.

"I call it identity building," Angie said. "I always ask, 'What is your identity as a couple?' Not Lisa. Not James. Lisa-and-James. I start positive. 'What are some qualities that made you fall in love?' *I love her shapely calves when she runs. I love when she uses cat emojis. I love that his eyes remind me of M&M's. I love how he puts those extra-fluffy marshmallows in my hot chocolate.*

"'What is your go-to activity as a couple?' *We do estate sales on Sunday and walk our dog down to the pier. We love a good taco truck and spitting watermelon seeds on the beach.*

"'What is your vision for your family?' *Touring the Great Wall of China, building a dream house in the Rockies, watching the boys jump on the couch as they rowdy cheer for the Cowboys.*"

But the real art of compromise, Angie said, is when she turns to the couple's vulnerabilities.

"James is Chinese; he doesn't believe in God. Lisa is Baptist; her father insists they get married by a pastor. James dreamed of a quiet ceremony; Lisa wants her sorority sisters by her side. James just lost his job; Lisa just lost a pregnancy.

"That's when the real work begins," she said.

That's when you need the four somethings.

Red Rock Canyon has a handful of approved locations for weddings. Ash Spring is limited to elopements, as the short hike is not ideal for grandparents, flower children, or harpists. The overlook is better for larger groups, as it has a paved parking lot, a toilet, and a view straight out of Ansel Adams.

Alyssa and Hunter chose the overlook for their twelve thirty microwedding. Hunter and his buddies arrived first. They looked like a country cover band, with boot-cut jeans, assorted blazers, and matching black cowboy hats. Hunter, who was built like a linebacker, wore a bespoke leather tuxedo jacket tattooed with garlands.

"Alyssa and I have been together for six years," he explained. "We met when I drove some horses up from Texas to deliver to her father's farm in Ohio. I basically never left."

Alyssa didn't want a "humongous wedding," he said. "She doesn't like being judged; she didn't want to spend a year planning; and she hated asking family members to fly across the country. We already come to rodeo finals every year; she said, 'Let's get married in six weeks!'"

Once the decision was made, though, their parents wanted to come, her grandmother insisted, siblings had to be included. So they ended up with thirty-five under the desert sun, followed by a private room at El Dorado Cantina on the strip.

McKenzi began moving everyone into formation. Red Rock limits folding chairs to twelve, so most guests stood. Two thirds wore cowboy boots, the rest sneakers; fleece was the most popular outerwear. A limo pulled into the parking lot. Alyssa, accompanied by a small entourage, began strolling along the incline—not so much down the aisle as up it.

The wind picked up, and no sooner did Alyssa reach the summit in her ankle-length lace dress and black-and-white cowboy boots than her black hair began to come loose from its bun. Unflustered, she grabbed her pink-and-orange bouquet in one hand, brushed back her hair, and issued a gusty laugh.

It would set the tone.

Welcome, everyone, to Alyssa and Hunter's wedding. Shimura, a native Las Vegan and family therapist who now conducts weddings full time for Peachy Keen, began the service.

Welcome to scenic Red Rock Canyon, where we have gathered under an open sky to witness two people embrace love as one of life's most fulfilling—

"Why are you frowning?" Alyssa interrupted, jabbing Hunter in the ribs. "Smile!"

Figure 9: The setup for Alyssa and Hunter's wedding in Red Rock Canyon, Nevada.

Everyone laughed.

The pattern continued. Shimura would say something earnest and sweet: *The evolution of love is found within a million tiny words; it's a promise to be patient, devoted, and forgiving.* And Alyssa would deliver a punch line: "Did you hear that?"

Shimura: *Hunter, have you come here gladly of your own free will?*

Alyssa: "We're in Vegas. Who doesn't come here willingly?!"

Alyssa may have demurred that she doesn't like standing out, but she turned out to be a rodeo clown. After exchanging their vows, she and Hunter didn't sob; they fist-bumped.

Watching the spectacle, I was struck by how even a small number of guests changed the experience. While Jana and Remington's ceremony felt private and self-contained, Alyssa and Hunter's felt more like a show, with performers and audience members feeding off each other.

I also realized that I had missed the point. I was so focused on how loving rituals have become more ornate and more bespoke that I had overlooked the far more pressing issue: Why have a ritual at all? The real question is not why people are having microweddings versus large weddings; it's why they're having microweddings versus *no* weddings. I put that question to Alyssa after the ceremony.

"I wanted to make today as easy as possible for everybody. My motto was less stress, more joy. But *no* wedding? Are you kidding? I'm way too old-fashioned for that!"

And therein lies the hope for life rituals: If we can find a way to reduce the stress and increase the meaning, if we can identify the most necessary of the unnecessary ingredients, we can ensure that collective celebrations continue. The challenge, as it always is in Las Vegas, is betting on the right number.

I choose four.

On our timeline of banner dates in the history of ritual, we should put an asterisk on 1871. That year, smack in the middle of the Victorian-era frenzy around invented rites, London's *St. James' Magazine* published the first known appearance of the most memorable ditty in the ritual canon.

In an article entitled "Marriage Superstitions, and the Miseries of a Bride Elect," an unnamed bride-to-be, let's imagine her to be the Joan Didion of her time, issues a scathing takedown of contemporary weddings. She ridicules the fuss over her clothes: "Such big discussions in which all my own ideas and opinions are silenced." She frets about "an old Welsh law" that "three blows with a broomstick on any part of the person, except the head," are fair. She sneers at the idea that the bride must toss a shoe into the crowd, with the expectation that whoever catches it "would shortly be married."

She also complains that "on the wedding day I must 'wear something new, something borrowed, something blue.'" Within a few years, that maxim had expanded into the legendary earworm, "something old, something new, something borrowed, something blue, a sixpence in your shoe." Within a century, that rhyme (minus the sixpence) had become the sine qua non of every pop cultural reference to weddings, from Emily Post to *ER*, Frank Sinatra to *Buffy the Vampire Slayer.*

And no wonder: Four seems to be the official number of life rituals. In my travels, I heard about the four elements (earth, water, air, fire), the four directions (north, south, east, west), and the four aspects (male, female, old, young). I would like to propose my own foursome: the four somethings—something old, something new, something borrowed, something you. This grouping represents what I believe to be the cleanest formula for how to plan a meaningful life ritual that balances tradition with progress, adaptation with personalization.

Let's consider this quatrain one couplet at a time.

Something old.

As we've seen, life rituals are shared, unnecessary acts that make us feel at home. A big part of feeling at home is feeling familiar. DIY rituals have their appeal, but if every element is plucked from Pinterest and scripted by AI, the resulting ceremony will seem soulless and shallow. The most enduring life rituals begin with tradition—a cultural keepsake, a valued prayer, a treasured memory, a beloved dish. For all the North African spices at our reception, the ceremony itself began with Linda walking down an aisle with a long veil.

The founder of the Purple Pundit Project has a simple test for picking something old. Sushma Dwivedi was born in Montreal into a long line of male Brahman pundits, a learned figure in Hinduism who also leads rituals. After moving to New York

City and working in corporate PR, Sushma became engaged. "Our wedding was a nightmare. I was estranged from my father; my husband had a transgender sibling who felt excluded; the ceremony started at midnight and lasted twelve hours."

Sushma asked her grandmother if she could become the family's first female pundit. "Even though she wasn't a pundit, she had all the knowledge to train me. And she was a tough coach—if she didn't like my Sanskrit, she'd made me do it over again."

The Purple Pundit Project focuses on "progressive, inclusive, LGBTQ+-friendly" life rituals including baby namings, housewarmings, and business blessings for people who are "straight, gay, having an interracial marriage, or just want a female pundit." "I knew if I could architect a thirty-five-minute express wedding where I cut out all the crap, got rid of everything offensive, and still made it feel Indian, I could help families." In her first seven years, Sushma performed a hundred rituals.

Her secret to navigating family sensitivities? "A ceremony has to pass the Auntie Sniff Test. The couple has to be happy, the parents have to be happy, but the real test is the aunties."

So how do you pass that test?

"In Indian weddings it's walking around the fire, putting vermilion powder in the bride's hair, and exchanging jewelry. But every culture has its own test. Stepping into the future means being willing to let go of what you don't need from tradition in order to preserve what you do."

Something new.

Every ritual, by nature, is new. It's not a replication of the past; it's a conversation with the past. It's not a reenactment of convention; it's a reinterpretation of convention.

Todd Shotz grew up in suburban Philadelphia surrounded by tradition. "There were five synagogues on one street." As a boy, he ate delicacies from his grandfather's shtetl in Moldova—beet borscht, kotleti beef and onion patties, potato bilkalach with egg and matzo. At ten, he joined the Torah club; at sixteen, he was confirmation president; at twenty-one, he moved to Israel.

Todd was on a fast track to being a rabbi, but after working on Broadway productions of *Kiss Me, Kate*; *Peter Pan*; and *Bring in 'da Noise, Bring in 'da Funk*, he realized the future wasn't in pure tradition but in blending traditions. He started Hebrew Helpers in Los Angeles, which runs modern rituals—mitzvah ceremonies, baby namings, weddings, memorial services—for interfaith and cross-cultural families. He has a staff of forty-two serving eleven regions.

"With couples in particular I start with a dry-erase board," Todd said. "I say, '*Let's write a mission statement for your wedding*. Not what your parents want; not what your rabbi or preacher wants. What resonates with you.'"

The ideas that emerge are breathtaking in their originality: decorating the chuppah with flowers, blankets, and calligraphy from each family; making a prayer shawl with quilted garments from the four grandmothers; anointing the couple's hands with holy water, henna, or spice blends; inscribing the rings in different languages; breaking shot glasses given by the fathers.

"We can't expect nineteenth-century rituals to fit twenty-first-century lives," Todd said. "People are used to curating their social media feeds, their streaming platforms, their Spotify playlists. We want to consume what we want, when we want. We need new rituals for new times."

The Las Vegas Strip is not actually in Las Vegas. The three-mile stretch of South Las Vegas Boulevard is just outside city limits. The glitziest part of the strip, containing the Monopoly board of ersatz wonders like the Great Pyramid, Eiffel Tower, and Venetian canals, is an hour's walk from the honky-tonk part. On this gap-toothed checkerboard of low-rent motels and fenced-in lots, across the street from Koolsville Tattoo and the Peppermint Hippo gentleman's club, and underneath the Elvis billboard with gyrating hips, is the world's most famous wedding venue.

The Little White Wedding Chapel was built in 1951 and expanded over the years to include a Drive Thru Tunnel of Love; outdoor gazebo; red-velvet chapel for sixty guests; and MJ Chapel, named after Michael Jordan, for six. That last name hints at why this bric-a-brac dollhouse has become so famous: all the famous people who were married here. A short list, annotated with their marital fate: Frank Sinatra and Mia Farrow (divorced); Joan Collins and Peter Holm (divorced); Bruce Willis and Demi Moore (divorced); Joe Jonas and Sophie Turner (divorced); Britney Spears and Jason Alexander (divorced); Ben Affleck and Jennifer Lopez (divorced). Oh, and the aforementioned Michael Jordan and Juanita Vanoy (divorced).

The Little White Wedding Chapel deserves an *Ad Age* award for Spin of the Century.

The chapel's check-in area is located across a parking lot in a building that also houses a photo studio and dress rental. The fluorescent waiting area reminded me of a car wash, complete with ATM, snack machines, and a wall-to-wall refrigerator with twenty bouquets. Signs were taped everywhere: SAVE YOUR LINGERIE FOR YOUR HONEYMOON, PROPER ATTIRE REQUIRED; LEAVE US A GOOGLE REVIEW AND GET A DISCOUNT! NEED DOLLY IMPERSONATOR.

In just over ninety minutes, I watched two dozen couples cycle

Figure 10: Elvis arrives at the Little White Wedding Chapel as a couple is photographed in front of the Tunnel of Love.

through and witnessed three weddings. Their package names tell their stories.

Tunnel of Love. Just after three, a female couple came dashing through the door. Both were around five feet tall; one wore a tuxedo with embroidered flamingos on the back, the other a poufy white gown above the knee that showed off a dragon tattoo serpentining up her left shin. The couple had booked the drive-through, which meant they recrossed the parking lot and entered a carport behind a white iron fence topped with hollow hearts. A photographer chronicled their every step.

The brides mounted the back perch of a pink Cadillac convertible with 4 LVIS plates that looked like it could have escorted John Travolta and Olivia Newton-John in *Grease.* A man in a threadbare tux poked his head out of a

McDonald's-style drive-through, hurried through the motions, and declared them married. The entire ceremony lasted less than ten minutes.

That's Amore. The next ceremony took even less time. It involved an elderly man in a wheelchair and ill-fitting brown suit and his twentysomething blonde nurse in a red dress. They chose Chapel Amore, which has red velvet love seats, six columns cascading with white plastic flowers, and a painted waterfall backdrop. The bride pushed her soon-to-be husband down the aisle, then scurried back and processed on the arm of her mother. A bored-looking officiant, a short script, and a peck on the cheek later, and mother and daughter were crying.

The King's Jubilee. The final couple looked like they had met at a furniture convention that week. He was slightly bald, slightly pudgy, slightly above fifty; she was the fun, flirty colleague who decorates her cubicle for Valentine's Day and drinks too much eggnog at the holiday party. They chose the Elvis tribute package for $495, which included a "12 Rose Hand Tied Bouquet," "Matching Boutonniere," and "3 Songs Performed by Your Impersonator."

This particular rent-a-king was Late Elvis in a white sequined flared pantsuit and an upturned collar stained with black hair dye. His three songs were "Love Me Tender" as the groom walked down the aisle, "Can't Help Falling in Love" as the bride did, and "Viva Las Vegas" after he declared them husband and wife. The photo shoot took longer than the ceremony.

By this point I was eager to flee this hunk of burning love. I have a high tolerance for kitsch; I spent a year performing as a circus clown.

But after the intimacy and charm of the morning, this afternoon's entire scene struck me as facile and fabricated. I could taste the bile of Joan Didion's ghost.

Stepping onto the street, I felt as lonely and depressed as I'd been on this journey. The Little White Wedding Chapel embodies the possibilities of ritual freed from long-standing norms; the couples, for their part, seemed thrilled with the dollar store glamour. But the venue also reeked of opportunism—less the feeling of home, more the feeling of flea market. I couldn't help wondering, if more and more couples view their weddings as stunts, would more and more marriages end up (divorced)?

The final two of the four somethings are trickier than the first.

Something borrowed.

Borrowing has become something of a flashpoint in recent years as appropriation has taken on a bad name. Defined as the adoption of rituals or traditions of one culture by a dominant culture, often for profit, appropriation is widely considered taboo. Native American groups have called the mainstream embrace of sweat lodges and vision quests a "direct attack and theft." Some designers I spoke with warned of importing rituals without context.

But far more pushed back on these concerns, pointing out that integrating ideas from other traditions has been the backbone of cultural evolution. Jews borrowed from Mesopotamians, Christians from Jews; Muslims from Christians; the Italian Renaissance from Ancient Rome; French impressionists from Japan; the Beatles from Chuck Berry and Bach;

Lin-Manuel Miranda from Eminem, Beyoncé, and Stephen Sondheim.

"Culture," writes Martin Puchner, a professor of comparative literature at Harvard, "is made not only from the resources of one community but also from encounters with other cultures. It is forged not only from the lived experience of individuals but also from borrowed forms and ideas that help individuals understand and articulate their experience in new ways."

Scarlett Mullikan had little choice but to borrow—the communities she designs rituals for have limited precedents. In the absence of an Auntie Sniff Test, she devised a Cool Uncle Exam.

Scarlett was born in rural Illinois to a five-time-married Korean War veteran turned sixties free lover and a thrice-married Christian who held church services at home. Scarlett married two weeks after her senior prom, had three children, and divorced at thirty; she worked as an ENT, a firefighter, and a truck unloader at Walmart.

Following her divorce, Scarlett dabbled in alternative communities—motorcycle clubs, tattoo parlors, swinging, polyamory. What she found were subcultures embracing non-traditional lifestyles but craving traditional rituals. When friends started asking her to draw on her church background to design "church-like" commitment ceremonies, Scarlett quit her job to open a barrier-breaking ritual design company.

In two decades, Scarlett has performed three hundred ceremonies for an alphabet of modern intimacy—LGBTQ, BDSM, ECNM (ethical and consensual non-monogamous). Ninety percent of her weddings are "alternative," including *Star Wars*, *Star Trek*, *Harry Potter*, Vikings; half are second marriages; a quarter use one of the fastest growing borrowed rites: handfasting.

"It started with my second husband, with whom I have an open marriage. He's Scottish, so we wanted bagpipes and kilts; I started researching other rituals when I discovered handfasting."

Derived from the Norse word *handfesta*, meaning "strike a bargain by joining hands," handfasting involves tying a cord or ribbon around the couple's clasp in a symbol of commitment; it inspired the English phrase *tying the knot*. From its roots in the British Isles, handfasting boomed in recent years and is featured in up to 15 percent of indie weddings in Britain and nearly that number in the US. Adopters include Angelina Jolie and Billy Bob Thornton, Daryl Hannah and Neil Young.

"I did a triad commitment ceremony recently for a married gay couple who was welcoming a third man into their relationship." The couple entered first; the new groom followed on the arm of one of the other men's moms, because his own mother had died. The men had chosen three satin ribbons—purple for royalty, blue for loyalty, and black for protection—each decorated with a charm. "The one nicknamed Papa Bear picked a bear paw; the Florida native selected a sailboat; the one who works at Disney chose *Fantasia*'s hat."

Scarlett wrapped their hands in a giant heart. *These are the hands that will love you*, she said. *These are the ties that will sustain you. These are the fingers that will wipe away your tears. These ribbons are a symbol of your souls, woven together forever, borrowed from others but bound by you.*

Something you.

The final something seems the simplest: You need an element that represents your life. Making that choice without seeming superficial, however, is challenging. Angie Kelly has a rule of thumb: no "thingies."

"Unity elements have become trendy," she explained, including unity candles (each person lights a taper that together light a third), unity stones (each person adds pebbles to a bowl), and unity sand ceremonies (each person pours different colored sand into a vessel).

"Where I draw the line is when a couple tells me they want 'that sand-blending thingy.' 'Thingy' is a dead giveaway that they just read about it on the internet. I tell them, 'Let's find something that represents you.'

"I had a couple who wanted to do a unity painting," she continued. "I told them, 'We're not letting paint anywhere near your dress.'" Then she asked them to share their love story. "Turns out they met when he sent her a shot of apple brandy at the airport. So we rolled out a cocktail cart, each poured brandy into a common glass, then they served each other sips. I called it a unity cocktail!"

Sometimes a cocktail can make you pucker up, she said. *Sometimes it can give you a headache. Just like marriage!*

The sun was setting behind Red Rock Canyon as I started walking up South Las Vegas Boulevard. I wasn't even sure where I was going. The wind picked up; the neon lights at Talk of the Town adult books flickered on.

A sign across the street caught my eye. It was bright pink with art deco hearts and diamonds: LITTLE VEGAS CHAPEL. The vibe said 1950s nightclub, though the building said 1980s Pizza Hut. A glutton, I walked in and asked if I could attend a wedding. Within minutes I was ushered into the Archway Chapel, with exposed beams, a barn roof, and seating for forty.

A groom was talking with a female officiant about his bride's "first look" entrance. Sergio was Puerto Rican, around twenty-eight, dressed sharply in a gray plaid suit, white shirt, and black patent leather shoes that looked rented. He was humble, handsome, and charmingly nervous.

"It's my first time in Las Vegas. We thought about having a big wedding, but I'm cheap."

By this point in my day, I was pretty sure I knew how the ceremony would unfold.

"We'll start the music," the officiant explained. "I'll signal for you to walk down the aisle. Then Jocelyn will walk through those doors."

We were merchandising "nice," as Didion said; we were "doing it right."

I was completely wrong.

Sergio had just graduated from MIT with a PhD in biological engineering. "During the SARS-CoV-2 pandemic," the university boasted in a commendation, "he played a leading effort to develop a recombinant subunit vaccine candidate that could be manufactured at a global scale." Sergio had just accepted a job in New York City at a novel antibody therapeutics company. That penny-pinching he referred to? He was saving money so that he and his bride, Jocelyn, who was from Ecuador, could buy their first apartment.

"Joss," Sergio said, after she made her entrance in a sleeveless white dress and hip-length veil, "sometimes I cannot believe that you and I, coming from two different parts of the world, coincided in the same place. But ever since meeting you, I have lived the best years of my life.

"You were my companion when the world went into lockdown, when I stayed late in the lab, when we lived thrilling experiences and heartbreaking losses. You're gorgeous, smart, and caring.

"I promise to support you on any path you want to take. I promise to be the sympathetic ear to all your thoughts and feelings. I promise to take care of you. After four years together, today, I can finally say that I choose you, my best friend, the beautiful Joss, as my perfect match."

There were four people in the room. All of us were crying.

"Sergio, I never expected to find the kind of love we have. I didn't believe it existed. The love I would see only in movies.

"To walk around every single day feeling like we were meant to be. To feel so connected that sometimes I feel like we read each other's minds. To love someone so deeply that it feels like home.

"Because that's what you are to me, Sergio. You're my best friend. You're my soulmate. You're my home. I can't wait to love you forever."

Three weeks after "Marrying Absurd" appeared in *The Saturday Evening Post*, the magazine published a letter to the editor from Barstow, California. "Where does Joan Didion get off running down Las Vegas weddings?" the writer scowled, noting that she and her husband had been married by a justice of the peace in Las Vegas and "are still happily married and the parents of three great kids.

"Not everyone who marries in Vegas is drunk, pregnant, mini-skirted or multi-married. Most are average people like us who don't care for the expense, the show, the planning and waiting for a traditional church wedding."

Nearly sixty years later, Boiling in Barstow's critique still holds. The lights might be brighter on the Vegas Strip; the kitsch might be kitschier; the weddings might be smaller, cheaper, and fewer. But the answer to why have loving rituals at all appears to be the same: because people need to clean their cowboy hats and polish their patent leather, slip on their lace and slide on their rings, rehearse some compromises and resolve some tension, stand before the saguaros and however many guests they choose and decide whether or not to approve a mention of God.

They need to make peace. They need to make nice.

They need to make love.

"I cry at every wedding," McKenzi Taylor told me. "When people hear what I do, the most common question I get is, 'Tell me about your Bridezillas.' But the truth is, we don't have any. Most of our couples are lovely. I feel so much gratitude being able to watch them live out their dreams. I hope we never abandon these rituals."

Now wouldn't that be something.

8.

CELEBRATION TRAIL

Seeing the Forest Through the Forest Bathing

"Before I explain what forest bathing is, I will explain what it is not."

Alfredo Herrera is sitting in a grove of some of the oldest vegetation on the planet—five-thousand-year-old cypress, carob, and monkey puzzle trees—on the banks of the Liucura River in the Lake District of south-central Chile. Nestled among the Andes Mountains to the east, the Pacific Ocean to the west, the Patagonian glaciers to the south, and the Atacama Desert to the north, this volcanic alley is what the ancient Greeks called a "crossroads," a location "between the worlds" where the paranormal becomes normal, where the Indigenous Mapuche tribe has a rich spiritual tradition, and where people come from around the world to experience nature rituals.

"Forest bathing is not an activity that requires physical effort, so we're not hiking to the top of a mountain. It's not a naturalist excursion, so we're not identifying plant or bird species. It doesn't involve soap or water."

Six participants from South America, Europe, and the Middle

East, dressed in light sweaters and loose-fitting pants, are seated cross-legged with their eyes closed on patches of damp grass on an early midsummer afternoon. A bumblebee buzzes. A woodpecker pecks.

"Forest bathing is a feeling. It's immersion in an atmosphere. It's a ritual practice that began in Japan in response to rising levels of anxiety, depression, and stress and quickly spread around the globe. It's about reconnecting with one another in our sacred surroundings."

Alfredo is a handsome thirty-five-year-old with an angular nose and shoulder-length black hair who was raised between the crowded capital of Chile and the jungles of Ecuador. His Spanish-born wife struggles with depression and had long found comfort being in nature; when she heard about the robust scientific benefits of forest bathing, she said, "Oh, that's why I feel better outdoors!"

The two became certified leaders in one of the world's fastest-growing ritual subcultures, with a global headquarters in Portugal, a network of training programs in seventy countries, and ritualized gatherings stretching from the Black Forest of Germany to the Himalayas in Bhutan, the redwoods of California to the Rift Valley of Kenya.

"Over the next several hours, I'm going to offer you a series of invitations," Alfredo said. "We call them invitations because they're opportunities to connect with nature—and with one another. You can walk around or lie on the ground; you can feel the texture of a flower or follow the call of an owl. The idea is to listen to your surroundings, then share what you feel with the group."

"And what if we don't feel like sharing?" asked a sixty-something woman from Sweden.

"Whatever you feel is right. We're not here to judge—or to ask questions. We're here to listen, because only when we discover what we've lost will we discover what we need. Now, I invite you to open your eyes and see what's in front of you as if for the very first time."

For years I've kept a running list of all the times I was visited by a ghost. Not a ghost in the white-sheet, black-holes, Casper sense. Nor the chilling, Hamlet, my-uncle-killed-my-father sense. More in the Dickens–Ebenezer Scrooge sense of an unexpected messenger from the past, present, or future.

The first was at my bar mitzvah. Standing at the pulpit of Congregation Mickve Israel in my itchy, navy pin-striped suit, my wavy blond hair looming over my ears, I was preparing to deliver a commentary on the Torah portion I had just recited in (poor) Hebrew about Abraham going forth from his father's house. Reading from green felt-tip ink on yellow legal pad paper, I looked over the crowd of three hundred people in the sanctuary my family had prayed in for nearly a century. As light shone through the stained glass windows, I suddenly felt myself floating over the pews, looking back on my boyish self becoming my future self.

The second was at our wedding, twenty-five years later, at the old stable converted into a Moroccan boudoir. (We got the hummus!) Linda and I were holding hands just off the dance floor as family members delivered toasts. When my parents took the microphone—my father in a tuxedo, my mother in a purple pantsuit—I suddenly flashed back to myself as a child looking at photographs of their wedding, then flashed forward to my own children looking at photographs of ours.

The third was the day I was diagnosed with bone cancer. I came home on crutches, lay down on my bed, when my three-year-old daughters, Tybee and Eden, came skipping into the room, laughing, giggling, twirling this ring-around-the-rosy dance until they tumbled to the ground. Suddenly I was the specter of my future self, watching my daughters do all the things without me that I had dreamed of doing with them, from walking through Paris to walking down aisles.

Not until this journey through ritual did I realize that each of these episodes happened during a moment of extreme emotional arousal—the great transitions of my life. Or that "ghost" isn't really the best way to capture what I experienced.

Instead, I think it's more accurate to say that I partook in a kind of time travel, a rupture in the ordinary laws of physics and space when I could ricochet from past to future and back again in a flutter of remembering and a phantom of foretelling. And that this seemingly paranormal experience is actually quite normal in moments of liminality.

Indeed, I now believe that this bursting of conventional restraints and lifting of the quotidian veil is the third great thing that life rituals do. They reprieve reality with virtual reality. They access what Indiana Jones called "the space between the spaces." They allow us, in the words of the Romanian mythologist Mircea Eliade, to "break the bonds of daily life," to pass "from plane to plane," to fulfill the "ultimate longing of the human body" to live "in the manner of a spirit."

They levitate. They consecrate.

They celebrate.

The idea that life celebrations might inspire a form of time travel has roots far deeper than I would have imagined. For starters, the concept of time travel, which the science historian James Gleick points out is a cultural phenomenon and not a scientific one, was "invented" in the nineteenth century during the same window that ritual was "invented" as a cultural force, as we heard the historian David Cannadine say. The Victorian era was the age when grandfather clocks and pocket watches became commonplace, when the industrial revolution put everyone on the relentless march of "efficiency," when "progress" became the benchmark by which all of life was judged.

Given how tightly the cult of time fastened its grip on the world's imagination, it's no surprise that some of the world's greatest imaginations tried to evade that grip. From H. G. Wells to Mark Twain, Western intellectuals were eager to break out of the tyranny that time was a "Rigid Universe," as Wells described it in a serialization of *The Time Machine*. In an era obsessed with optimization, time travel offered optimism that you could escape the monotony of a rigid life and replace it with the dream of what William Blake called a "winged life."

"Only the Time Traveller can call himself free," Gleick writes.

Sure enough, once time travel caught on, observers saw the same impulse of escape in other cultural inventions, from theater to music to dance. One of those creations was ritual. Society draws strict distinctions between power and status, Victor Turner observed; ritual "eradicates these distinctions." It is a way to make everyone equal. Eliade went further. Working in the wake of Hiroshima and the Holocaust, when the world came face-to-face with annihilation, the European refugee to Chicago set out to analyze what premodern societies considered a meaningful life. It is "useless" to study their languages, Eliade wrote; it is essential to study their rituals.

Not what they say, what they do.

One characteristic of those rituals stood out above all: "Their revolt against concrete, historical time, their nostalgia for a periodical return to the mythical time," their longing for "the 'Great Time.'" Societies embrace celebration because it is a conduit for time travel, a passport to a primeval past when all humans were equal, an opportunity to fulfill the spirit of the Latin word *celebrāre*, "to honor, to praise, and to throng."

If our premodern ancestors needed ways to relieve suffering, if our Victorian forebears needed techniques to escape time, if our twentieth-century elders needed methods to prevent annihilation, then we need those solutions even more. In our 24/7/365 world, when we're all "on the clock" "around the clock," when our "timelines" are a "time suck" and our "screen time" a "time sink," we need fresh means to "stop time" to "find time" to "make time."

We need rituals.

Rituals connect the group, as we've seen; they correct imbalances within the group. The third essential thing they do is create opportunities to celebrate the group—to pause the onrush of obligations, to enter time outside of time, to tap into what Aboriginal Australians call "Dreamtime."

Rituals are a means of collective time travel. And there's no better place to begin those trips than from our original home: nature.

Here's what I noticed when I opened my eyes in the forest:

Everything was moving: trees swayed, flowers bobbed, bamboo weaved back and forth like a boxer.

A spiderweb drooled dew.

The weather was changing. It had rained in the morning, leaving a slight chill in the air, but the grass was drying now, succumbing to the sun.

A kingfisher swooped low over the riverbank and settled on a piece of driftwood midstream.

The clouds had parted, clearing a view of a snowcapped volcano that reminded me of Mount Ararat.

White morning glories the shape of gramophones blared toward the sky even as the branches above tried to block their light.

Everything was clamoring even if no one was listening.

When I moved to Japan in the 1980s, the country was the envy of the world—the "Japanese miracle" had turned the vanquished World War II loser into an economic superpower. But the country was also wilting from within, with overcrowded cities, overextended workers, and overstressed families. Six in ten Japanese complained of anxiety, worry, or fatigue.

The Land of the Rising Sun also faced a geographic anomaly: Two

Figure 11: Before forest bathing in the Andes Mountains outside of Pucón, Chile.

thirds of the country is covered in forest, meaning 120 million people crammed into a remaining land mass the size of Mississippi. Among countries that are not cities, Japan is the only one that ranks in the top twenty of both most populated and most forested.

Japan had trees, but nobody was seeing them.

In 1982, the director general of forestry, Tomohide Akiyama, hatched a plan to address this problem. His goal was to encourage people to heal through nature. Akiyama coined the term *shinrin-yoku* out of three Japanese characters 森林浴—the first meaning "forest," the second "interconnectedness," the third "bathe." The English name that stuck: forest bathing.

The ministry began a pilot program in a national park on the old samurai trail that connected Edo, the forebear of Tokyo, and Kyoto, a patch of land known for its emerald-green rivers, hundred-foot cypresses, and the Japanese Rip van Winkle. One member of the organizing team was Qing Li, a medical professor in Tokyo who cared less about trees and flowers and more about cortisol and adrenaline. Anticipating the coming wave of tech-enhanced biometric research, Li initiated what would become one of the most comprehensive scholarly investigations of a ritual practice ever undertaken. The results were mind-boggling.

The idea that spending time in nature is good for humans is hardly new. Pliny the Elder wrote that "the smell of the forest" is "extremely salutary." The Garden of Eden is built around the tree of life and the tree of knowledge and forgetting; the Hebrew prophets imagined a time when "everyone will sit under their own vine and under their own fig tree"; the Buddha achieved enlightenment under a Bodhi tree; Hindus venerate "forest dwelling" as an essential part of any life transition.

What Li and his peers added were thousands of studies with reams of data. Participating in forest bathing can increase energy and immunity while decreasing anxiety and depression; it can boost the parasympathetic system that helps with rest and recovery while suppressing the sympathetic nervous system that produces fight or flight; it can amp up "natural killer cells" while tamping down stress.

And the rewards of forests aren't limited to immersion. Just *looking at trees* through a window speeds recovery from illness and allows patients to require less pain medication; just *smelling healthy soil* increases cognition, energy, and quality of life; just *living on a street with ten trees* decreases blood pressure, reduces the need for antidepressants, and makes residents feel as good as being given a $10,000 raise; when the number of trees rises to eleven or more, the benefits are the equivalent of a $20,000 pay raise and feeling a year and a half younger. By contrast, the US Forest Service found that residents of communities decimated by emerald ash borer—an invasive forest pest that has wiped out 100 million trees—died at higher rates than those in non-affected areas.

As Dacher Keltner, the psychologist at the University of California, Berkeley, who pioneered the study of awe, sums up this research: When we partake in forest bathing, we don't just sleep better, derive more pleasure from food and drink, and feel more alive, we also connect more deeply with others and take more joy out of "an uplifting gathering with friends or family."

Maybe we should host all of our life rituals outdoors!

"Now that we're back together," Alfredo said, after he'd summoned us back to the circle with a birdcall. "I'm going to place this talking stick in the middle and invite you to share what you witnessed."

I watched flies and mosquitoes floating around.
I found the sound of the river soothing; it reminded me of home.
The smoke above the campfire created these cool vibrations.
I thought I saw a rattlesnake, but it was green.
I followed this black-and-white bird, which led me to the hydrangeas, my favorite.
I noticed the verticality—low grass, high grass; short trees, tall trees; flowers close to the ground, flowers stretching toward the sky. Everything felt like a continuum between heaven and earth.

Listening to these observations, I was reminded of my first visit to the desert, in the Sinai Peninsula. I steeled myself for the silence of such a barren terrain. Instead, once I stepped into the open, I was amazed by the din—wind whipping through the mountains, sand tinkling against my face, rocks crunching beneath my feet. The desert may be empty, but it's the least quiet place I've ever been.

I had a similar experience while forest bathing. Surely the trees, grasses, and flowers would be still, a break from the cacophony of buzzes, beeps, pings, and vibrations. Instead, everything was agitating—glade, grove, overhang, underbrush. Everything was striving—for food, water, oxygen, attention. Everything was alive.

To forest bathe is to bask in aliveness, to rediscover a natural world every bit as in flux as the modern world around it. Two worlds dancing side by side, revealing themselves to be one.

When I first heard about forest bathing, I had the same skepticism I had about Grieving & Weaving. Forest bathing is not ritual; it's mindfulness; it's ecotourism; it's a walk in the park. But as I soon discovered, I needed to keep up with the times.

At its simplest, forest bathing is not done alone; it's done in groups, with guides, with the specific purpose of connecting participants not just with nature but with fellow nature seekers. As a forest bathing instructor in Maine told me, "I go on plenty of walks with my dog in the woods; that's not forest bathing. What makes it forest bathing is the intention—the pausing, the breathing, the goal of developing relationships through the living world. It's like the difference between a Pop-Tart and a ravioli: On the surface they're similar, but deep down they're not."

But the bigger reason that forest bathing, like breast cancer walks, butterfly releases, or block parties, qualifies as ritual is that it forces us to do what humans used to do naturally: spend time together outdoors. What was once obligatory has now become voluntary. Americans spend 87 percent of our time indoors and only 7 percent outdoors. The rest we spend in vehicles: We spend more time car bathing than forest bathing. As three researchers wrote in a review of 127 studies of forest bathing, "When one ponders humans existing less than 0.01% of the species' history in modern surroundings and the other 99.99% of the time living in nature, it is no wonder some humans yearn and are drawn back" to where life began.

Today, with our attachment to those origins severed, our only recourse is to set aside time to restore that attachment. And we are. A stunning number of contemporary rituals have direct links to the natural world: Earth Day, solstice parties, polar plunges, tree plantings, water blessings, hunting parties, carbon pledges, mandala makings, community-cleanup days.

Hawaiians, Californians, and Australians all held renewal ceremonies after wildfires; West Papuans, Peruvians, and Bhutanese all convened "climate grief" rituals. Finns hosted a "forest funeral" after ancient trees were clear-cut; Icelanders organized a "glacier funeral" after the country's first ice cap was declared "dead" from climate change. Japanese Buddhists revived a seven-hundred-year-old rainmaking ritual during a drought; Thai Buddhists hosted a cat processional during a dry spell in which they carried Siamese cats in baskets and sprinkled them with water. Pope Francis's 2015 encyclical "Laudato si'" called for a "Sabbath for the Earth," inspiring pilgrimages and reconciliation events; the UN called for an "Environmental Sabbath/Earth Rest Day."

And these events aren't limited to remote areas; they thrive in urban centers, too. Brazilians painted giant Band-Aids on sidewalk potholes to reduce the 18 percent of hospital visits caused by falls, then opened "sidewalk storytelling" stations to encourage slowing down; Ghanaians convened drum circles for library openings, anti-hunger campaigns, and conflict reconciliation ceremonies. In 1997, the German artist Gunter Demnig began placing concrete cubes bearing brass plates with the names and dates of victims of Nazi extermination in front of homes in Austria where the deceased lived; one hundred thousand "stumbling blocks" have since been installed in thirty-one countries, including Germany, Hungary, Poland, Norway, France, and Ukraine.

In 2008, the Swiss designer Tina Roth Eisenberg started a free monthly breakfast for creatives in New York City; within fifteen years, CreativeMornings was hosting "laughing yoga" resets, knit togethers, grief cafés, "PhotograPals" photo outings, "sun your buns" picnics, and spontaneous flower giveaways at busy intersections in 248 cities across seventy countries serving twenty thousand members a month. All events have the same structure. At the revival-like meeting I attended at the Morgan Library in Manhattan, the 350 guests were greeted by signs (EVERYONE IS CREATIVE; YOU LOOK GREAT TODAY!); asked to fill out name tags (*What's your punk anthem?*); serenaded with a live R&B tune ("Lovely Day"); galvanized with a game of Stand Up If (*you have recently made something you're proud of*; *you've been low-key eyeing someone you'd like to chat with*); mythologized with the creed (*We believe in the power of community—face-to-face connections, learning from others, hugs and high fives*); roused by four 30-second pitches (*I was a New York City cop for twenty years and quit to take better care of myself, now I do outdoor calisthenics in Madison Park; please join me this Saturday!*); and cheered by a talk from a barrier-breaking female cartoonist at *The New Yorker*.

"The gatherings are pure ritual," Tina told me after her fiery closing call to "elevate your ROF—return on friendship." "They're synchronized campfires of kindness, born of generosity, designed to welcome you into community. The idea is you can show up anywhere in the world and it feels like home because you *make* it home."

A few weeks after forest bathing, I received an unsolicited email inviting me to "a BYO-picnic at a block-long community table for hundreds" around the corner from my home. "We'll supply the tables and chairs; you bring the food and beverage of your choice." The event was organized by the Longest Table, a growing New York City initiative akin to similar outdoor dining events around the world. These gatherings include the "dinner of the thousand" in Parma, Italy; the "longest table" in Paris, organized by the Republic of Super Neighbors; and the "world's longest table" across the Vasco da Gama Bridge in Lisbon that stretched three miles, seated fifteen thousand guests, and earned a place in *Guinness World Records.*

The first Longest Table in Manhattan's Chelsea neighborhood welcomed five hundred neighbors. The next year it grew to six hundred; the year after, a thousand. Similar events were organized in Virginia, New Mexico, Missouri, California, and Oklahoma. As Maryam Banikarim, who cofounded the group with her husband, Andy, said, "The desire to be connected is the greatest human need. All we've done is unlock it."

What all these grassroots-and-asphalt gatherings make clear is that at the exact moment when humans seem most disconnected from the larger world and one another, the human response has been to repair those connections.

In Cape Town, I met Jess Tyrrell, a South African ecotherapist and ritual entrepreneur with three decades' experience running "nature-allied experiences" for young people, career changers, or anyone hoping to "walk into the unknown of the next chapter of their lives." Her offerings include wellness walks, survival retreats, point-of-human-origin cave immersions, workplace interventions, biomimicry bush camps, and, yes, forest bathing.

"What you learn being in nature is that everything is relational," she said. "Plants are a community of relationships just as humans are. Together we embody the African philosophy of ubuntu: I am who I am because of my relationship with all beings."

The more time you spend in nature, Jess said, the more you access that spirit of connectivity.

"On our expeditions, a lot of people find that they start talking to trees, talking to rocks, talking to animals. In the Western world, that kind of behavior is considered certifiably crazy, but in the natural world it is entirely normal. It's a mindfuck, really, a quantum, nonlinear collapse of time where everything exists in one moment. You have full access to yourself as a child, to your ancestors, to your descendants.

"And what happens in those moments," she continued, "is that life is experiencing itself through us. We become a vessel for nature's story, not the other way around."

In Copenhagen, I joined an early morning session of saunagus, the Danish version of the booming global sauna movement that alternates heat therapy with cold plunges, mixed with music, breathwork, and Burning Man–style bonding. For some, saunagus is a frat party; for others, it's a ritual of renewal. For Hjalte Wieth, it's both.

Hjalte grew up in Copenhagen playing drums and hosting house parties. "I was very extroverted, high-energy, and loved bringing people together." He parlayed his love of partying into a startup that built the loudest battery-operated speaker in the world, which could play nonstop for days. He called it the Boominator.

"When I was twenty-one, we had a hundred employees, $50 million in annual revenue, and the fastest growing hardware company in Danish history."

He also had a drinking and drug problem, was diagnosed as bipolar, and was shaken by two grandparents dying by suicide. The crash came suddenly. Hjalte was pushed out of his company, joined a twelve-step program, and traveled the world seeking enlightenment. What he discovered was a world embracing the healing power of nature gatherings. He returned home and started Plugin Heat Club, which now runs a hundred saunagus sessions a week in two locations.

At the one I attended, twelve of us squeezed our mostly naked bodies onto two cypress benches in a steel barrel about the length of two coffins. Hjalte locked the door, poured lavender-infused water over the sizzling stones, and pumped Coldplay on a Boominator. He led us through breathing exercises, fanned our faces to increase the heat, and then counted the seconds until he released the door.

We stepped into the freezing cold, tiptoed nervously toward four elevated wooden tubs filled with ice water, held our breaths, and lowered oohing and arghing into the arctic soup. It was baptism by ice. "Everybody prefers either the heat or the cold," Hjalte told me later. Count me on the heat side. I was blue and rueful when I climbed out of the slush.

We repeated the cycle twice more.

Like so many contemporary rituals, saunagus has deep roots. Romans were doing hot-and-cold baths in the second century BCE; in Scandinavia especially, thermal baths assumed a place of pride. "These stubborn people," wrote a Swedish economist in 1776, "even connect the sauna with their theology and think the sauna building is some kind of shrine." A Finnish saying goes, "In the sauna one must conduct himself as one would in church." Saunas became popular places for rites of passage. "In the sauna children were born," writes one historian, "women went through the purification ritual before marriage, and old people often dragged themselves there to die."

After declining in the twentieth century, saunas boomed in the twenty-first, rallied by a craving for shared gatherings and a wave of research that, like forest bathing, articulated the benefits for mind, body, and soul. "Saunagus improves circulation and reduces blood pressure," Hjalte boasted. "It relaxes your muscles and boosts your immune system. It also spikes your dopamine as much as cocaine, only cocaine comes with a crash while saunas don't."

He asked me what I experienced.

"In the first session, I was very self-conscious. Everyone seemed younger, thinner, fitter, blonder. And I've never seen so many tattoos!" Hjalte himself fits all those descriptions and said I wasn't alone: "Everyone spends the first session checking out everyone else."

"In the second session, I felt claustrophobic—all these bodies around me, all these voices in my head."

By the third session, when Hjalte played the haunting ballad "Sacre Coeur" by the Danish folk singer Tina Dico, who mused that she could return home to her love and the life she thought she wanted—"Or I could go running off / Into the night, lonely and haunted"—something ignited within me and brought me to tears.

"Boom! That's the magic of saunagus," Hjalte said. "Your veins constrict, your heart dilates, and you catapult out of your body into a state of love. Nature is the best drug in the world."

Alfredo's third invitation is when the "ghost" appeared.

We were lying on the grass as Alfredo guided us through an exercise.

"I invite you to reflect on how it feels to be here, in this place, at this moment."

"Breathe through your mouth as if you're sipping the air from a straw."

"Bring your attention to the natural symphony around you."

"Notice the smell of the grass or the flowers."

"Ask yourself if there's anything in this environment that brings you pleasure."

Alfredo's story has parallels with Hjalte's. Feeling lost after leaving his father's home in rural Ecuador to live with his mother in the Chilean capital of Santiago, he came down with severe depression in his late teens. "I think I was homesick for nature," he told me later. "A friend said, 'I want to invite you to something that I think will help you.'"

The two traveled deep into the Andean jungle where a shaman took them to a sweat lodge.

"For two hours we were in a tent so stifling I felt like I was dying." Afterward, they held a peyote ceremony, drinking tea from a psychoactive cactus laced with mescaline that is known to induce altered states of consciousness. "And something happened. My heart, my mind, everything gave me this overwhelming feeling of home."

So what does he think transpired?

"I don't really need to know," he said. "As human beings, we suffer when we think there's an explanation for everything—we have too much science, not enough spirit. I came from a broken home. There is no external medicine that can fix that; the only thing that can fix it is ceremony, the internal medicine that allows you to invite in the spirit of the trees, the rivers, the ancestors. That experience is when I decided to help others make those connections."

Which is exactly what happened to me.

(I think.)

I was flat on my back, half smelling the citrusy tang of cypress, half hearing the throaty croak of a duck, half pondering the scientific oddity of how the ground could be holding me down while simultaneously holding up the trees. I almost fell asleep.

I was jolted awake as a body reached out to touch me. It wasn't a physical body, more of a spectral one. I'd say a ghost, if I hadn't talked myself out of their existence. It was an arm, a hand, the side of an unseen face. Somebody standing over me, looking *at* me, looking *for* me. I felt a weight of pressure on my chest, a warmth, then nothing.

I didn't want to open my eyes; I wanted to close them even tighter. To see. To know.

Who is that?

What is that?

Why is that?

I'd never remotely experienced this kind of feeling before. I was pretty confident that I hadn't traveled through time; I was also pretty confident that someone else had.

Alfredo issued the call to return to the circle. I was breathing heavily by this time, and sweating. I knew I should probably keep this moment to myself. But we were asked to share, so I shared. I braced myself to be judged. But no one said a word.

"We are not here to ask questions," Alfredo reminded us.

Still, I had questions.

The next day Alfredo drove me into the mountains to meet a Mapuche shaman. No peyote; just muday, a cloudy alcoholic drink made from fermented wheat and corn. The drink of ritual.

A once-nomadic people who settled in the Andes in the first millennium BCE, the Mapuche are a storied Indigenous community, having fought off colonization by the Incas, Spaniards, and Chileans until the 1880s. Named for a combination of *mapu*, meaning "land," and *che*, meaning "people," the 1.8 million "people of the land" comprise 80 percent of Chile's native population and nearly 10 percent of the overall population.

Machi Jorge is not a typical machi, an honorific that encompasses healer, diviner, medicine man, and ritual leader. A portly thirty-four-year-old with thinning black hair, a mustache, and an injured left leg, he looked like a retired baseball player in his blue jeans, gray sweatshirt, and Adidas slip-ons. The biggest clue to his exalted status was his intense, alert green eyes.

Jorge welcomed us with a short ceremony. Using wooden sticks, he beat on a shallow goatskin drum that had been decorated with symbols of earth, fire, air, and water; shook a leather strap of bells; then blew a shofar-like horn.

Guardians of this land, we call upon the spirits. Let these instruments carry forth our prayers to heaven. May our offerings be received.

Finally, he poured out a tin cup of muday on the roots of a foye tree, a native evergreen that is considered the symbolic axis connecting heaven and earth. The decanting of homebrew was the same gesture that had opened the wedding of Lillian and Jeffrey in South Africa.

Mother Foye, I am calling on your path to the high sky, I am drawing on your knowledge of the world. Send us from above the waterfalls and deep in the earth the wisdom of the ancestors.

Jorge led us into a traditional circular hut, or ruka, with grass thatching secured to bamboo crossbeams; chickens fluttered in and out. Machis employ a variety of Indigenous practices, including exorcisms, herbal remedies, and dream interpretations, though usually as supplements to Western medicine. "Most machi are Christians," Jorge explained; "we work in rukas alongside public hospitals." Long a symbol of resistance to outside influence, the Mapuche today are a symbol of how no place can resist the integration of traditional and modern.

Jorge took an unconventional path to becoming a machi. Born into a home with no electricity or plumbing, Jorge always preferred his grandmother's life on the farm. To fulfill his parents' wishes, he enrolled in agricultural college, but a few weeks in he attended a family funeral.

"Standing under a foye tree, I felt surrounded by the past. My spirit left my body, flew around in a circle, then reentered through the back of my head. At that moment I knew my calling."

Jorge trained for the next five years, then moved to this village to begin serving the community. His cases ranged from heart disease and respiratory problems to grief and depression. "Usually someone comes to see me complaining about a stomachache, but really what they're experiencing is a spiritual imbalance. In our culture, you can't separate being a doctor for the body with being a doctor for the mind."

I asked how he decides whether to treat a condition with medicine or ritual.

"There is no distinction. For us, everything is ritual. In the morning, we have rituals for sun and the earth, in the afternoon for home and body, in the evening for food and sleep. Even a conversation like this one can be a ritual."

I told him about the imbalance that sent me on this trip—my father, my mother, my children. "I feel homesick. I came on this journey because I want to feel at home again."

For the first time since I arrived he unfocused his eyes. He didn't stop looking at me so much as start looking through me. After a minute, he locked back in.

"All right, I will tell you your problem: You ask too many questions. Too much thinking, not enough feeling; too much mental, not enough spiritual. The way to cure homesickness is to ask your ancestors permission to feel at home. If you don't have their blessing, you will continue to suffer."

Now it was my turn to unfocus for a second.

"Yesterday I received a visit that I think may have been from an ancestor," I said. "But I didn't hear the message that was being conveyed. It didn't fully download."

"Because you're not ready," he said. "You're too busy insisting that what you're feeling is wrong when in fact what you're feeling is right. It's perfectly natural that your father would die, that your mother would get old, that your children would grow up. All these things happen in nature. But you're not thinking about nature, you're thinking about yourself."

"So what should I do?"

"You can continue to think about what you're missing. You can think about good times from your life. You can think about how grateful you are for what those experiences taught you. Then you must accept that those times are gone but that they'll always be part of you. Remember what I told you: Everything is ritual. It is the antenna that allows you to connect to the past so you can move on from the past. Once that happens, you will be prepared for the future."

The final invitation was to stroll around the forest until you felt called by a tree. "Stay with it, interact with it, maybe just watch it."

I wandered aimlessly for a bit, still mystified by my earlier encounter. I glanced at some stalks of bamboo and a few monkey puzzle trees, tall, enigmatic pines with spiny, cactus-like branches that look like medieval maces. But it was a rather bland trunk of an ordinary-looking tree that drew my attention. The trunk sloped gently up from the ground and had a weathered patchwork of gray-and-brown bark, mottled with lichen, that vaguely reminded me of my childhood backyard.

As I approached, I realized that the trunk was actually split; there were two trunks coming out of the same root system. My first thought was, *Oh, the dual trunks represent our children.* Then I paused, *Maybe it represents our family, that we are irredeemably split.*

Arriving at the tree, I stepped over some ankle-high grass and reached to touch the rutted bark, when I discovered that there weren't two trunks, after all. There were four. Not a tree, a tree system. A family.

As the trunks climbed, their separate origins mattered less and their unity prevailed. The lower branches were largely dead—bent and brittle—but they gave architecture to their younger relatives above, a crinoline offering ballast for the generations that followed. At the top of the tree, the supplest branches melted into the sky, lush, green,

Figure 12: A family of Dombey's southern beech trunks spotted while forest bathing in Chile.

expansive. A celestial canopy. *I will make of you a great nation*, God says to Abraham. *I will make your descendants as numerous as the stars.*

As my gaze slid downward, I noticed a feather stuck in a sprig. White at the bottom, black at the top, its upper wisps fanning like a cartwheel, the feather had the same shape as the tree that caught it. Birds of a feather stuck together.

Alfredo later broke the rules of forest bathing and told me the type of tree it was: in Latin, *Nothofagus dombeyi*; in Spanish, *coihue*; in English, Dombey's southern beech. A broadleaf evergreen indigenous to Chile, this tree is known for having main shoots, called parents, and offshoots, called siblings. Faced with external threats, parents and siblings unite, trade chemical warnings, share nutrients, and reposition branches to ensure that everyone has access to light in what scholars call an "extraordinary resilience to exogeneous traumatic factors."

"We call it the 'family tree,'" Alfredo said. "It recovers faster after infestation and regrows faster after fire. It's a miracle of cooperation."

Encountering this miracle in a random act of ritual was a reminder that the world is a theater of synchronicity. I had seen in nature the reality I wanted to see, only to discover that the reality had been there all along. I had projected onto the forest the wisdom I needed to hear, only to find that the forest had projected onto me the wisdom it wanted me to know. As the Potawatomi biologist Robin Wall Kimmerer captures that wisdom in *Braiding Sweetgrass*: "When times are easy and there's plenty to go around," individuals can go it alone. "But when conditions are harsh and life is tenuous, it takes a team sworn to reciprocity to keep life going forward."

Rituals thrive in the harsh and tenuous, which is why they flourish in the harmony and reciprocity of nature. When we fear that we can't see through the trees, the universe speaks to us through the forest. "It is quite characteristic in peak-experiences," writes the legendary psychologist Abraham Maslow, "that the whole universe is perceived as an integrated and unified whole." Ritual is our most effective tool for reaffirming that whole, bathing us in gratitude as it transports us in time.

It was exactly that feeling of being transported that pervaded the first Longest Table in Brooklyn. At 1 p.m. on the first warm day of spring, more than seven hundred people gathered at a six-hundred-foot-long table in the heart of Brooklyn Heights, overlooking the Statue of Liberty. One group decked out in white and carrying parasols seemed like they stepped out of an impressionist painting; a family from Texas wearing black cowboy hats held a baby shower; a swarm of cheese-and-waffle lovers celebrated Norway's Constitution Day with mini flags and yogurt shots. Some parents whose kids were making chalk drawings on the street offered me a piece of a Funfetti cake while some Gen Z women in matching sun hats insisted that I take a taco. "We're from another neighborhood," they whispered. "We decided to crash last night while texting in our WhatsApp group chat."

What jumped out to me about the motley, even giddy, gathering is that everyone was cosplaying as characters from a bygone time and place, though it was different times and different places for different people. Still, the varied ritual narratives shared a common theme: a Saturday afternoon on a Brooklyn grand street where everyone could act out a parallel fantasy . . . together.

"When I was an only child growing up in Iran," Maryam, the cofounder, told me at the end of the afternoon, "my happy place was when my grandmother would spread out a tablecloth under a tree, the family would gather around, and we would eat together.

"When I first had the idea for the Longest Table, it was to celebrate community—the people we barely talk to in the place we call home. What I didn't expect is that it would *improve* the community; just being out here feels like we've traveled to a different era and in doing so improved our lives today."

To dine, dance, bathe, plunge, sing, sweat, and gather together, indoors or out, is to retouch our shared roots and reclaim our common origins. Though we may not be able to understand all the signals we receive or the messages we hear on such occasions, to open ourselves to the wisdom of the ritual is not to ask, to judge, or to know, but to honor, to wonder, to summon.

To celebrate.

9.

BLESS THE BROKEN ROAD

How to Create a Ritual, Volume 3

Some people believe the beginning of a life ritual is the most important part; Ezra Bookman believes the end is. That philosophy may be why the thirty-year-old wunderkind hailed by *The New York Times* as the public face of ritual entrepreneurship found it so difficult to devise a ritual for the most important beginning of his life, his engagement.

His answer was to turn to his favorite tip for rituals of all kinds: "Humans like to go full circle."

Ezra was born into a petri dish of ritual exploration: He is the youngest of four sons of a hippie rabbi and a Jewish educator in Miami. "A tradition that shaped who I am today is that we would eat dinner together every single night as a family without fail. Sharing that table was bigger than consuming calories; it was the anchor of where relationship happens."

After earning a degree in theater and then training with Indigenous healers in Ecuador and Colombia, Ezra moved to Chicago to become an actor. "I was in my boxers with a snake on my chest doing my best drag version of a shaman when I realized my soul was decaying." He fled to Israel, farmed in the desert, and then accepted a job as the artistic director of an avant-garde synagogue in Greenwich Village called Lab/Shul, an "artist-driven, everybody-friendly, God-optional, pop up, experimental community for sacred Jewish gatherings."

Basically it was a ritual reinvention factory, the Skunk Works of meaning, and Ezra was its mad scientist: Kaddish Club grief circles, "Saturday Soul" spas, "Raise the BAR" mitzvah classes, "Wrestling with Transitions" weekends, "Pass/Age" personal growth retreats, and "GENerate," a "year-long rite of passage experience for a small cohort of seekers, 60ish and above."

Just as the pandemic brought the perils of isolation into sharp relief, Ezra quit Lab/Shul over the objection of his boss to start Ritualist, "a creative studio that believes better rituals build more conscious companies & connected communities." Offerings include rituals for design sprints, a good quarter, or shutting down a division.

"I looked around and realized that the ideas and practices I had developed were applicable way beyond religious communities. The crisis of meaning, purpose, and belonging is everywhere. Ritual, this tool we've used through all of human history to build culture and create connections, deserves a place in the conversation on how to fix these problems."

As the *Times* summarized the moment in its profile of Ezra and others ("God Is Dead. So Is the Office. These People Want to Save Both"): "spiritual consultants" blend the obscure language of the sacred with the obscure language of management consulting to provide clients with a range of meaning-inflected services. "Their larger goal is to soften cruel capitalism, making space for the soul, and to encourage employees to ask if what they are doing is good in a higher sense."

The ritual entrepreneur, already a novel concept, now came forward with an even more novel invention: the ritual startup. For Ezra, however, becoming the figurehead of a movement came with a dilemma: The unflappable guru who helps others say goodbye was unable to say goodbye himself. He was paralyzed by his messy departure from Lab/Shul.

He needed a ritual.

Going full circle is one of the oldest stories in the ritual playbook, especially when that circle involves lots of twists and turns. In ancient Crete, the Minoans represented those oscillations with a double-headed ax ( ), or *labrys*, a word that became the foundation of one of the most storied ritual archetypes in history.

A princess gathers flowers by the sea, when she eyes a beautiful white bull with golden horns. Europa mounts the bull, who swims her to the island of Crete, where he unmasks himself and mounts her in return. Europa gives birth to their son, Minos. Zeus honors his beloved by lending her name to the continent of her birth; Minos grows up to become the king of Crete and lends his name to their people, the Minoans.

Minos's wife, Pasiphaë, also falls in love with a bull. She asks the artist Daedalus to create a simulacrum of a cow with mechanical legs, fur, and eyes—a "cow machine," the bards tell us—which she rides to seduce the bull. Their offspring has the lower half of a boy and the upper half of a calf. He's known in history as the Minotaur.

King Minos is so enraged that he makes Daedalus design a mazy skein to hold the hybrid bastard, a prison of crinkles and puzzles. When Minos and Pasiphaë's eldest son, Androgeos, is killed in war by Athenians, the king insists that every nine years, three Athenian sons be sacrificed to the Minotaur.

On the third such anniversary, Theseus, the son of Athens's king, volunteers. Minos is so impressed with the boy's courage that he invites him to his palace and asks his daughter, Ariadne, to host him. Infatuated, she filches a ball of red thread from Daedalus, enters the Minotaur's maze, and hides a sword. With whispered instructions the next morning, the prince threads a spidery escape path, slays the beast, and then whisks his beloved Ariadne away.

This story was told for hundreds of years, all the way back to Homer, before its most enduring legacy was attached to it. In the fifth century BCE, Herodotus first uses the word *labyrinth*, borrowing the Greek word for *double ax*, to describe a similar mazy complex in Egypt. It was Pliny the Elder, writing in the first century after Christ, who first applied *labyrinth* to the Minotaur's prison. Spiral designs had been used on coins as early as 2500 BCE, but no architectural labyrinth has ever been unearthed. Sir Arthur Evans, who excavated Minos's palace in the last century, found a network of corridors but no dungeon or maze.

But as history repeatedly reminds us, intangible archetypes sometimes take on tangible form. Early Christian thinkers, who had access to Pliny, latched on to the labyrinth as a metaphor for the unstraight roads and nonlinear paths that believers often take to salvation. The earliest Christian labyrinth ever uncovered was square and paved into the floor of a fourth-century basilica in Algeria; the earliest round labyrinth was carved into a church wall in Italy in the ninth century.

But it was the Middle Ages that gave us the labyrinth as we know it today. The popularity of the Crusades and other pilgrimages to the Holy Land piqued interest in drawing closer to the kingdom of Israel. Circular pathways (they're not technically mazes because there are no dead ends) modeled on the ancient myth but using numerological dimensions from Solomon's Temple in Jerusalem were installed in cathedrals from Amiens and Reims in France to Ravenna and Lucca in Italy.

Figure 13: The labyrinth in Chartres Cathedral.
Courtesy of Jeff Saward/Labyrinthos Photo Library.

By far the most famous was laid into the nave near the entrance of Notre-Dame de Chartres, southwest of Paris, following the great fire of 1194. It is forty-two feet in diameter; its sixteen-inch-wide path stretches eight hundred sixty-one and a half feet. The labyrinth contains eleven rings and thirty-four turns, six of which are 90 degrees, the rest 180 degrees. The U-turns are decorated with ten double axes that together form a cross. The original center was made of copper, brass, and lead, which was converted into a cannonball during the Napoleonic wars.

Chartres unleashed a torrent of emulators. Scores of labyrinths were installed in the following centuries in ecclesiastical buildings across Europe, with hundreds more in nonecclesiastical buildings. The once mythical design had become a real-world, physical embodiment of the cosmos, a place to make a spiritual pilgrimage and draw closer to the divine. But as rationalism descended on the West, just as quickly as the symbol rose, it just as quickly disappeared. For the next half a millennium, no labyrinth was built in the Western world, until a little-known pastor in San Francisco in 1991 named Lauren Artress had an idea that would redirect the path of ritual 180 degrees.

Ezra Bookman is a wiry, kinetic bundle of contradictions, the most excitable yogi at the retreat. He quotes anthropologists and evolutionary biologists the way some people quote sports GOATs: *Collective effervescence is hard. We have an evolutionary need to end where we start.*

He likes categorization. "I collect two things: rocks and definitions of ritual." His two favorite definitions: "Ritual is attention and intention"; "Ritual is something that if you take it away, the moment feels less important."

He keeps a running list of what distinguishes ritual from routine and habit:

- Rituals are intentional, symbolic, elevated actions.
- Routines are intentional, repeated actions.
- Habits are automatic, repeated actions.

"Take my family dinner," he explained. "We always sat in the same seats; that's habit. We had the Clean Plate Club, which had the clear intention of making sure our parents didn't do too many dishes; that's routine. We held hands at the beginning of every meal and said a prayer of gratitude; that's ritual."

When it comes to his own life, however, Ezra struggles to implement his own theories.

"Leaving Lab/Shul was messy as fuck. I realized after a while that I needed a mourning ritual, but I couldn't think of one. I was staying at a farm in upstate New York that had a giant Stonehenge circle. One night it was pouring, gloomy, and cold. I went out into the rain and climbed onto this altar in the center of the stones. I knew that for the ritual to work I had to expunge my anger and hurt. I could burn it, I could release it in the water, or I could exhale it.

"But what came to me in the moment is that I could let it fly away. So I opened my arms and imagined these beautiful, cream-colored wings coming out of my back; I tried to receive whatever message the world sent me. Like a bell, I heard these words: *I will lead with my values no matter how people treat me.*"

Ezra held his breath for a second, then released the air.

"A few weeks later I bought a bottle of champagne, along with some cheese and crackers, and invited friends to a rooftop in Brooklyn, where I re-created what happened. I still get sad from time to time, but when I do, I reconnect with that moment—and that message—and feel a little less lonely."

Ezra had gotten good with rituals of goodbye. Could he do the same with rituals of beginning?

In the early 1990s, I made my first visit to Nashville, for what would be three years of traveling with Garth Brooks, Wynonna Judd, Willie Nelson, and others, writing a book about country music. On that initial trip, I met a young songwriter named Marcus Hummon, who was recording a new ballad he'd written with two friends. "Bless the Broken Road" describes someone who sets out on a narrow path hoping to find true love, only to get lost a time or two before finding his way.

The song had the indelible hook "God blessed the broken road / That led me straight to you."

Marcus's wife, Becca, is an Episcopal priest and the founder of an organization that helps female survivors of human trafficking, for which she was named Nashvillian of the Year and a top ten CNN Hero. In addition to Marcus's version, "Bless the Broken Road" was recorded by the Nitty Gritty Dirt Band and the contemporary Christian singer Melodie Crittenden.

None of those recordings found an audience. "Bless the Broken Road" was just another sad moment on an artist's boulevard of broken dreams.

But sometimes archetypes work in mysterious ways. Around the same time, Lauren Artress, the canon pastor of Grace Cathedral in San Francisco, was experiencing her own brokenness. "I was in the midst of a transition," she writes in the opening of her 1995 memoir, *Walking a Sacred Path*. Hired to build a "bridge of understanding" between the traditional church and the nontraditional forms of spirituality that were springing around it, she felt deflated and burned out.

Hoping for inspiration, she enrolled in a spiritual retreat where attendees were invited to walk through a temporary labyrinth taped to the ground. "As soon as I set foot into the labyrinth I was overcome with an almost violent anxiety," Artress writes. "Some part of me seemed to know that in this ancient and mysterious archetype, I was encountering something that would change the course of my life." She organized a pilgrimage to Chartres with friends, where they stealthily moved aside chairs on the little-used labyrinth, held hands, prayed, and stepped inside.

"I received the embrace of Mary," Artress recalls.

And she knew exactly what to do. At 6 p.m. on December 30, 1991, Artress strode to the center of Grace Cathedral on San Francisco's Nob Hill and unfurled six bolts of canvas containing a forty-two-foot labyrinth painted in purple. Visitors lined up for six hours to walk through it. Twice a month for the next three years, the church spread out its labyrinth. Walkers included those struggling with divorce, recovering from incest, or simply feeling lost, uncertain, or alone.

"Why does the labyrinth attract people?" Artress writes. "It enlivens the intuitive part of our nature and stirs within the human heart the longing for connectedness." It "calms people in the throes of life transitions." They "realize that they are not human beings on a spiritual path but spiritual beings on a human path." The labyrinth transports us from "clock time into dreamtime."

Recognizing that it had tapped into a larger need, the cathedral opened a full-time, outdoor terrazzo stone labyrinth in 1995. Artress called it "the first labyrinth to be installed in permanent form" in the West in six hundred years. The following year, she created the World-Wide Labyrinth Project, "to pepper the planet with labyrinths."

To her awe and gratification, "that is exactly what our work has done."

Not long after Ezra Bookman upended his work life, he decided he was ready to settle down in his personal life. "We made the decision to propose to each other," Ezra said of his girlfriend, "which meant that we committed to design our engagement together."

They started with the question he poses to all clients at the outset of a ritual design process: *Why am I doing this?* "Actually, it's a cheat because it's really three questions in one," Ezra said. "'*Why* am I doing this?' As in what is my intention. 'Why am *I* doing this?' As in what are the stakes for me. And 'Why am I doing *this*?' As in, why am I taking this particular action."

The two lovers spent months trying to answer the questions. They selected a date, their two-year anniversary. They picked a location, Hawaii, because it was meaningful for her. They agreed to give each other presents. But they couldn't agree on what the gift should be.

"Finally, a few days before the appointed date, we were in a shop when my girlfriend saw this ceramic vase. 'What about this?' I thought about it for a second and said, 'That's brilliant!' It's connected to our past, because the first time she visited me long distance I bought her flowers and said, 'Welcome home.' It's connected to our future, because a vase symbolizes the part of our relationship that needs to be constantly refreshed."

Hours before the deadline, they had their gift. But they still didn't have a plan. "By this point she was exhausted," Ezra said. "'You're the ritual designer,' she sighed. 'You figure it out.'"

And he did.

He chose the oldest archetype in the book.

Linda and I met on a blind date in New York City the week my book on country music was published. We dated for a year and a half, broke up for a year and a half, then started dating again. A year later, on the eve of our trip to Puerto Rico, I tried to find a creative alternative to an engagement ring. On a scouting trip on Fifth Avenue, I chose a necklace made from a fossilized ammonite, a coiled cephalopod with a mesmerizing spiral that reminded me of my favorite shell, the chambered nautilus, as well as the circuitous history of our relationship.

Fortunately, the one person who didn't think it was weird was Linda. As she tells the entrepreneurs she advises, "Know your target market!"

But I wasn't done with circuitousness. When the time came to discuss our first dance, I floated this long-forgotten song I'd heard on my first visit to Nashville. Linda loved the idea. We hired a Broadway choreographer to design a dance that had us spiraling solo around the dance floor and then meeting in the center as the chorus crescendoed, "God blessed the broken road / That led me straight to you."

I wasn't the only person who remembered that song. Reba McEntire promised the songwriters for years that she would cut it, as did Faith Hill. But recording failed songs is not customarily done in Nashville. The year after our wedding, the flailing country trio Rascal Flatts were desperate for a hit. They released a simple, stirring rendition of "Bless the Broken Road." It exploded, spending five weeks at number one on the Hot Country chart, selling four million copies, and earning a Grammy Award. The recording was named Song of the Year by the Nashville Songwriters Association. A Christian version released two years later won the identical award, the first song in history to win the same award twice. Marcus Hummon was elected to the Nashville Songwriters Hall of Fame.

"I hear from people wherever I go," Marcus said. "*It's our recovery song. It's our wedding song. We played it at Mom's funeral.* I once performed it at a women's prison with my wife. I got so verklempt that I forgot the words. When I looked up, all the inmates were singing them back to me."

The same year "Bless the Broken Road" won its Grammy, Lauren Artress reissued her memoir. The book has "been like the Energizer Bunny," the otherwise humble pastor wrote, "not only in sales," but in kick-starting what *The New York Times* "coined 'the Labyrinth Movement.'"

A quarter of a million people had walked the Grace Cathedral labyrinth in its first decade, spawning copycats in hospitals, hospices, schools, and prisons. A Girl Scout in Pennsylvania won a Gold Award for building a labyrinth in a lakeside park; the famed *Washington Post* Watergate editor Ben Bradlee commissioned a fifty-foot labyrinth on his Maryland estate for his wife, Sally Quinn; a professor in Indiana received a $500,000 grant to study the psychological benefits of labyrinths. The pandemic supercharged this momentum. *Today* aired a segment; the BBC ran a report; *The New York Times Magazine* published an article, "I'm Lost All the Time. So I Went on a Labyrinth Vacation."

Artress's World-Wide Labyrinth Project set up a locator to track all the new constructions. In 1995 the locator had one entry; by 1998 it had ten; by 2025 it had 6,600 in ninety-five countries. The top five locations were the United States (4,780), Canada (381), England (261), Australia (192), and Sweden (91). There's even a labyrinth in Santiago, Chile, built by a nun from Ohio named Judith Ress who took me for a visit on my final day in the country.

"When you walk the labyrinth, you walk your own story," Sister Judy told me. "You start at the beginning, you often lose your way for a while, and you end up in a place you can never anticipate."

The remarkableness of this story cannot be overstated: We have no evidence that walking labyrinths even existed in the ancient world; we have plenty of evidence that they blipped in the Middle Ages, before dying out for half a millennium. The one thing we can say for certain is that labyrinths are *more popular* today than at any time in history. Why on earth would this be?

The answer, I believe, goes back to the original conundrum that Lauren Artress was asked to address: "building a bridge" between religion and spirituality. Labyrinths are one of the few archetypes that have the mystique of the classical world, the imprimatur of religion, the affirmation of spirituality, and the validation of social science. They are a perfect poster child of the modern ritual—short, simple gestures in iconic, elevating third places that are easily accessible, physically undemanding, and deeply rewarding both personally and interpersonally.

What's more, they're especially effective in times of transition, doppelgängers for the twists and turns of our lives, blueprints for the lifequakes that keep upending our dreams of straight paths and straightforward achievements. Labyrinths are immersive crucibles that allow us, in redirecting our paths, to redirect our emotions—from fear to hope. From loneliness to love.

It was raining on the morning of the proposal; Ezra didn't have time for a haircut; he had a pimple on his face. "Everything was wrong. I had to remind myself that there is beauty in imperfection."

Ezra woke up early, went down to the beach, and drew two giant spirals on the sand.

"One of our earliest conversations was about time being nonlinear; how it curves, bends, expands, then doubles back on itself."

The two lovers stood side by side, then set off down their respective paths.

"We basically did a slow, walking meditation toward the center as the sun rose over the water," Ezra said. "The idea was to drop in, bring our attention to the present, and hone our intention. You have to prepare the surface before you prepare the art."

At the center of each spiral, Ezra had drawn a line connecting the two routes. "We met in the middle. I said some nice things I had written about her; she said some nice things she had written about me. We asked a more mystical version of the question, 'Will you marry me?'

"And what struck me in that moment is the thing that I love most about rituals—and why they've been such a sticky, behavioral quirk of our species. Time seemed to disappear. It felt like we were in every moment of love that had ever happened. That we were part of something infinitely bigger than ourselves. That we had entered this giant vortex where everything came full circle and we were starting the story all over again."

Then they turned, faced the ocean, held hands, and crossed the threshold.

They had completed the labyrinth. They had jumped the broom.

They had renewed the archetype.

God bless the broken roads that lead us straight to home.

10.

A TIME TO HOLD

RIP.ie, Where Irish Eyes Go to Cry

I had never seen a dead body before. Within five minutes of arriving in Waterford, the oldest city in Ireland, I had seen three.

Saturday was shaping up to be the busiest day of the week at R. Thompson Funeral Directors at 19 Barrack Street, one of Ireland's oldest family-run businesses, having served this seaport town since 1786. Drizzle had just begun to fall as I approached the rickety three-story building with two front doors painted the same bright red as Paddington's hat. I rang the bell. A dashing man in a black suit and tie opened the door.

"Excuse the smell of embalming fluid," he said. "I'm almost finished with Mrs. Fitzgerald. She's having her hair done now. Come, let me show you around. Then I have to get my motorcycle ready for the funeral."

Michael Thompson is a fifty-something former fashion model in Dublin who returned to his hometown, the birthplace of Waterford crystal, to take over the business started by his great-great-great-grandfather. I ducked my head to accommodate the low ceilings and followed him through a warren of oak-paneled rooms.

First, a former pub. "Ireland is a small country," he said. "Most funeral directors used to have other sources of income—they were solicitors, auctioneers, publicans. My family grew timber, so they made coffins on the side. The funeral was just an add-on."

Next, a reception area with a display rack full of brochures: *A Celebration of Life: When a Loved One Dies*; *Island Crematorium: We'll Take Care of Everything.*

We climbed the stairs to the showroom, where I learned the difference between a coffin and a casket. The former is a tapered hexagonal receptacle that's narrow at the head and feet and wider at the shoulders and arms; the latter is a rectangular box with hinged lids and long handles. "All of our offerings are solid oak and mahogany," Michael said. "You go to Dublin, they'd be chipboard. In the US, they're reinforced with steel. The Irish could never afford such luxury. Plus, we bury up to eight people in one grave, so we need everything to decompose quickly."

Finally, we passed through a kitchen so old it had an operating fax machine and stepped into an embalming lab so new it was started by Michael's father, the first embalmer in eastern Ireland. In the center was a stainless steel table with a plastic headrest, gutters to catch bodily fluids, and plastic containers for tubes, clamps, hooks, and plugs. Along one wall was a grocery store refrigerator crowded with cavity fillers, tissue restorers, mouth formers, bone putty, color-correcting creams (yellow for bruises, purple for paleness, green for blotchiness), and eye caps, flesh-colored discs that get tucked under the eyelids to prevent them from sinking, sagging, or opening during a viewing.

"This is Mrs. Fitzgerald," Michael said, gesturing toward the remains of Josephine "Nanny" Fitzgerald, who was resting in peace in her oak coffin in a periwinkle-blue suit reminiscent of Queen Elizabeth II, and a matching blue hat currently covering her knees. A makeup artist was adding blush to her waxen cheeks. "Her hair looked awful when she came in," Michael added. "We needed to ensure that her family would not be upset."

Michael introduced me to Mrs. O'Brien, whose service was scheduled for that evening, and Mr. Melay, a former groundskeeper at the local hurling pitch and a devoted Liverpool soccer fan. He was wearing a dark suit, a white shirt, and a red-and-white-striped tie with a gold Liverpool logo.

"His son is a friend of mine," Michael said, wheeling over a retractable rolling stand. "We ride Harleys together. The local Freewheelers club are bringing their hogs to the funeral. Now—" He grabbed the head top of the wicker coffin. "Do me a favor."

He gestured to the coffin. I lifted the handle closest to the feet, we rested the wicker container on the stand, I opened the door behind me, and Michael pushed the body into the small chapel across the hall, where a famed Irish wake was about to begin.

Or at least what's left of the famed Irish wake.

In May 1946, amid the still-smoldering ashes of World War II, forty-two-year-old George Orwell, reeling from the sudden death of his wife, Eileen, and now the sole parent of their two-year-old son, moved to the remote Isle of Jura in the Inner Hebrides of Scotland to write a novel he'd been pondering for years. "Writing a book is a horrible, exhausting struggle," he complained, "like a long bout of some painful illness."

In Orwell's case, the writing became even worse because he was soon diagnosed with an actual illness, tuberculosis, for which there was no cure. In and out of sanitoriums, fighting blood-filled lungs, and looking increasingly cadaverous, Orwell wrote feverishly for the next two and a half years. He typed the final chapters of his "Utopia" in bed.

"I am not pleased with the book but I am not absolutely dissatisfied," he wrote a friend.

That book, *Nineteen Eighty-Four*, was published on June 8, 1949. Six months later, Orwell was dead. The dystopian masterpiece, which BBC voters would rank the eighth most-loved book in British history, is remembered today as a chilling depiction of totalitarianism, thought control, and doublethink. Less remembered is the book's even more ominous portrayal of a world in which death is completely dehumanized. When citizens expire, they are immediately erased by Big Brother.

"People simply disappeared," the narrator says. "Your name was removed from the registers, every record of everything you had ever done was wiped out, your one-time existence was denied and then forgotten. You were abolished, annihilated: VAPORIZED."

No weeping. No pining. No praising.

No ritual.

In the grim imagination of a dying George Orwell, grief became a thoughtcrime.

While Orwell got many things dead right about the future—mass surveillance, loss of privacy, misinformation—on the topic of death he was dead wrong. If anything, because the novel became required reading worldwide, what was once the least discussed of life rituals—*mourning*—has become the most discussed. Long swept under the rug, grief now receives red-carpet treatment.

The rethink has been building for decades. The 1960s gave rise to the attack on what the muckraking journalist Jessica Mitford called "the malarkey" of Big Funeral; the 1970s gave rise to the academic discipline of thanatology, the study of death and dying; the 2000s gave rise to the green funeral business. But nothing could have prepared the world for what social media has done to death: made it low-key cool.

#DeathTok, where influencers talk about everything from how to embalm a pregnant woman to why hospice patients don't need to drink water to the dating woes of crematorium workers, has a quarter of a billion views. The Reddit thread r/askfuneraldirectors has seventy thousand members, ranking it among the top 3 percent of the site's one million communities. The most popular query:

> My daughter passed away suddenly last week. Since we opted to have her cremated, I requested a lock of her hair. The funeral director gave me two generous Ziploc bags of her hair. She'd had an autopsy and had been in the cooler for three days. There was a smell. I need to wash and dry it but I'm afraid of ruining it. She was 24 and had thick shoulder length curly red hair. I'm still in shock. Any advice?

The most upvoted of the four thousand answers:

> I'm so very sorry for your loss. Put the hair into a clean Ziploc bag then add a little warm water & your daughter's favorite shampoo. Shake it up good. Drain. Rinse. Repeat if necessary. Lay it out to dry in a safe place.

As this exchange suggests, mourning rituals have a high degree of granularity. Grieving is the opposite of one-size-fits-all; it's every griever for themselves. Depending on where you live and what you believe, corpses are burned, buried, smoked, or pickled; funerals are private affairs or lavish celebrations; graves are unmarked and unremembered or enshrined and enthroned. Saint Peter's in the Vatican, Saint Paul's in London, the Duomo in Florence, the Parthenon in Athens, Grand Central Station in New York, and the Lincoln Memorial in Washington, DC, would all fit inside the footprint of the Great Pyramid of Giza, the third-millennium BCE burial spot of Pharaoh Khufu.

And we wonder, *Who's in Grant's Tomb?*

Organized religion assumed the responsibility of teaching people how to cope with death, which is one reason so many scriptural figures struggle with grief. Adam and Eve lost a son, David lost a son, Mary lost a son, Confucius lost a son, Shiva lost a son, Muhammad lost three sons, Joseph Smith lost six. What these stories have in common is showing that death compels the bereaved to slow down, scale back, seek meaning. Compassion, from the Latin root for suffer, infuses all faiths; the Hebrew word *selah,* which suggests "to pause, reflect, and feel," appears seventy-one times in Psalms.

Funerals, the front door of grief, are designed to ease private pain with collective solace. "We are not accustomed to thinking of grief as a process of finding comfort," writes the Columbia University psychologist George Bonanno, "but this is precisely what resilient people tend to do." They "consistently fare better" when they have other people to turn to. The more comfort a mourner receives from the living, the easier they find it to make peace with the dead, and the closer they grow with the living. The cycle of death, in other words, is a cycle of life. "By following acceptable ritual routines," Bonanno writes, "ordinary citizens participate in the process of cultural unification."

A time to weep becomes a time to laugh. A time to mourn becomes a time to dance. A time to fear becomes a time to hold.

Michael Thompson rolled Mr. Melay to the front of the modest chapel that had been added as an extension to the eighteenth-century Thompson building. The coffin came to rest in front of a curtain, alongside a table with a photograph of the deceased, a large candle, and a red-and-white Liverpool scarf. A small number of family members were seated in the front pew. As mourners arrived, they would pay their respects to Mr. Melay, then greet the family with the iconic Irish expression of condolence, "I'm sorry for your trouble."

Not *sorry for your loss*; *sorry for all the trouble that comes with it.*

What followed was an hour of the kind of performative sharing of grief, intimacy, neighborliness, and gossip that has been the hallmark of life rituals for thousands of years. Not until I stepped outside did I appreciate the strong undercurrents of change that were shaping the event.

"A funeral is a celebration of someone's life," explained John Thompson, Michael's eighty-seven-year-old father, who has attended upwards of twenty thousand funerals. "We take care of things that the family doesn't want to—the priest, the organist, the flowers. But ultimately we are at the service of families, and families want something different these days."

For centuries, Irish funerals followed a well-established script. When someone died, a group of neighbors known as handy women would arrive with soap and water to clean the body, candles to ward off evil spirits, and keening shawls for lamentation. The deceased would lie in repose with round-the-clock company for up to forty-eight hours, the period known as the wake. The body would then be removed to a church for a requiem mass, accompanied by a procession. Afterward, the body would be interred in a graveyard, and the family would host a feast.

But as with everywhere around the world, nearly every aspect of that ritual has been upended. Take Mr. Melay. His family opted against a home wake and chose a repose at the funeral home. Though he remained deeply religious, his children had soured on the church, largely because of the priest sex abuse scandal that ensnared thirteen hundred molesters in Ireland alone, along with the forced adoptions and Magdalene laundries that traumatized 56,000 women. The Melay children considered forgoing a service and going straight to cremation but ultimately decided to honor their father's wishes with a mass. But even that decision proved problematic, because plunging church attendance

Figure 14: Members of the Freewheelers Motorcycle Club in Waterford City, Ireland, set off for the removal of Michael Melay.

has decimated the priesthood, forcing the Thompsons to scramble to find a rent-a-priest to conduct the funeral.

The removal to the church also reflected generational tensions. John Thompson, looking straight out of an Evelyn Waugh novel in a morning suit, crisp bowler, and with a black umbrella, would normally lead the cortege, but because Mr. Melay's son, Anthony, was a serious biker, the local Freewheelers Motorcycle Club had brought their Harleys. "One percenters," as they're known, earned their nickname for being the minority of riders willing to embrace the label "outlaw." They have their own initiation rites, grooming customs, and gang-like dress, which meant that around two dozen bikers arrived at the funeral home wearing ruddy leather jackets decorated with skulls, wings, and chains.

The Freewheelers boast on their website: "The Freewheelers Motorcycle Club took a 'Don't Fuck with Us' attitude which still holds strong today."

I'm sorry for your trouble, which I will now go out of my way to make worse.

After the wake, Michael rolled Mr. Melay into the parking area. Some pallbearers lifted his coffin into the hearse, the motorcycles revved, and off we went. Four Harleys with blinking lights led the way, followed by John Thompson, the hearse, the family, and finally a caboose of graying Freewheelers bringing up the rear.

You are very welcome to Ballybricken Church, the oldest congregation in Ireland's oldest city, where today we gather to celebrate this funeral mass for the happily reposed soul of Michael Melay.

The bored-looking priest stood in front of the two-thirds-empty sanctuary that reeked of sadness and past-its-primeness. Requiem masses were part of the original ritual infrastructure of Catholicism, and their focus was almost exclusively on the salvation of the soul. Instead of eulogies for the deceased, there were homilies for Christ. But as the church came under intense pressure in recent decades to adapt to changing expectations around ritual, a number of more personalized elements were added. Mr. Melay's service included a presentation of personal objects—a photograph, a Bible, a soccer ball—and a short eulogy by his son.

"I'd like to thank all of you for coming," Anthony began. The gray-goateed son spoke of his father's upbringing in World War II, his industriousness, and his love of sport. "One of the greatest moments in Dad's life was when we traveled to America for the World Cup. Dad

Figure 15: John Thompson leads the funeral procession of Michael Melay to Ballybricken Church in Waterford.

was a plain man; he didn't like much food. We found a place that had solid fish and chips, and he lived on that for three weeks."

Following the service, as Mr. Melay's coffin was wheeled down the nave, a scratchy version of "You'll Never Walk Alone" played on the sound system. Written by Rodgers and Hammerstein for *Carousel* in 1945, the ballad, in which one character tries to comfort a cousin on the suicide of her husband, took an unlikely turn in 1963, when the version we were hearing, performed by Gerry and the Pacemakers, became the official anthem of the Liverpool Reds. Sixty years later, it's still sung before every home game and following every major victory, making it one of the most recognized fight songs on the planet. A number of guests started singing along; several cried; more than a few booed.

Walk on, walk on, with hope in your heart.

"That was my favorite moment," John Thompson said as the family gathered in the small graveyard out front. "And it never would have happened when I started in this business. In the past, funerals were for the dead; today, they're for the living. That's why I still dress this way, why I walk in front, why I played that song. I'm the funeral *director*. I can't direct your feelings, but I can direct the show."

Located a short river ride from the Celtic Sea, Waterford was founded by Vikings, became a Norse settlement, a Norman stronghold, a Gaelic outpost, an English colony, then a leader in Irish independence. Today it embodies the country's attempt to emerge from decades of stagnation—the Waterford crystal company went bankrupt and was bought by Finns; the once-Catholic monopoly is now dotted with Muslims, Hindus, and Orthodox Christians; the legalization of same-sex marriage inspired a thriving Gaelic Pride.

One of the city's most ambitious initiatives is the Viking Triangle, a tourist hub that includes sites devoted to armor, silver, and timepieces, along with the first-ever Irish Wake Museum—Rituals of Death. The eleven-pound ticket-and-tour fee includes a one-pound donation to Waterford Hospice.

Please be aware this tour will include mention of death, injury and illness, as well as realistic depictions of the recently deceased. We greatly appreciate that the subject matter of this museum may be upsetting for some.

At the entrance, I met up with Kevin Toolis, a journalist and

BAFTA-winning filmmaker who was so moved by how residents on his home island of Achill responded to his father's death that he plunged into the history of Irish mourning rituals, which led to a memoir (*My Father's Wake*), a TED Talk ("What the Irish Wake Teaches Us About Living and Dying"), and a stage show (*Wonders of the Wake*). Kevin is the poet laureate of the fourth rule of life rituals: They hold space for the emotional spectacles of our lives.

"Death has a louder voice in Ireland," Kevin said. The two of us were making our way through the three-story, six-hundred-year-old almshouse that includes a welcome desk made from a coffin, a Bronze Age funeral urn, the death mask of the sixteenth-century friar who inspired Saint Patrick's Day, and a handwritten condolence acknowledgment from Jackie Kennedy following the assassination of her third-generation Irish American husband.

"Four hundred people came to my father's wake on an island of twenty-three hundred people," Kevin continued. "If you ask a middle-aged Irish person how many dead bodies they've seen, the answer would be at least two hundred. In England or America, only a medical professional would have seen that many."

The earliest descriptions of wakes appear in the ancient world. In *Gilgamesh*, the eponymous hero initiates public mourning over his beloved companion Enki; in the *Iliad*, the Trojan King Priam leads a nine-day public lamentation for his son Hector. The modern "merry wake" emerged in the 1600s out of a mix of mourning, playing, drinking, and troublemaking. An Irish synod in 1614 issued an edict against misbehavior at wakes, including "obscene songs and suggestive games," among them mocking priests, stringing potatoes into rosaries, and dealing rounds of cards to corpses. One peasant recorded all the sex games he'd played at wakes, including Frimsey Framsey (a kissing game), Weds and Forfeits (a flirting game), and Croosting (a matchmaking game involving pelting romantic targets with pieces of turf). In a world where boys and girls were strictly segregated, he noted, more than half of marriages were "runaway unions" kindled at wakes.

"The biggest fear around death is that the dead overwhelm the living and disturb the normal order of life," Kevin said. "That's what happened to Hamlet. Funerals are designed to make the dead dead and the living live."

The biggest surprise of his father's wake, he added, was hearing "I'm sorry for your trouble" over and over. "But it wasn't the words that stuck with me; it was the handshakes. Four hundred people shook my hand in a few hours. It's as if they were reinforcing the physical reality—*he's dead; he's dead*—pulling me through the catharsis of grief. It's why so many rituals involve walking, marching, dancing, parading: Nonverbal communication can be more powerful than verbal.

"And that's why I believe the wake will survive in some way: the power of physicality. People *turn up*. They *give strength*. Because in the end, we're all Hector's children, a chorus of sons and daughters, weeping, wailing, caring, knowing that when we mourn together, we never stop singing our song."

Holding space is the single most common phrase I heard in the scores of conversations I held with ritual entrepreneurs. More than a third invoked the idea as the ultimate goal of a well-run ritual.

The expression has roots in 1960s psychotherapy but surged in popularity following a 2015 blog post from the Canadian ritual designer Heather Plett. Plett defines holding space as being "willing to walk alongside another person in whatever journey they're on." Honoring their feelings even if they're different from your own, giving them support without imposing solutions. Amy Wright Glenn, a ritual teacher in North Carolina and the author of a book called *Holding Space*, told me that the key is "listening more than speaking, feeling more than acting, being more than judging."

Two designers I met who work closely with death capture the breadth of how holding space is being expressed today.

Katrina Spade grew up in New England in a family obsessed with nature and dying. "My parents worked in medicine; they would come home every night, change clothes, and go into the garden. Nature is the closest thing I have to spirituality." Afterward, the family would eat dinner and talk about mortality. "My parents both had patients who were dying, so we talked about it openly."

Katrina attended a Quaker college, worked in finance, started a T-shirt business, and remodeled kitchens, before landing in architecture grad school. For her final project, she returned to her childhood roots. "I did a huge dive into the funeral industry, which hadn't changed meaningfully for centuries. I kept coming back to a simple question: *What do I want to happen to my body when I die?*"

Her answer: "I want it to return to nature."

"From steel caskets to toxic chemicals to titanium urns, everything about burial seemed designed to postpone decomposing. I thought, *Why not bury bodies directly in the ground so they decompose more quickly? Farmers have composted livestock for decades.*"

Katrina plunged into the science, earned her degree, wrote a business plan and, five years later, dressed in a three-piece suit and flew from her home in Seattle to New York, where she won a grant for $80,000. And she launched Recompose.

Welcome. We're a green funeral home specializing in human composting to transform your loved one's body into soil. This soil can then be used to regenerate the earth that supports us our whole lives. We're available to consult online, in-person, or on the phone.

And people clicked, and visited, and called. In its first five years,

Recompose helped legalize human composting in twelve states, including Washington, Oregon, New York, California, Colorado, and Arizona; legislation was introduced in a dozen more. Katrina was profiled on NPR and the BBC; she was featured in *People* and *Newsweek*; she was invited to give a TED Talk and named a fellow at Harvard.

Only then did she realize that she'd made a huge mistake: She left out the ritual.

Recompose uses a multistep process: The body is wrapped in a biodegradable shroud and placed in an aerated steel container; that container is buried in the ground, where bacteria and fungi break down the remains; after sixty days, the family receives a cubic yard of soil, about the size of a pickup truck. But over time, the company faced pushback, even from families willing to take the risk.

"They needed ritual," Katrina said. "They needed a space to process what they were experiencing."

So she went back to the design board.

"We built a nondenominational chapel at our headquarters in Seattle that's warm and nature-y. We wrote a carbon-cycle ceremony. We renamed the container 'the vessel,' because vessels carry you through thresholds. As we lay the body in, we invite family members to surround it with wood chips, alfalfa, and flowers—even letters—anything that can decompose. One family added a pizza! All these gestures are designed to help the family say goodbye."

But even these steps weren't enough.

"What was cool is that everyone asked if they could come back and have another ceremony when they picked up the soil." So Katrina built a special pavilion, where loved ones can place their hands in the dirt, parcel out portions into pots, share a few memories, and sing a few songs, all before driving the soil home. Recompose was voted Best Funeral Home in the Pacific Northwest for two years in a row.

"What I've learned," Katrina said, "is that a funeral is not just about how you hold the dead; it's about how you hold the living. We created a ritual to speed up returning the body to nature, but it didn't succeed until we created another ritual to slow down how the family appreciates it."

I took an Uber to Mrs. Burke's funeral at St. Agnes Church in southwest Dublin, which meant that I had no easy way to get to her burial in Bohernabreena Cemetery in the nearby Dublin Mountains.

"Why don't you just ride with us!" said Mary Cunniffe, the manager of a Massey Brothers funeral home and the president of the Irish Association of Funeral Directors. Mary was dressed similarly to John Thompson, only instead of a bowler she wore a top hat and instead of practical shoes she wore stilettos.

"Sure," I said without thinking.

And with that she opened the back door of the hearse, popped up the jumper seat, and invited me to ride to the cemetery alongside the happily reposed soul of Marjorie Burke.

Dublin, from the Gaelic word for *black pond*, is the cultural, political, economic, and rock and roll capital of Ireland, with a quarter of the population though nowhere near as many burials, because many Dubliners return to their rural roots when they return to the ground. Mrs. Burke's funeral was simultaneously more bustling, more fashionable, more religious, and more personal than Mr. Melay's. It didn't hurt that the priest actually knew her.

"Dear Marjorie had a great sense of fun," began Father Tom, fondly recalling her love of ice cream, penny opera, and her husband of sixty-plus years, Tony, whom she outlived by a decade. One of Mrs. Burke's fourteen grandchildren, dressed in Prada, invited family members to present her personal objects. "To represent her faith: a prayer book. To represent her voice: the score of *My Fair Lady*. To represent her playfulness: a singing teddy bear that she took to every birthday party."

One of Mrs. Burke's five children, Isabelle, shared stories of her mother's uncanny ability to make friends. "Mom chatted to everybody, from all races, genders, and religions. I recall coming home from school one day to find three Jehovah's Witnesses in the sitting area having tea, while Mom converted *them*." I literally laughed out loud. Isabelle concluded with how her mother was crooning her favorite song, "I Could Have Danced All Night," until a few weeks before she died. On cue, the organist played the final bars as Isabelle returned to her pew.

I was gobsmacked by the beauty.

"The Irish know how to throw a party," Mary said. The hearse was pillowy and plush. A modified Mercedes E-Class that had been cut, stretched, and heightened; outfitted with a rear deck that included rollers and hydraulics; then customized with walnut, leather, and ambient lighting, it was the most luxurious ride you'll never feel.

"We fiercely value being together. It's why you saw people fly in from America for the funeral of a ninety-five-year-old woman. Everybody wants to reaffirm their Irishness."

That pride around *turning up* helps explain one of the more illustrative examples of how rituals are evolving in the digital age. In 2005, Dympna Coleman, one of five children of two farmers in the northeast town of Dundalk (the same place where the hearse was fabricated), returned home from abroad to visit her family. After bumping into a school friend, she was embarrassed to learn that her schoolmate's father had died a few months earlier. "It was so tense," Dympna remembered. "I hadn't known, which meant I hadn't acknowledged his death." That night, drinking wine around the kitchen table, Dympna and her brother, Jay, who had taken over the family farm, hatched an idea.

In a country where attending wakes is a backbone of civil society, informing people of those wakes is a centerpiece of civic life. In the Middle Ages, deaths were announced by town crier; later, newspapers took up the role, followed by radio. In Waterford and Dublin alike, death announcements are still read on the radio four times a day—at nine, noon, six, and nine. "Somebody always shouts, '*Shush!* The death notices are on.'" Mary said.

The Colemans' idea was to take this service online. "With the wonders of the web and the power of the internet, we should bring notices into the twenty-first century." They wrestled with HTML, brokered with skeptical funeral directors, and in 2006 opened a site with the iconic Irish URL RIP.ie. "It's short. It's easy to remember. It speaks to the subject matter," Dympna said.

And the public agreed. Overnight, RIP.ie transformed resting in peace in Ireland. Today, the site has 60 million page views a month from 185 countries. It has two types of visitors, Dympna said: "searchers," who look for individuals, and "browsers," who visit every day. Mondays are the busiest, Saturdays the slowest. Nine a.m. is the peak when people get to work.

After their initial suspicion, funeral directors embraced the site, which is searchable by name, date, county, and town, largely because it made their lives easier. But one aspect made their lives harder: Just as diplomats rely on euphemisms for tense meetings ("Our conversations were frank, open, and constructive"), funeral directors had to devise a new code for cause of death that would live in perpetuity on the web.

"We use three phrases," Mary explained: "'died peacefully,' 'died suddenly,' or 'died tragically.' 'Peacefully' means of natural causes; 'suddenly' means of a short illness or accident; 'tragically' means of suicide or overdose."

"So you're not allowed to tell the truth?" I said.

"We strongly hint. We write that donations can be made to Pieta

House, which helps with suicide, or St. John of God's, which helps with mental health or addiction. Everybody understands."

Bohernabreena Cemetery stretches across the side of a treeless hill that's home to fourteen hundred graves in a variety of shapes, designs, and colors. The atmosphere seemed more like an amusement park than a solemn place of perpetual peace. I saw yellow, pink, and even rainbow-colored headstones; grave markers carved into guitars, crosses, angels, and cherubs; plots decorated with garden gnomes, flying eagles, prom photos, and beauty pageant satin sashes adorned with DAD or BEST DAUGHTER EVER.

The hearse stopped in front of a stately headstone that read "Precious Memories of Anthony (Tony) Burke," but with an open grave for the addition of his wife. Mrs. Burke's coffin was rested on two steel beams. Father Tom led a short service that included the Lord's Prayer, a singalong of "The Bells of the Angelus," and the benediction *ashes to ashes, dust to dust.* He concluded: "It has been hard for us to imagine a world where Marjorie and Tony could not talk about all things. Now they will be reunited. The country we have today is here because of their generation."

The pallbearers lifted the coffin with leather straps, attendants removed the beams, and Mrs. Burke was lowered into the loving grasp of the first man with whom she ever shared a dance. As the body descended, I couldn't help wondering if we were watching not just the passing of a couple but the passing of an era.

In the final gesture, each of the children, grandchildren, and great-grandchildren, followed by the in-laws, cousins, and neighbors, stepped forward one by one and tossed a long-stemmed yellow rose into the grave. Suddenly, I was Ezra Bookman at every engagement that ever was, McKenzi Taylor at every wedding, Brother Agnello at every baptism.

I was myself, holding a bag of Tybee Island sand and a long-stemmed yellow rose, standing over my father's grave.

Crying all over again.

Like Katrina Spade, Sarah Kerr became a roundabout expert in holding space. Sarah was born into a close-knit family in British Columbia. "I'm deeply wired for the collective. When my mom slammed her finger in the washing machine, my finger swelled up." She earned a master's degree in environmental studies, became an activist, and felt called to spirituality in her forties. For the next decade she worked on a PhD in ritual healing, then opened the Centre for Sacred Deathcare in Calgary, "a vibrant community of learners and seekers" who are "committed to creating a death-positive culture." Her signature course: Holding Space at a Deathbed.

"One definition of trauma is 'too much, too fast, without enough support,'" Sarah said. "It's a crisis of meaning. A primary function of ritual is to slow us down so our insides can catch up with our outsides."

Sarah shared a story about a family she worked with, including a terminally ill man in his sixties, his wife, and their two grown daughters. "The father died at three in the morning. When I arrived, the room was a swirling gray, backwash-y eddy of murky energy. One daughter was standing, the other was lying on his body, crying. The wife was wandering around the room in shock."

Sarah went to work. She opened a window; cleared out the medicines, the machinery, the sippy cups, and the juice boxes; and then walked the family through a ritual.

"The archetype of what happens when we die is that there's a village of the living and a village of the dead—and a river that connects the two. Our job in the village of the living is to build a canoe to convey the soul to the village of the dead. That canoe is built by love and fueled by grief."

Once she opens the ritual, Sarah asks each family member to call out an ancestor on the other side that they want to receive the soul.

"Grief is all-consuming. It feels like all there is and all there ever was. But once you start remembering all the relatives who've crossed over—*Grandma died. So did Uncle Peter. Don't forget Bonzi, the dog!*—you start thinking, *Oh, I lived through this before, I can live through this again.*"

Then she guides the family through a cleansing, taking warm water and essential oil and tenderly washing the body. "By this point the brain knows the person is dead, but the soul has yet to accept it. The simple act of touching his body helps persuade our body that he's gone."

She then suggests that the wife remove his wedding ring. "Think back to when you put this ring on his finger. Think back on the love you felt, the commitment you made. Now remove that ring with the same love and commitment. As you did the first time, you can seal those feelings with a kiss."

When the mother finishes, one of her daughters offers her a chain, and she suspends the ring around her neck.

Finally, Sarah pulls out a drum and begins to beat—*boom, boom, boom.* She hands each person a perfume bottle, sterling silver, antique, "straight out of a Harry Potter movie," and invites them to anoint the forehead of the deceased.

"Then, with their hands on his head and their hearts in their throats, they gently push him across the river. His body remains, but his soul is departed. They've held him as long as they can, now they give him permission to go."

Sarah slowly pulls the sheet over his head.

"What happens next may be the most magical moment of all:

Everyone looks around and realizes, *We are the family now.* They take the same oil they used on the father and anoint one another. The circle has been remade. The village has been reborn."

On my last day in Ireland I made my first visit to a crematorium. Mount Jerome Cemetery squeezes 225,000 graves into forty-seven acres in South Dublin. Opened in 1836, it has nearly five times the density of Green-Wood in Brooklyn. Since 2000, it's also had the country's first crematorium.

"Ireland is very much America's fifty-first state," explains Alan Massey, the third-generation head of the cemetery. He was dressed in the traditional morning suit and top hat, but instead of an umbrella, he carried a cane. "Our trends mirror the US. Twenty-five years ago, cremations were rare; today they're 20 percent of the country and 70 percent in Dublin."

He led me into a large concrete room with tile walls and two giant green machines, each the size of a one-car garage. Alan pressed a few buttons on a computer screen, and out slid two shiny platforms that popped up like ironing boards. "The coffin goes on this platform," he said. "We remove the handles, then everything disappears into the incinerator."

The temperature reaches up to 1,600 degrees Fahrenheit, and the first combustion lasts around ninety minutes. What emerges is a chunky mixture that's 85 percent crushed skeletal bone, 15 percent coffin ash. The staff then picks out the metal remnants, from coffin nails to artificial hips, which are sent to the Netherlands to be recycled.

"So my titanium femur might end up in someone's cell phone?" I asked.

"Probably a carburetor."

The remaining char is then fed into a cremulator, which grinds it

Figure 16: Alan Massey demonstrates how to use one of the crematoria in Mount Jerome Cemetery, Dublin, Ireland.

into around four liters of powdery ash. Those cremains are placed into a container of the family's choosing, usually an urn, box, shaker, clock, hourglass, tealight, necklace, or pendant. Cremains these days are also launched into space, submerged into reefs, pressed into vinyl records, molded into garden stones, sealed into time capsules, sewn into teddy bears, or sometimes just left in the closet for descendants to figure out.

"Funerals are still popular in Ireland," Alan said, "but we're expecting that a quarter of deaths will soon be direct cremation, meaning no service whatsoever. For funeral homes, those numbers would mean devastation."

Of the funerals that do happen, about a third are nonreligious, which has spawned the rise of a new class of alternative celebrants. Mary Cunniffe introduced me to one of the most popular, Karen Dempsey, a former hospice nurse turned interfaith minister, who was leading a funeral that afternoon in Mount Jerome's modern Garden Chapel. Karl was a theater artist who had died by suicide.

Karen is one of the more colorful ritual designers I met; her Instagram username is @BaldPriestess, and it's an apt description: She has snow-white skin; dark, anime eyes that she sometimes makes up with smoky black eyeshadow and other times with rainbow sparkles; and, because of alopecia, no hair.

"I come from a family with lots of trauma and lots of grief," Karen said by way of introduction. "Deaths by suicide, drowning, alcohol, and homelessness. The core being my mother's mother, who was struck by a truck in Dublin when she was forty-seven, leaving behind an absent husband and eleven children, the oldest of whom was my mother, who had just given birth to me. I became the twelfth child, so to speak, raised on the cusp of two families."

Karen has never left that cusp of trauma and grief—and believes that liminal space explains the Irish affinity with death.

"Our biggest tragedy is our language, which was taken from us by our invaders. I didn't know what I was missing until I learned Gaelic as an adult—each word contains so much nuance and poetry. When you can't express your pain for fear of being killed, all that trauma gets repressed."

The biggest reason the Irish are obsessed with death, she continued, is the potato blight of the 1840s, which killed more than a million people and led a million more to emigrate; in the span of five years, a quarter of the population disappeared. "Think of all the wakes people went to! They even held elaborate vigils for people who emigrated, since most would never have the money to return home. They called them 'American wakes.'"

In English, that period is known as the great famine; in Gaelic, it's called the great hunger. The difference in wording is an epic of pain.

"We still hunger for what we lost," Karen said, "Every time I perform a funeral, I try to identify the underlying anguish. You can't offer compassion until you understand the suffering."

Karl's funeral was no exception. The ceremony was largely similar to the others—it had a welcome, personal objects, eulogies, music. "A ritual can't be entirely bespoke," Karen explained. "The psyche has to recognize it as ceremony." It passed the Auntie Sniff Test.

But the tone was radically different; it also aced the Cool Uncle Exam. The overture was "The Pink Panther Theme"; the personal objects included a skateboard, a sack of rock climbing gear, and a fairy wand. Karen's remarks did not sugarcoat:

We are gathered here today to honor the life and love of our dearly beloved Karl. We also want to join together in our grief, anger, shock and sadness at the terrible suddenness of his death, and our confusion and heartbreak over how he chose to leave this life.

A clue was offered when a colleague read Karl's own words from an autobiographical documentary he had been making: *Society asks so much of us. . . . Social media puts so much pressure on my generation. . . . Mental health these days is getting worse and worse.*

"From the moment I start working with a family," Karen said, "I'm holding them in some way. Offering boundaries, providing shape. When I met Karl's family, they had no boundaries. They were wide-eyed, reeling, adrift. Feeling unmoored is the opposite of feeling held, which is why the one essential function of a ritual is to provide the container to hold us, to protect us."

We are reaching the end of our time with Karl, Karen said. *You see before me a jar of stones. These stones were collected last night from the mouth of the river where Karl was living. We invite you to take one of these stones as you leave to hold on to as long as you like. And when the time comes to let it go, please return it to a beautiful place in honor of Karl.*

Karen placed the container in front of the coffin, which would soon be carried to the crematorium.

As we say goodbye, let us send Karl on his way with a piece of music he loved from his time on the stage. Everyone, please join in.

The curtains in front of the coffin began to close. The canoe pushed off from the shore. The time to weep became a time to sing. And Frank Sinatra came onto the speakers crooning Karl's favorite song, "You'll Never Walk Alone."

11.

THE PLACENTA CHRONICLES

How to Tell the Story of a Birth

If ritual were going to be revived, of course moms would lead the way. I'm thinking of two moms I met, in opposite hemispheres, on separate continents, in different generations, connected by little more than a desire to restore emotional richness to one of life's most enriching experiences.

The first mom is Mahina Rapu Tuki, born in the middle of the Pacific Ocean on the most isolated inhabited island on the planet, a Paris-educated midwife, and a fighter dedicated to protecting ancestral traditions while dragging a few backward men into the present, including me.

The second is Megan Sheldon, born in one of the most cosmopolitan cities in North America, an Edinburgh-educated cultural mythologist, and a tech entrepreneur behind "the first-ever guided ritual and ceremony app."

What divides these two mothers is ocean, land, language, religion, and technology.

What unites them is that they fulfill the fourth essential thing that life rituals do: They help us to narrate the ups and downs of our lives; they allow us to craft enriching life stories that convert our most precarious moments into annals of collective affirmation.

They chronicle.

In the case of contemporary childbirth, they empower us to balance scientific wisdom with ancestral wisdom, physical safety with emotional safety, and medical precision with spiritual precision. The emerging ritual landscape around having babies includes inventive ways to celebrate fear and joy; creative ways to honor moms while integrating dads, donors, and surrogates; and sometimes startling ways to pay tribute to the least romanticized parts of the process—the umbilical cord that turns out to make great necklaces, the creamy coating covering newborns that turns out to make great skin cream, and the placenta that turns out to make, well, great smoothies.

On a parched summer afternoon, I stepped off one of the few flights a week to Mataveri International Airport, "the most remote airport in the world," on the miniscule volcanic speck known as Easter Island in English, Isla de Pascua in Spanish, and Rapa Nui (Great Rapa) in the language of its nearly ten thousand inhabitants. Located twenty-three hundred miles west of Chile, twenty-six hundred miles south of Tahiti, and forty-three hundred miles east of New Zealand, the "South Pacific's loneliest terminus" has a remarkable constellation of nicknames: "the Mysterious Island," "the Land of Giants," "the Island at the End of the World," "the World's Museum," and, using the Rapa Nui word for *placenta*, "the Navel of the World."

"Aloha!" said Mahina as she draped an orchid lei around my neck. With the grandmotherly warmth of a Polynesian and the hardened edge of an activist, she was standing alongside a carved tiki signpost. "Welcome home."

Figure 17: The Tahai Ceremonial Complex on the western edge of Rapa Nui.

Mahina suggested that we drive to the western edge of the island to watch the sunset. Fifteen miles at its widest, Rapa Nui is so tiny compared to the Pacific (0.0001 percent of its surface area) that it's the equivalent of a slice of pie in the Superdome. Everything is close to everything else, yet it took us forever to get anywhere. In my twenties, I spent a week traveling by public bus across the South Island of New Zealand. Multiple times a day, the road would be blocked by sheep. "A New Zealand traffic jam!" the driver would joke . . . every single time.

Mahina is a Rapa Nui traffic jam. One of the oldest living descendants of the island's royal family, Mahina is related to, has mentored, or has delivered nearly everyone alive. They swarmed her car, offering hugs, tagging along, or simply piling in. By the time we arrived at the grassy archaeological site, our party had swelled to ten.

The Tahai Ceremonial Complex has three elevated stone platforms topped by seven giant head-and-torso statues, or moai, the signature feature of the island and the unofficial public face of the South Pacific. The extraordinary rise of the civilization that produced these singular human achievements, followed by the equally rapid fall of that civilization, is a large reason for the island's fame. No one can agree on why Rapa Nui collapsed.

As we approached the platform, a group of high schoolers was practicing a hula dance for the upcoming Tāpati cultural festival. The girls wore grass skirts and coconut-shell bras; the boys wore loincloths made from mulberry bark and headdresses made from feathers. The dance coach tried to wrangle the uneven performers, but once Mahina and our entourage appeared, the students followed us like ducklings.

A one-hundred-ten-year-old woman in a wheelchair appeared, carried by some men. The attendants set the woman down in front of a small stone altar. Mahina and her minions encircled her. One beat a drum, another lit some dried leaves, a third blew a call through a stone. A dance broke out as the woman began to rock back and forth, chanting toward the cloudless sky in an uncommonly arid spell, praying for rain.

As the sun dipped behind the silent colossi, hearing everything but saying nothing, an impromptu, intergenerational nature ritual played out.

Afterward, I peppered Mahina with questions: *What happened? Why? What did it mean?*

"Take a deep breath, son," she said. "Feel the wind on your face, the soil beneath your feet. Appreciate being uncomfortable. These are your ancestors, too, you know? Don't be in such a hurry.

"Let the story come to you."

A story I never dreamed of telling came to me uninvited on the eve of my fortieth birthday. Linda and I had been married the previous year; after canceling one honeymoon in Mongolia because of SARS and another in Bali because of a bombing, we ultimately went to Morocco. The following year I took her on a second honeymoon to Iran.

That summer we tried to get pregnant. When the first test showed a half-pink strip, Linda went to three drugstores and brought home five backups.

A few weeks later we went to an ob-gyn. A young doctor walked in, handed us a thick folder, and patiently answered our questions. Linda mounted the sonogram chair, and within seconds a gauzy image appeared. The doctor was quiet for the longest time, then said, with a worrisome catch in her voice, "Well, my dear, you're having, um, twins."

Seconds later, after Linda was cleaned up and we were seated next to each other, the doctor looked at us and announced, "We need to talk about selective reduction."

Neither of us had ever heard that term, but it wasn't hard to decipher its meaning. The sonogram had shown that Linda had two embryos, one placenta, and what appeared to be one amniotic sac, an extremely rare condition that all but guarantees that one fetus would cannibalize the other. The doctor dispatched us across Central Park to the most sensitive sonogram in the city to see if it could detect a membrane that would protect one child from the other.

As soon as we walked out of the office, Linda turned to me and said, "It's time to selectively reduce that doctor."

One way of looking at the history of life rituals is as a battle between life stories: the story others tell about your life versus the story you tell about your life. You're going through a life transition—you're losing a loved one, you're getting married, you're having a baby. That experience comes with a variety of emotions and a host of decisions. Who gets to make those decisions? Do you choose how to bury your parent, marry your lover, deliver your baby? Or do the people around you choose—your parents, your religion, your country, your doctor? For most people across time, others made those decisions. They chose how you celebrated the turning points of your life.

Childbirth is as good a case study as I know of how that balance of power has shifted over the last century, from others controlling our decisions to each of us seizing greater control. The surprising turning point in that evolution is the rise of the hospital.

Historically, women gave birth at home under the care of other women. Birth rituals reflected the risks. Egyptians waved hippopotamus ivory wands for good fortune; Greeks hung bronze or gold amulets to ward off spirits; the Yoruba in Nigeria rhythmically clapped to welcome babies into the world; the Hopi in North America locked mothers in darkened huts for weeks.

The Industrial Revolution overturned this calculus as workers crowded in filthy cities had no room to give birth at home. Working-class women were forced to seek out newly opened hospitals, while wealthier women enjoyed the comforts of their drawing rooms. The introduction of chloroform as an anesthetic in 1847 fed the rise of medicalized birth. That ubiquitous trendsetter Queen Victoria, though she gave birth to all nine of her children in palaces, used "that blessed chloroform" for her last two births. Most people needed institutions for such benefits. By the 1930s, half of Americans were delivered in hospitals.

But not everyone was happy with this trend. In 1933, the British obstetrician Grantly Dick-Read coined the term *natural childbirth*, insisting that delivering a baby was inherently pain-free, but that "overcivilized" women *caused their own pain* with needless anxiety. If neurotic, Western women just trusted their bodies like "primitive" women, they wouldn't have to fall back on anesthesia, he insisted. The work of eliminating labor pain is "in the mind."

The mildly eugenic Dick-Read was hardly the best messenger for this message, and natural childbirth went nowhere. It took the second wave of feminism, notably the Boston Women's Health Book Collective's 1971 bible *Our Bodies, Ourselves*, to bring women-centered birth back into vogue. In 1972, the midwife Ina May Gaskin opened a birthing center on a commune in rural Tennessee. Instead of relying on painkillers, Gaskin invited prospective fathers to nurture, encourage, even fondle and French-kiss their partners during labor; she introduced the "Gaskin maneuver" that positioned pregnant women on their hands and knees; and she trumpeted that, when done right, natural childbirth would stimulate orgasm.

Birth would be not just pain-free but pleasure-rich!

While some of her wackier ideas disappeared, Gaskin's influence was monumental. In 1970 certified midwives attended 1 percent of American births; by 1990 it was 3.3 percent; by 2000, 7.6 percent; today it's 12 percent. And these weren't the only women remaking childbirth. In 1970 female ob-gyns numbered 7 percent; by 1990 it was 18 percent; by 2000, 38 percent; today it's 62 percent.

But while the gender dynamics of childbirth were changing, the rituals of childbirth were not. If anything, the notion that drug-free, vaginal deliveries were more "meaningful" and "fulfilling" created a backlash, as the vast majority of women who either chose to—or were forced to—rely on medical assistance felt shamed and belittled. A cry went out: Why can't hospital births have more meaning?! It took the rise of mommy bloggers and Facebook posters sharing their stories online to burst these frustrations into view and lead to a revolution in rituals around childbirth.

Rapa Nui is a poster child for the ebbing and flowing of stories. On my first morning, Mahina took me to a volcano in the southeast corner that's home to nearly four hundred of the surviving nine hundred moai. The sloping UNESCO World Heritage site was the quarry for 95 percent of the volcanic ash that was used to carve the armless, legless creatures. Up to thirty-five feet tall and eighty-six tons, moai look like enormous petrified prairie dogs sticking their heads out of the ground.

Who made these creations—and why did they stop?

Rapa Nui was settled around nine hundred years ago. Oral tradition describes two canoes arriving from western Polynesia, with a chief, his captain, and their families. When the wives gave birth to heirs, the captain bit off their umbilical cords, giving rise to a long tradition of birth metaphors in the culture. Mahina's adolescent rite of passage was going on a long canoe trip to a faraway island. "When you're paddling home, Rapa looks like a placenta floating in the ocean, its umbilical cord stretching to earth. That's why we call the island 'the umbilical cord of the world.'"

The first European visitor, the Dutch explorer Jacob Roggeveen, arrived on Easter Sunday 1722, giving rise to the island's international name. During his weeklong stay, he observed a thriving culture of four thousand people centered on "remarkably tall stone figures" that "caused us to be filled with wonder." When James Cook landed fifty years later, some of those statues had already fallen, malnutrition was rampant, population decline had begun. Within a century, Rapa Nui was deforested and depopulated. In 1892, the number of residents was one hundred and one.

What happened?

The American biologist Jared Diamond, who won a Pulitzer Prize for *Guns, Germs, and Steel*, wrote a bestselling follow-up arguing that Easter Island collapsed because of self-inflicted wounds. After reaching a "golden age" of moai construction around 1500, the fifteen thousand islanders committed "ecological suicide," he wrote, ripping down forests, decimating food supplies, triggering tribal warfare and cannibalism.

The theory has generated near-unanimous blowback. Forty years of research drawing on bone pathology, satellite imagery, pollen sediments, radiocarbon dating, dietary isotopes, DNA sampling, and experimental archaeology showing that moai could be moved without tree trunks has concluded that the population remained steady for most of its history, ecocide is a myth, and cannibalism never happened. The biggest early threats to Rapa Nui were rats and tuberculosis brought by outsiders; the biggest later threats were Peruvian slave traders who abducted a third of the island's residents in 1862. As one scholar wrote, "there is no conclusive evidence" of a Rapa Nui "collapse."

Mahina went even further: "Fuck Jared Diamond."

Still, as important as this cautionary tale is in understanding how we tell stories of decline, what happened next is far more important for our purposes—understanding how we use ritual to tell stories of recovery. In that tale, Mahina plays a central role.

Megan Sheldon knows a thing or two about painful birth stories. "In the year that I was born, three of my grandparents died," the Vancouver native told me, "including my mother's mother, who was killed by a drunk driver. I was breastfed by a grieving mom, which I'm 100 percent sure shaped who I am."

As a child, Megan loved rituals. "Every Sunday we would gather as a family and eat pancakes. My dad had very specific rules: You had to use the same mix of berries, the same kinds of toppings, in the same order. My friends all wanted to stay over on Saturday nights."

Megan was majoring in cultural studies at McGill when her mother was diagnosed with breast cancer; the two started a long-distance ritual book club. "We read about Jungian archetypes, sacred rites, the divine feminine." After graduation, Megan moved to Scotland to earn a master's in cultural mythology. "My dad said, 'What the hell are you going to do with that?'" The answer was work in book publishing, community building, and marketing for UNICEF and Sarah McLachlan, before starting a "brand mythology" company in Vancouver.

Then she fell in love.

"We didn't believe in marriage," Megan said of her boyfriend, Johan, a Swedish engineer. "All those empty rituals like walking down the aisle, tossing the bouquet, 'giving your hand.'"

Then a friend told her about an Irish myth in which young lovers are unsure whether they want to marry. One morning, they gather on either side of a hill and climb up alone. Along the way, they're invited to think about where they've been and where they want to go, what obstacles they've faced and how they overcame them. Two chairs await them on the top of the hill. The lovers sit and share what they felt during the walk. As the sun sets, they face a choice: walk down apart and the relationship ends, or walk down together and the village celebrates their marriage that night. If they choose to stay together, the following year they must perform the ritual all over again.

Megan and Johan found a ritual they could embrace.

"We gathered twenty-four guests on the beach. We each went for a walk by ourselves and acknowledged that we were letting go of our singlehood." Then they came together for a ceremony. "We had rings engraved with mountain symbols; we placed them in an abalone shell and passed it around the circle so everyone could warm them. My sister-in-law is blind and found it especially moving. Afterwards we handed out heart-shaped stones and asked everyone to inscribe them."

Every year on their anniversary, Megan and Johan go to a beach, start out walking alone, then meet together and finish the walk, making a new vow for the year ahead.

That ritual proved to be lifesaving when the years started getting hard.

"We had a very linear path laid out for ourselves," Megan said. "We got pregnant quickly, which we appreciated because so many of our friends had difficulty. Seven weeks later I miscarried. The way the hospital negated my experience was horrifying; not having a ritual made it worse.

"I was walking around my house in a daze, crying. I found my way to the beach and picked up some stones. I had a Sharpie in my purse, so I wrote down names we had been thinking, dreams we had been sharing, anger I had been holding. Then I threw the stones into the ocean. I'm pretty sure people were thinking, *What the hell is she doing?* but each plunk released more emotions."

Then Megan had another miscarriage.

And a third.

"By this point I was being even more intentional. With my third pregnancy loss, I went into the forest and found this beautiful grove. I brought paper, pens, matches, and a bowl of water. I wrote down all the things that had been weighing on me—timelines, due dates, expectations. I burned them and dropped the ash into water."

Then she did what many millennial women would have done: She went home and told her story online. That's when she found her people, her purpose, and the answer to her father's question of what the hell she would do with her life.

I was handpicked by my grandmother at age four," Mahina said.

We were standing on a thousand-foot cliff overlooking the waves crashing against the rocks. This part of the island, a World Monuments Fund site, is home to Rapa Nui's most storied ritual, the Birdman, central to its decline and its recovery. "The idea was that I would learn the art of childbirth. She taught me how to make fire, boil water, and catch the baby."

Part of that training involved preparing ricin from native castor plants to induce labor. An even more valuable medical discovery on the island came in 1972 from a soil bacteria that's now used to coat coronary stents, treat cancer, prevent organ rejection after transplants, and slow aging. It's called rapamycin in honor of Rapa Nui.

"The key to human longevity is to learn what our ancestors already knew," Mahina said.

After Rapa Nui hit bottom in the 1880s, recovery was slow. An English businessman bought up most of the land and repatriated workers enslaved in Peru; Chile annexed the territory; a sheep-farming conglomerate tried turning the island into a mini New Zealand. During the Cold War, the United States invested in Rapa Nui, building the airport as an emergency landing spot for NASA. By then, the Indigenous rights movement, led by Mahina's family, was well underway.

Mahina's mother, Analola, was born in 1928 and forced to marry an older man at twenty-one. "I wasn't in love," she told an oral historian, "but over time I learned to love him." Analola gave birth to seventeen children with her husband and an eighteenth with a Norwegian ship captain. "I had them all at home," she said. With her first delivery, she got on all fours and pushed out the baby into the arms of her mother. "With that experience, I was able to have the others by myself. I cut their cords; I measured four fingers, tied it firmly with three knots, then cut it with an obsidian blade."

After training with her grandmother, Mahina was sent to Chile for school, then Paris, then Oxford. She married an American lawyer, had children, and moved to Hawaii, where she helped establish the Oriental Medical Institute. She eventually returned to the island to help her family rebuild Rapa Nui. Their strategy: comb the stories of the past to "invent" new rituals for the future.

The strategy worked. The first moai was restored in 1956. The "Rapa Nui manuscripts," a canon of oral traditions, was published in

1958. The Tāpati festival was started in 1969. It revived elements of the Birdman ritual, in which young men would climb down the cliff, swim the straits, and then wait weeks on a nearby islet until a sooty tern laid its eggs. Whoever swam back first and climbed the ledge with an intact egg was named Birdman, enabling his clan to rule the island for the next year. Though the sometimes-bloody ritual ended in the 1870s, the boat races and dance contests of today continue the rivalry.

Mahina's family was central to this renewal: One brother started the dance troupe; another was governor; a nephew made a film about the island. Mahina's role was to codify traditional birth rituals. Her message: The whole family must be involved.

"How do you tell the story of a birth?" she asked me. "Did you just fall out of your mother's vagina, for example? Did you hurt her? You especially, with your big head. Your poor mother!"

"My wife delivered two heads," I said.

"Ouch!" She slapped her head like a Borscht Belt comedian.

"But pain is the heart of any story," she continued. "When you make love, the father and mother enjoy that fully. But then the father disappears, and the mother does all the work. I teach fathers how to make soup and peel sea urchin; how to boil water and catch the baby; how to cut the cord.

"And then, after the baby arrives, I take the father to bury the placenta underneath an avocado tree, just like my father did for me." I raised my eyebrows. "You don't believe me? Come, I'll show you."

As soon as Megan Sheldon started blogging about her miscarriages, she began to hear from readers.

I just had my fourth miscarriage.
I just had a stillbirth.

My child was just diagnosed with cancer.
My baby is two months old, and my mother just died.
Can you help?

Megan had never designed a ritual for anyone else, but she drew from her own experience. "For that new mom who just lost her mother, I gathered her family in the backyard and created a storytelling ritual around life cycles. She offered to pay me, and I was shocked. *You mean this is something you can get paid to do?*"

The baby who was breastfed by a grieving mom designed her first ceremony for a grieving mom who was breastfeeding.

"I went on to have two daughters of my own," Megan said. "When my first, Hannah, was two months old, we lost Johan's dad. Suddenly *I* was the grieving mom who was breastfeeding."

Perhaps the most moving part of Megan's story is how closely it aligns with tens of thousands of other moms who flooded online in the early years of the internet to share their harrowing birth stories: *Screaming in Agony During a Traumatic Birth. Six Horrendous Minutes of Silence from My Son. I Gave Birth in an Elevator—and It Was Caught on Security Footage. I Think We Brought the Wrong One Home: One Mother's Search to Find Her Lost Son.*

Lynn Callister, a professor of nursing at Brigham Young University, studied online birth narratives on five continents and identified multiple benefits for women who share them: integrating a pivotal event into your life story; connecting your story with those of others; sharing fears, letdowns, and unresolved questions; seeing yourself as a hero.

Researchers at Cornell used natural language processing to analyze 2,847 birth stories from r/BabyBumps on Reddit. "The popularity of these stories speaks to the need for a narrative outlet for women who have undergone a surveilled and sometimes traumatic experience." Two thirds of moms framed their story as positive; they were most complimentary of their partners and their babies. A third framed their story as negative; they were most upset by the pain and postpartum side effects. The most striking finding: moms "consistently frame themselves as having the least power," while framing doctors and nurses as having the most.

These studies reveal how deep the frustration around childbirth remains. If the proliferation of novel birth narratives is an expression of that frustration, the proliferation of novel birth rituals is a response—a bid to claw back agency. The ritual revival has spawned a host of alternative childbirth rites, a veritable next-gen rebrand: sonogram photo reveals, baby bump postings, nausea tea parties, craving recipes, babymoons, mother blessings, dadchelor parties, push presents. Even gender reveals, which are sometimes mocked online and off for their exploding excesses of pink or blue regalia, at least normalized mixed-gender showers.

What Megan found most encouraging in this outpouring is how the craving for ritual stretched beyond successful pregnancies to unsuccessful ones. After her miscarriages, she founded Seeking Ceremony, a community of women who create ceremony boxes for mothers who've had pregnancy loss. "We include a letter from a woman who's been through the same experience, river stones and permanent markers, wildflower-seed paper and matches, and a 'ritual jar' with inspirational quotes you can pull out at any time. One woman puts a stuffed bunny in every box in honor of her stillborn son."

But even that initiative was just the start. After Johan lost his job, he and Megan took their annual beach walk and decided to create a ritual design app. Be Ceremonial's "signature framework" allows you to pick and choose elements from "traditional rites of passage" to make your own rite of passage. Their offerings include fertility and birth, lifestyle and relationships, end of life and grief. The single most surprising outcome: the ceremony that proved to be most popular.

Surprising, that is, until Megan discovered that her daughter needed one, too.

Mahina drove cautiously through a metal gate into the overgrown apiary and fruit orchard of her childhood home. Dogs swarmed the car; rusted metal chairs offered cover for a hen and her chicks; a Jenga tower of lavender and green wooden boxes teetered with beehives.

"Grandpa lived here," Mahina says. "We lived next door. Now we rent it to a honey maker."

We stepped around the dogs, over the chicks, and alongside the bees into a tangle of orange, pineapple, and papaya trees. The center of the island is the one area that still boasts abundant vegetation. After some effort, Mahina located an avocado tree that sloped to the right and then burst through its neighbors into the light.

"My father planted this tree over my placenta the day I was born."

She described a process that she still teaches: first, the father "milks" the cord, squeezing any remaining nutrients into the bloodstream of the baby; then he clamps the cord; finally he takes the placenta home and buries it underneath a fruit sapling.

"The tree that grows is used to diagnose the child," Mahina said. "When I was living abroad, my mother would check the tree. If it was healthy, I was healthy. If it was unhealthy, she would call me in the middle of the night."

Placenta rituals have a long history. The mysterious one-pound organ, the shape of a Frisbee, supplies oxygen, filters toxins, and disposes of waste. Cultures across time viewed it as the child's spiritual twin (Egypt), doppelgänger (Mexico), or guardian angel (Iceland). The Navajo buried the placenta on tribal land, believing it would ensure that the child returned home; the Japanese washed the placenta in sake,

Figure 18: Mahina Rapu Tuki peers up at the avocado tree that her father planted on the day of her birth on Rapa Nui.

wrapped it in silk, and buried it in a wooden box with calligraphy brushes or a needle and thread; the Maori placed the placenta in hollowed-out gourds that were planted in ancestral ground. Two anthropologists at the University of Nevada investigated 179 cultures and found 169 different ways of ritualizing placentas.

Given this cultural tailwind, it should hardly be shocking that placenta rituals would make a comeback in any ritual revival—yet the return of such rituals still seems surprising. News feeds burst with stories of dads stealing placentas to bury, moms pressing placentas into "archival paper" to create "tree of life" prints. Some hospitals became so outraged that they banned the removal of "afterbirth." In Hawaii, an Indigenous couple sued the state in 2005 after it labeled placentas "biological waste." When their case was bogged down in the courts, the dad simply plucked the placenta from the fridge, stuck it in his backpack, and carried it home. The following year the state passed a law declaring placentas the property of the couple, the first of ten states to do so.

Burying placentas was only the beginning. By the 2010s, celebrities started ingesting them. In a 2015 social post sent to her four hundred twenty-five million followers called "Eating My Placenta," Kim Kardashian wrote that she had the placenta of her first child freeze-dried and turned into a pill—"not actually fry it like a steak and eat it (which some people do, BTW)." Her explanation: "I really didn't want the baby blues, and thought I can't go wrong with taking a pill made of my own hormones. . . . I totally recommend it for anyone considering it!" Her sister Kourtney, with two hundred sixty-five million followers, followed suit: "Yummy . . . PLACENTA pills! No joke. . . . They are life changing! #benefits #lookitup."

Women's Health did look it up—and more. They asked the author of *DIY Placenta Edibles* to share recipes for placenta lasagna, placenta chili, placenta truffles, and placenta smoothies. The smoothie recipe instructs new moms to don gloves, then "place your placenta on a tray, and see where you feel called to remove a piece. . . . Using your scissors, take out a half dollar–sized chunk from . . . the maternal side, the fetal side, the cord insertion point." These chunks are tossed into a blender with orange juice, yogurt, and strawberries; puréed for one to two minutes; then served "in a gorgeous glass with a colorful bendy straw."

The arguments for placentophagy, as consumption is called, is that four thousand mammals do it, and for humans it speeds recovery and reduces the blues. Scholars disagree. Researchers at Northwestern reviewed ten published studies and "found no data to support the common claims that eating the placenta either raw, cooked, or encapsulated offers protection against postpartum depression, reduces post-delivery pain, boosts energy, helps with lactation," or any other alleged benefit. The CDC issued a warning about bacterial infections and respiratory distress among babies whose mothers had consumed placenta capsules. *The New York Times* published a plea: "Thank You for Not Eating Your Placenta."

But placenta rituals are not about science; they're about pushing back on centuries of medicalized, meaning-free births, grasping at half-remembered rituals from the past to form sometimes half-baked rituals for the present. By the 2020s, those rituals had become big business. Today.com touted $200 gold-plated umbilical cord jewelry; Artnet heralded $600 pink or blue umbilical cord prints; Etsy sellers offered 928 umbilical cord items, including umbilical cord keepsake jars ($16.95), breastmilk and umbilical cord rose gold rings ($170.66), and solid gold placenta rings with umbilical cord and baby hair ($379.00).

The ultimate frontier was vernix caseosa, the milky coating that covers newborns. While most hospitals wash off "the divine moisturizer," the wait-to-wash movement has parents leaving it untouched for twenty-four hours, hiring photographers for "golden hour" photo shoots, and honoring Grandma with the "first bath." No less a mainstream source than Pampers devotes an entire web page to the rituals: "Although you might think it's a little icky and sticky to leave the vernix on, its beneficial properties are important for your baby, and it won't be long before you have your freshly washed baby skin to kiss and cuddle." Biologique Recherche sells Crème Masque Vernix VG, a "botanical biomimicry" of the body's natural creation to "help recondition the epidermis so it feels practically 'born again.'"

When I rushed into the bathroom of our Brooklyn home one night to tell Linda how much birth rituals had changed since our girls were born, she paused, then looked sheepishly at her hands. She was holding a dropper of Iso-Placenta Sérum Authentique. On the counter was a jar of Crème Masque Vernix.

The ritual cry for help was coming from inside the house.

Which is exactly what happened to Megan Sheldon.

In the first four years of Be Ceremonial, the app facilitated four thousand ceremonies. Megan ranked the top five, in reverse order: blessings before birth, death anniversaries, celebrations of life, then croning rituals, or celebrations where aging women reclaim the archetype of the wise, older woman. The number one category, however, caught her off guard: "mother loss ceremonies." Rituals that mark a failed pregnancy, stillbirth, or death of a child.

"We have a ceremony-shaped hole in our lives," Megan said. "What I discovered by giving people an open platform where they can create their own ceremonies is that they create ceremonies no one ever realized they wanted. All these new rituals, from birth to death, are just ways to shift narratives. They're intentional, symbolic actions that make us feel like we have some control over our own lives."

Megan came up with a name for rituals that reframe traumatic pregnancies; she calls them birth closing ceremonies. The first one she did was for herself.

"After years of miscarriages, I was overjoyed when I passed twelve weeks of my first successful pregnancy. I enrolled in hypnotherapy classes, hired a naturopath, wrote out my birth plan. I'm a ritual designer! I prepared for the most awe-inspiring experience a woman can have.

"Then my doctor told me I had placenta previa, which meant that the placenta was blocking my cervix. I could no longer deliver naturally. And I was devastated. After so much loss, I was not going to get the one thing I thought would initiate me into motherhood."

The scheduled caesarian went smoothly. Hannah was a healthy, beautiful baby. Megan released her disappointment—or at least she thought she did.

"The night before Hannah turned seven, we were having a ritual where we said goodbye to being six. I asked what excited her about getting older. 'When I grow up, I want to marry a girl,' she said. 'That's lovely,' I said. 'That way she can have the babies. I don't want to have my tummy cut open like you did and all the problems that you had.'

"I thought, *Oh, shit,*" Megan said. "I have passed my traumatic narrative on to my seven-year-old. Without thinking, I said, 'Tomorrow, we're going to hold a ceremony!'"

Megan took Hannah for a walk on the beach, just like her annual ritual with her husband.

"We talked about her birth story. I explained in gruesome terms that I hadn't used before what happened, why I needed to have the caesarian. We thanked our shared placenta for keeping us both alive; we expressed frustration with where it ended up. 'You stupid placenta!' Hannah said."

Then they went for a swim.

"It was January. I do a lot of cold-water swimming, but this was Hannah's first experience. It was magical.

"We came upon a ball of red kelp," she continued. "I laughed and said it looked exactly like a placenta. It had a long stringlet that reminded me of an umbilical cord. Hannah and I held either end and floated for a few minutes. We talked about how as we get older we will always have this connection. Then we let the kelp float away."

On my last day in Rapa Nui, Mahina drove us to the island's ultimate spectacle, Ahu Tongariki, the largest ceremonial platform, with fifteen massive moai, their backs to the ocean, standing shoulder to shoulder like an oversize chessboard.

Mahina wanted to know my story of becoming a father.

Within hours of our chilling encounter with selective reduction, the hi-fi ultrasound provided the relief that our girls were in different sacs; within days we had moved on to a specialized doctor; within

Figure 19: The fifteen majestic moai statues at Ahu Tongariki in Rapa Nui.

weeks Linda was on bed rest. "Tushy on the cushy!" we called it. Linda ran her global organization from our couch, which left me to do the shopping, cooking, and cleaning. For decades I've tried and failed to elicit sympathy for this husbandly burden. Mahina was the first to offer at least some grudging appreciation. "That's what a father's supposed to do!"

By thirty-eight weeks, Linda had gained fifty pounds and our doctor was ready to induce. Linda delivered Tybee Rose at 6:14 p.m. on the second Friday of April. I whispered in her ear the poem that her mother and I had recited ritually every night for months. But the moment was cut short because her sister was in trouble: Her heartbeat was crashing. "Time to scrub!" the doctor announced.

For months Linda had said that she didn't care whether her children were born vaginally or by caesarian, but she didn't want one of each.

"No!" barked the head nurse, who was wrapped around Linda's neck. "I think she can do it."

Eden Elenor arrived at 6:42 p.m. I whispered the same poem in her ear; Linda held up two triumphant fingers; the doctor looked at his watch. "April fifteenth. Tax Day. Early Feiler and Late Feiler."

It is still the greatest ending to a story I've ever heard.

"What I love about your story," Mahina said, "is all the people who are in it. Your wife; your daughters; the doctor, who was probably bluffing to get her to push, by the way; the nurses. Even you!"

She winked.

"My grandmother had a saying," Mahina continued. "'Everyone is welcome here. Everyone is needed here.' On Rapa Nui, when anyone goes through anything, everyone knows they have to do something. If somebody died right now, the whole island would stop what they were doing, walk toward the home, and start performing rituals uninvited. They would clean the body, they would cook the food, they would paint the house.

"In the West you have this idea that you can stand by yourself; here we know better. Do you know how many times those statues have fallen? They washed away in the last tsunami; we needed help from Japan to raise them. That's the real secret of Rapa Nui: In the end, we're all like babies; none of us can stand alone."

Mahina went to pray to her ancestors; I sat for a while at the feet of the moai. What struck me about Rapa Nui was the ever presence of story—family, island, civilization. And the critical role of turning points in those stories: rise and fall, boom and bust, birth and death. Rituals thrive in such moments; they flourish in the cauldron of plot. They are a "shield against terror," as the Austrian sociologist Peter Berger writes, offering us the sacred canopy of protection that allows us the time and space to do what we do best—convert our scariest moments into coherent narratives that satisfy "the human craving for meaning."

But something else stands out about this island at the end of the world: Those rituals all involve movement—paddling, planting, dancing, diving, carving, climbing. Why would humans, the one species on earth most effective at using words, ground our coherent narratives in acts so minimally reliant on words? The "obvious answer," writes Roy Rappaport, is that physical storytelling communicates what words alone cannot.

Rituals are embodied storytelling. Sure, they have critical utterances: *I do, I pronounce, rest in peace, peace be with you.* But as the stories of Mahina, Megan, and so many others prove, words alone are not enough: You must plant the tree, climb the hill, knit the cap, take the walk, swim the straits, boil the water, beat the drum, pay the lobola, push the canoe, release the kelp.

You must do the deed in order to tell the tale.

You must circle the stones, summon the spirits, dance the dance, so that in the hottest hour of the driest season, far above the splashing seas, in the cloudless skies looking down on the peerless moai, the keepers of secrets and placentas of peoples that have risen and fallen and risen so often that no chronicle can fully capture, it suddenly starts to rain.

12.

THE GARDEN OF LOST CHILDREN

How to Create a Ritual, Volume 4

Moms aren't the only ones who are changing the world of ritual; sometimes it's grandmoms. That dynamic was certainly true for one of the more vexing problems in the history of ritual: how to honor dead children.

Jan Chozen Bays was born in Chicago on the day—August 9, 1945—when Nagasaki was destroyed by an atomic bomb. "That day was very distressing for my parents, who were Protestant pacifists committed to making the world a better place," Jan said.

"But that day was significant for me, too. Tens of thousands of people were vaporized—including children and priests. The dust cloud spread around the world. In my first breath, I probably inhaled some of both. I'm sure that's why I became a medical doctor and a Zen priest dedicated to serving children."

Jan grew up straddling North and South, East and West. As a child, she was the only white girl in her elementary school in Alabama, where her father worked at an HBCU. "The KKK burned crosses in front of our house." When she was fifteen, the family moved to South Korea, where her father took a job teaching library science. "One morning, we climbed a mountain before dawn to witness a Buddhist ceremony. It was dark; there was chanting. But when the sun came up, the rays struck an icon in a cave. I still choke up at the memory."

Jan was in the first class of women at the medical school at the University of California, San Diego, where she also started meditating, learning acupuncture, and exploring ways to integrate Eastern practice into Western medicine. "I was like a duck discovering water."

After graduating, Jan moved into the Zen Center of Los Angeles, where she first encountered the story of Jizo, a bodhisattva, or enlightened being, who is the guardian of deceased children, unborn babies, and travelers. A teacher placed a statue of the childlike Jizo beneath a lemon tree. "I was unexpectedly drawn to this figure, planted a small garden of moss around it, and arose every morning to place a stick of incense in front of it. My attraction made little sense to me."

A distinguished pediatrician at the clinic where Jane worked asked if she would be willing to evaluate children for signs of physical, emotional, or sexual abuse. "I was so naive. I said, 'Sure!' I had no idea of the horrors these children face—violence, drug abuse, neglect. I thought, *There must be a better way to treat them.*"

Jan devoted the next three decades to answering that call while running Zen centers in California and Oregon, raising three children, and, with her second husband, welcoming eight grandchildren. "I don't think I could have done this work without my meditation practice. It clears your mind of all the terrible things you see during the day."

And they were terrible.

"In one year, thirty-two children died of child abuse in Oregon. I knew all of them. I had examined their limp, pale bodies, gently run my fingers through their downy, soft hair. I had talked as gingerly as I could to frightened, aggressive parents who had beaten these children.

And when no one was looking, I held each baby's hand to pray for its transition out of suffering into peace."

Until one day she hit a wall.

"I was on my way home one night after a rape case. This sappy country song came on the radio. I started crying . . . and couldn't stop. It triggered a surge of grief—all the autopsies I had performed, the child pornography I had seen, the suffering I had witnessed."

That's when Jan remembered that mysterious statue she had been drawn to twenty years earlier. Maybe what she needed was the spirit of Jizo. Maybe what anybody who's grieving a child needs is a way to plant a few seeds of remembrance.

They need ritual.

On the afternoon of Sunday, November 25, 1922, Howard Carter, the frustrated British archaeologist who had spent the previous fifteen years searching Egypt's Valley of the Kings for the lost tomb of Tutankhamen, made "a tiny breach in the top left-hand corner" of a plastered doorway. Carter was accompanied by his patron, Lord Carnarvon, who had given Carter one final year of funding.

Carter poked an iron rod into the darkness, then lit a candle to test for oxygen and poisonous gas. "It was sometime before one could see," he later wrote in his journal, "the hot air escaping caused the candle to flicker." But once his eyes adjusted, they took in one of the most extraordinary spectacles in the history of archaeology, a chamber twenty-six feet long and twelve feet wide filled with a "strange and wonderful medley of extraordinary and beautiful objects," the "property-room of an opera of a vanquished civilization."

As the world would soon learn, those five thousand three hundred and ninety-eight objects included the mummy and golden death mask of Tutankhamen, the Eighteenth Dynasty pharaoh who came to power suddenly at age ten and died equally suddenly at age nineteen. But what the world would not learn for many years, largely because Carter kept it secret, is that those objects also included the mummies of two stillborn girls, possibly twins, the pharaoh's only biological heirs.

King Tut, the boy wonder pharaoh, was not immune from one of the more confounding quandaries plaguing life rituals: what to do with dead boys and girls.

Ever since cultures have held funerary rites for humans, they've been unsure whether those rites should apply to the youngest humans. In ancient Athens, infants who died before their naming ceremony on their seventh day were discarded in pits; in Rome, babies who died before their "solemn day" (forty days for males, eighty for females) were denied funerals; in ancient China, Confucian texts insisted that a baby's death "should occasion little or no mourning."

These laws weren't limited to antiquity. The Ifugao in the Philippines hung dead babies in trees; the Inuit in North America laid deceased children under stones; the Xhosa in southern Africa wrapped departed infants in leaves and discarded them in abandoned fields. The anthropologist Stephanie Jo Fox of the University of Nevada, Las Vegas, studied more than forty cultures around the world and found that more than half held no burial rituals whatsoever for children and two thirds banned mourning. As one scholar put it, children's deaths were "nonevents" for "non-persons."

Jews and Christians took these customs and codified them for a third of the world's believers. The famed twelfth-century rabbi Maimonides insisted that babies who died before thirty days had never lived and could not be mourned—a policy that was still observed among Jews into the 1970s. Saint Augustine wrote that children who died unbaptized were damned. As late as 1992, official Catholic catechism was that such children were not guaranteed access to heaven. "The Church can only entrust them to the mercy of God."

A number of things might explain these seemingly inexplicable laws. Child mortality was common—as high as 50 percent in the ancient world, 30 percent in the Middle Ages, and 25 percent in 1900. Rituals are often resource intensive, a cost that communities could not always bear. But even if families had means, they were *specifically forbidden* from hosting mourning rituals. For most of history, families were ghosted over the ghosts of their children.

This gaping pain surely explains why it was family members who led the charge to overturn these laws and introduce new rituals.

After her breakdown in the car, Jan Chozen Bays called her "dharma sister" Yvonne Rand in San Francisco. Rand had been experimenting with hosting a Jizo water ceremony she imported from Japan in remembrance of unborn children. Rand set one condition: "no observing." Jan had to participate.

"At first I thought I would go for *my* miscarriages," Jan said. "Then I realized, *Oh, I have seen all these children who died. I'll honor them.*"

Jizo is a quasi-divine being who emerged in India in the fifth century CE, then passed into Japan via China and Korea. Considered the savior of vulnerable beings, Jizo especially protects children, from those sick or disabled to those facing stressful entrance exams. Like *Rapa Nui*, the name *Jizo* in Sanskrit means "womb of the earth." As Jan characterized his reputation, Jizo is "wide-eyed and openhearted toward humanity's griefs, mistakes, broken hearts, and hurting wounds."

Though Jizo is old, the Jizo ceremony is new. In the lead-up to World War II, Japan aggressively promoted having babies; birth control was banned. "After Japan lost the war," Jan said, "the government reversed its policy and made birth control and abortion legal. The primary means of family planning were the rhythm method, which was unreliable, and condoms, which were unavailable." By 1960, two in three pregnancies ended in abortion.

"Buddhist temples also suffered during this period," Jan continued. "Priests saw an opportunity in helping families honor their aborted fetuses." They developed a ceremony where you could buy a statue of Jizo and place it next to a nursery school. "Though the temples made a lot of money, the ceremony brought a lot of comfort to families."

On a learning trip to Hiroshima and Nagasaki, Jan witnessed the impact firsthand.

"I met a woman who every year on the anniversary of her abortion would make a meal that her child would have liked at that age—in the early years it was juice boxes and candy necklaces, in the teenage years it was hamburgers and french fries. She would knit a red cap, place a bib on the statue, and serve the meal. It was an ocean of love."

Jan returned home determined to spread this ritual to anyone reeling from the death of a child of any age.

When Howard Carter entered Tutankhamen's tomb, he found an undecorated wooden box containing two miniature coffins nesting in opposing directions. Inside were two mummies, which he labeled 317a and 317b. Both were covered in black resin and decorated with gold bands. He stuffed them in storage, where they remained for the next fifty years. Egyptians cared little about dead babies, why should he?

In 1978, the two mummies were x-rayed and discovered to be stillborn girls who had died at twenty-four and thirty-six weeks. They had congenital abnormalities related to spina bifida that are consistent with inbreeding—Tutankhamen's parents were biological siblings, which explains his twisted spine, elongated skull, and clubfoot; his wife was his half sister. In 2001, the British medical historian Geoffrey Chamberlain argued that the mummies were identical girls who suffered from twin-to-twin transfusion syndrome—the same condition Linda and I had been warned about—which led to their premature deaths.

Those deaths produced a succession crisis. With no heirs, the Eighteenth Dynasty ended with King Tut's death, propelling the kingdom into a power vacuum for the next three decades. A similar nightmare played out in ancien régime France after Louis XIV outlived his son, grandson, and great-grandson, leaving his five-year-old third-born great-grandson his heir; when Louis XVI and Marie Antoinette lost two sons to illnesses and a daughter to stillbirth, their deaths symbolized the termination of the monarchy.

The English had their own dead-child crisis when Princess Charlotte, the only legitimate child of the future King George IV, died in childbirth in 1817 while delivering a stillborn son. With no direct heirs, her uncles launched a "royal baby race" to secure a successor. The Duke of Kent won that race with the birth of his daughter on May 24, 1819. She became Queen Victoria. The world might never have embraced the white wedding dress if not for her stillborn first cousin.

These twists of state notwithstanding, the real legacy of lost children is the personal cost for the millions of families who were never allowed to grieve. One expression of that cost is the countless parents who circumvented authorities and crafted their own gerrymandered life rituals. King Tut's daughters likely ended up in that grave because their mother hoped they could piggyback off their father's access to the afterlife. In ancient Rome, parents buried unbaptized children in secret graves outside of town; by the Middle Ages, unauthorized cemeteries popped up in abandoned baptisteries and churches.

In Ireland, scholars have identified fourteen hundred children's burial grounds, known as cillíní. Frantic fathers performed lay baptisms before interring their babies, ladling water from streams, even burying corpses under the roofs of churches, a practice known as eaves-drop burials, so that dripping water might stealthily baptize their unprotected children.

The folklorist Robin Flower witnessed one such ceremony on Great Blasket Island in the North Atlantic in the early twentieth century after a desperate father asked where he could acquire wood to build a coffin for his newborn. The entire village walked through the rain, "all in a speechless trance of sorrow and respect" until they reached "the unkempt space of dank, clinging grass, with stones scattered over it here and there," where the child would be laid to rest in anything but peace.

The silent trauma of unritualized children is almost immeasurable. But what if we took a stab at measuring it? In 2000, a year for which there were reliable numbers, there were around two hundred ten million pregnancies worldwide, according to the Guttmacher Institute, which has tracked birth trends since the 1960s, and around one hundred thirty million births. These numbers mean that around eighty million pregnancies ended through miscarriage, stillbirth, or abortion; another million babies died in the first year.

In 1989, the American gerontologist Kenneth Doka, the author of *Grief Is a Journey*, coined the term *disenfranchised grief*, which showed how the unacknowledged death of a child affects not just parents but also siblings, grandparents, and caretakers. Using a conservative estimate that every death bereaves six people, the total number of individuals influenced by the loss of a child in 2000 approached five hundred million. This figure suggests that even in a world of modern medicine, as many as one in ten people in any given year were affected by a loss that almost no one was addressing with a life ritual. The legacy of anguish cannot be exaggerated.

If there is a hopeful coda to this story, it's that within the span of a few decades, this wrong had been righted in nearly every corner of the world in a ritual reversal of epic scope, led largely by unsung heroes like Jan Chozen Bays.

Jan's Jizo Remembrance Ceremony has three parts. The first is arts and crafts. "Our ceremony is a little broader than the one in Japan or even Yvonne Rand's," she said. "We include people who lost pregnancies, young children, or adult children. I find the adult cases to be harder. When a child grows up and dies by suicide or in a plane crash, the impact can be devastating."

Jan welcomes everyone into a circle, explains the intention of the ritual, then invites guests to a craft table covered with cloth, yarn, needles, beads, and origami paper.

"Then we make remembrance tokens. Some people bring photos; I have patterns for a bib or hat. I find that women get busy very quickly; men usually help their wives awkwardly for a while, then break off and make something on their own. One man built a kite with wood, paper, and a tail. Every piece had a message: *Aunt Susie sends her love*; *Daddy misses you.*"

The project takes an hour.

"After a while, people enter in a state of timelessness," Jan said. "A woman came to honor her son who was a sharpshooter in the army. He killed himself with his own gun. She had a picture of him in uniform and said he was there with her while she was sewing: 'It's like he reached out through time and space.'"

Jan then leads everyone along a stone path to one of the first Jizo gardens in North America, filled with soaring pines and foot-high bald statues.

"The space is designed to look like a meditation room," Jan said. "It's the most sacred spot in the monastery." Guests take turns ringing a bell, they chant, they do a heart sutra. "Emptiness is not a void," Jan says. "Emptiness is a furnace. We may not be able to hold or speak to our child, but that child has not disappeared. When we feel ourselves in the darkness, creativity emerges."

At the end of the ceremony, mourners light a stick of incense, carry their remembrance tokens into the trees, and lay both at the foot of a Jizo. "The spirit of the child picks their own statue."

I asked Jan what she believes is the most important part of the service.

"That it's done in a group. There's so much shame around losing a child. The only medicine strong enough to counter that pain is the blessing of not being alone."

The Jizo ceremony opened the floodgates on a wave of new rituals around disenfranchised grief. In a now-familiar pattern, NPR aired a piece about Jan; *The New York Times* ran a story on the ceremony; Reddit subgroups appeared; replica ceremonies popped up in Houston, Austin, Buffalo, Brooklyn, Toronto, Bangkok, and Taipei. Jessica Zucker, a Los Angeles psychologist, attended a Jizo ceremony in Japan following her own miscarriage. She launched the #IHada Miscarriage campaign, built an Instagram following of four hundred thousand, and partnered with an artist to photograph mothers who painted poems about their pregnancy loss on their naked bodies.

As happened with similar emergent life rituals around divorce, forced adoption, and other long-taboo topics, first came a truth-telling phase when laypeople demanded to be heard. As early as the 1970s, British parents formed Sands, the Stillbirth and Neonatal Death Society; in the 1980s, American parents pressured Ronald Reagan to create Pregnancy and Infant Loss Awareness Month; in the 1990s, Irish parents identified scores of cillíní and other mass childhood graves; in the 2000s, scholars released studies showing that parents who see, hold, sniff, dress, kiss, and comfort their stillborn children have better mental health outcomes than those denied the privilege.

Next, a debate erupted around how to respond to this legacy. In the 2020s, Canada plunged into a national uproar over thirteen hundred child graves uncovered near former Indian schools; Ireland passed a national law to exhume eight hundred infants buried in a septic tank behind a Magdalene laundry; New York City agreed to disinter babies on Hart Island, a potter's field where prisoners had buried a million unidentified bodies since 1869, a third of whom were stillbirths.

In time, an outpouring of ritualized healing burst forth. A great number of these responses, like Jan's Jizo ceremony, involved gardens. Germany opened "gardens of star children"; Canadians constructed "spirit gardens"; England built a hundred "remembrance gardens," including the National Memorial Arboretum. "It's not hidden away, everyone can see it, and that's the whole point," said the organizer of the arboretum, who lost a daughter at twenty-nine weeks to preeclampsia. "Having it more out in the open leads to discussions." Americans planted "memorial gardens" in a dozen states, honoring victims of the Holocaust (New York, Tennessee), murder (Oregon, Georgia), even school shootings (Connecticut, Colorado).

The ritual outpouring has not been limited to outdoor gathering places. Hospitals started offering "cuddle cots," bassinets with refrigerated mattresses to preserve the baby long enough to allow families to hold mourning rituals. Pinterest features custom keychains, Christmas ornaments, and tattoo designs with stillborn footprints. Walmart sells angel charm bracelets, "Perfect Little Angel in Heaven" frames, and "An Angel in the Book of Life" acrylic heart paperweights with handprints.

As we've seen with honor walks, divorce registries, and labyrinths, the most consequential of these new rituals often grow out of personal experience.

On February 4, 2005, Cheryl Haggard of Evergreen, Colorado, gave birth to her fourth child. Maddux Achilles was born with myotubular myopathy, which prevented him from breathing, swallowing, or moving. Cheryl and her husband, Mike, spent days by his side, "asking questions that had no answers." Cheryl documented the experience with her digital camera, but when she looked at the images, they "contained only tearstained cheeks, red swollen eyes, forced smiles, and fear."

On Maddux's sixth day of life, the Haggards made the "heartbreaking decision" to remove their son from life support. They invited their three older children for their first and only meeting with their brother. "The mother in me knew that I needed to have my son's photograph hang alongside those of his older brother and sisters."

The hospital had heirloom-quality images of plump, healthy babies on its walls. Mike called the local photographer who had taken those images, Sandy Puć; her first opening was in two days. "That will be too late," Mike said. Sandy met the couple in the hospital that night.

A ritual was born.

Several months after Maddux's death, the Haggards started Now I Lay Me Down to Sleep, a nonprofit that offers free, professional remembrance photos to families. In its first twenty years, the organization's seventeen hundred volunteer photographers gifted seventy-five thousand portrait sessions in every US state, the District of Columbia, and fifteen countries. The images have been shared more than a million times on social media.

What I take from this story is what I've taken from nearly every garden path I've stumbled onto on this journey: An army of motivated moms, dads, grandmas, and grandpas can turn back thousands of years of silence and shame. A century after Howard Carter looked at two mummified children in the greatest archaeological treasury of all time and thought, *They don't matter*; thirty-two centuries after a mother looked at those same babies and thought, *The best possible outcome is that they hitch a ride to heaven on the golden chariot of their father*; in our century, we look at similar children and think, *They do matter; there is possibility.* There is ritual.

As Cheryl Haggard observed, "Some may look at us and think we photograph dead or dying babies, my perspective is: We don't photograph death, we capture love. And the love between a parent and a child can never be broken."

13.

A MOMENT OF HOPE

The Missing Ritual

I remove the ecru sheet wrapped toga-like around my body and hang it on a hook on the wall. I carefully peel off the fleck of tissue I dabbed onto my cheek after a razor cut, step onto the bathmat, and peer down at the seven stairs spiraling to the right.

At just after ten o'clock on a lightly snowing, late-winter morning, I am standing naked above the immersion pool at the "living waters community mikveh" in Newton, Massachusetts. Adapted from the Hebrew word for *gathering*, a *mikveh* is a ritual bath used in Judaism for spiritual purification, renewal, and transition. The Hebrew Bible ordains "washing in water" to regain "ritual purity"—for women after menstruation or childbirth, for men after nocturnal emissions or sexual intercourse, for anyone before entering the temple or after handling a corpse. The story of Jesus's immersion in the Jordan River bears all the hallmarks of a mikveh.

Most purity laws were abandoned after the destruction of the Second Temple in 70 CE, but the Talmud doubled down on the ones surrounding menstruation, childbirth, and conversion. Like many religious rituals, mikvehs fell out of favor in recent centuries as the majority of Jews favored integration into secular society and viewed the cumbersome rite as outdated, invasive, and sexist. Despite growing up in an active Jewish family (both my parents were synagogue presidents), marrying a Jewish woman (Linda studied Hebrew through high school), raising engaged Jewish daughters (both were leaders of their synagogue youth group), and writing five books on the Hebrew Bible, I had neither seen nor set foot in a mikveh before this visit.

What drew me to Mayyim Hayyim, "a 21st century creation . . . rooted in ancient tradition, reinvented to serve the Jewish community of today," is its gobsmacking and, to me, unfathomable role in taking a niche, all-but-dead custom and turning it into a thriving symbol of the worldwide movement to reclaim outdated rituals for contemporary audiences.

Started in the early 2000s by Anita Diamant, the daughter of Holocaust survivors and the author of eleven books on Jewish life, including the international bestseller *The Red Tent*, Mayyim Hayyim, or "living waters," has hosted twenty-five thousand ritual immersions and run programs for hundreds of thousands more. It also inspired a global network of fifty modern mikvehs in two dozen states, including Kentucky, Louisiana, Texas, Oklahoma, Nebraska, and Arizona, as well as Australia, Brazil, Canada, and England. Israel relocated a two-thousand-year-old stone mikveh to a kibbutz in the Galilee, where it now welcomes Jews, Arabs, and Christians.

Mayyim Hayyim led this revitalization by opening up the once limited practice to include a wider array of human experiences.

"From day one, we always welcomed people for the traditional reasons—weddings, births, deaths, bar mitzvahs," Anita told me. "But the big four leave out so many important transitions in women's lives especially—menarche, menopause, the loss of a child, the end of fertility. All these experiences that men never wanted to acknowledge."

And it's not just women's transitions that went ignored.

My immersion guide for the morning, Seth, a former Quaker turned Jew by choice who runs technology at a local prep school and is married to a rabbi, told me that two thirds of his immersions are men going through nontraditional transitions. These events include depression, divorce, losing a job, becoming a grandparent. "I guided for a man who had been called up by the army reserve. He came in his civilian clothes, did his immersion, then walked out in his uniform."

Seth's role is to help participants fulfill religious law but also personalize the experience.

"I'm technical," Seth said. "I like process—where to stand, what to say, how to submerge. But it turns out that what's actually fun is the teaching part—helping people identify what transition they're in, what's making them feel alone, and how we can help them feel supported.

"Nobody has a mikveh in their basement," he continued. "By definition the experience is communal. My job is to help customize it."

I took a breath, grabbed the rail, and stepped into the water.

In the early 2010s, I was invited by PBS to host a series in which I accompanied Americans on six pilgrimages around the world. We spent a year debating which journeys to cover. The final list had a notable division. Half the episodes focused on land-based rituals: the harvest festival in Jerusalem and Jesus Trail in Nazareth; the hajj in Saudi Arabia; the eighty-eight-temple Shikoku path in Japan. The other half focused on water-based rituals: the Osun-Osogbo river festival in Nigeria; the fifty-million-person Kumbh Mela bathing celebration in India; the yearly visit of American wounded warriors to the healing waters of Lourdes, France.

Our selections reflect the disproportionately large role that water has played in the history of ritual. In Africa, the Dagara in Burkina Faso plunge in holy waterfalls while the Akan in Ghana dunk in redemptive rivers. In the Americas, Mayans cleansed in sinkholes, Incas in streams. In pre-Christian Europe, Minoans, Mycenaeans, and Romans built lustral baths. In the ancient Near East, Egyptians purified in the Nile; Mesopotamians in the Tigris and Euphrates; Jews, Christians, and Muslims in any desert water hole—well, spring, or oasis.

It's hardly a surprise, then, that contemporary seekers looking for rituals with deep spiritual resonance disproportionately turned to water. Like Mayyim Hayyim, many of these rituals are reinterpretations of older practices. Buddhist centers from Scotland to Cambodia run "water blessing" or "wild swimming" retreats; Hindu centers from Mexico to Michigan host "aquatic therapy" or "Naquaste" gatherings. Unitarian Universalist churches hold "water communion rituals" in which members pour vials of water they've brought from personal travel into blended mixtures that are used for life celebrations.

Christian groups have been especially inventive in using Instagram-ready baptisms to attract lapsed believers. Members of the Ohio State Buckeyes football team, backed by a campus-based mission from Auburn, Alabama, led multiple outdoor baptisms in the backs of U-Haul trucks. The first of these revivals, at the beginning of the 2024 season, attracted a thousand people and baptized sixty; the second, after the team won the national championship, drew sixty-five hundred people and baptized two thousand.

And it's not just students. In "Horse Troughs, Hot Tubs and Hashtags: Baptism is Getting Wild," *The New York Times* reported how "in some evangelical churches, a once-staid ritual is returning to its informal roots—and things sometimes get 'a little rowdy.'" Viral inducements include blaring music, flashing lights, and custom T-shirts in dark colors ("for the sake of modesty when wet"), emblazoned with "#washed," "Best day ever," or "Meet the new me." As the pastor of a

Baptist church in Linwood, Kansas, that consecrates members in an inflatable hot tub explained, "We live in an age where people like experiences."

Some of these reimagined rituals move so far from their religious roots that they create quasi-religious communities of their own. Misogi is the medieval Shinto ritual of standing under a freezing waterfall or plunging into a cold river or ocean to shock the body into controlled breathing, meditation, and other restorative responses. In 2012, the Harvard-trained physician Marcus Elliott resurrected the idea to help athletes develop mental fortitude. He asked NBA players to team up, dive ten feet underwater, and take turns lugging an eighty-five-pound boulder as far as they could along the seabed (usually around twenty feet) until the boulder traversed three miles. Following a similar outing in which the all-star Atlanta Hawk Kyle Korver paddleboarded twenty-five miles across the Santa Barbara Channel, Korver set a record for most consecutive games with a three-pointer.

The journalist Michael Easter popularized Elliot's "misogi challenge" in his bestselling book *The Comfort Crisis*, attracting boosters like the podcaster Joe Rogan, the entrepreneur Jesse Itzler, and other icons of the manosphere. Modern misogi, sometimes called sufferfests, invite people to do periodic quests in nature to mimic the challenges of early humans. There are two rules: (1) make the experience so challenging that you have a fifty-fifty chance of failure; (2) don't die. Hundreds of thousands of devotees in thirty countries anonymously post their exploits (bragging is off-limits), with many honoring misogi's water-based origins—cutting ice holes in Finland's Lake Saimaa and then swimming ten yards underneath the sheet while holding your breath; braving a twenty-mile channel swim across New Zealand's treacherous Cook Strait; enduring a two-day, twenty-seven mile Rio Negro Challenge in the murky "black water" of the Amazonian jungle.

Elliott believes that misogi fills the hole left by the decline of traditional rites of passage. "The idea of a rite of passage is that the elders are seeing in you the potential to rise up and achieve this really important, challenging thing that is going to benefit you and everyone around you," he said. "Misogi is an emotional, spiritual, and psychological challenge that masquerades as a physical challenge."

What all these new age rituals share, along with many of the indoor, outdoor, secular-minded, and spiritual-minded rituals we've encountered, is that they are cocreated by practitioners. They're not top-down directives forcing people onto predetermined trajectories; they're bottom-up invitations that encourage people to follow their own bespoke assortment of loops, curves, and whorls, then create moments of ritual connection at whatever curve they face.

Maybe you were baptized as an infant or child, then drifted, got bored, or were beat up by life and want to reengage your faith; a traditional church ceremony might hold little appeal while one in a swimming pool or bowling alley would feel more relevant. Maybe your career stalled, you got cancer, or you overcame addiction and want to honor the confusing feelings that accompany such lifequakes; a meditation retreat or misogi challenge might feel more bespoke.

The clear through line is that lifequakes need their own life ritual. Let's call it the fifth ritual, the missing ritual, the versatile ritual.

Renewing.

Renewing rituals have all the hallmarks of other life rituals except they're not tied to specific life events. I witnessed that flexibility on my journey to Lourdes with forty American veterans for the annual "military pilgrimage" held since 1947 in the grotto where a fourteen-year-old peasant girl said she had eighteen encounters with the Virgin Mary. Today, the healing baths of the Sanctuary of Our Lady of Lourdes attract five million visitors a year.

On the opening day, the veterans gathered and shared their reasons for coming—blindness, amputation, traumatic brain injury, quadriplegia, losing friends, losing marriages, losing the will to live. Private First Class Zach Herrick grew up in a small town in Kansas and was three months into a deployment in northeast Afghanistan when his face was blown off by the Taliban. He had thirty-one surgeries between the tip of his nose and the tip of his chin, including having his tongue sewn back on. He experienced depression, PTSD, and suicidal ideation.

"I learned that life isn't a fairy tale," he said. "The prince doesn't always get the princess."

After three days of bonding with fellow soldiers and a morning immersion in the sacred baths, he also learned the power of camaraderie and ritual.

"The shock of the water wasn't as bad as I feared," he told the group on the final day. "I experienced relief. As I got out of the icy water, I felt something leaving me.

"But mostly I'm happy that I came here with all of you," he continued. "Watching you guys smile, that's my religion."

I was barely two steps into Mayyim Hayyim on the day before my immersion when I was reminded of the first rule of water rituals: You get wet. The CEO, Julie Childers, welcomed me to the homey space that looks more like the model apartment in a gated community in Boca than a stuffy religious shrine. To the right are two mikvehs about the size of small plunge pools; to the left are a kitchen and conference room with snacks.

Two millennial women with moist "mikveh hair" had just completed their immersions. Davinica and Cassia had driven down from Maine. Davinica is a mindfulness teacher, a forest bathing guide, and the founder of a death café. "I came for the ritual experience not the religious one," she said. "Not to get super vulnerable, but I'm not in contact with my Jewish family anymore, so during scary times, I sometimes feel alone. My friends are my chosen family, so sharing this experience with Cassia is very meaningful."

Cassia, who also works in wellness, called her immersion the most spiritual thing she's ever done. When she signed up, she hadn't identified her intention, but in the interim she dislocated her shoulder. "Stepping into the water, I thought about people who had done this across time and space. I felt more connected to my ancestors."

Their guide, Bev, first came to Mayyim Hayyim when her cousin threw her a mikveh wedding shower; she returned years later when she became a vegetarian. "It felt like a huge shift in my relationship with food that I wanted to pause and honor."

Anita Diamant may not have known these specific reasons when she first had the idea to open a modern mikveh, but she certainly understood the growing craving for fresh life rituals. In the late 1990s, Anita, a columnist at a Jewish newspaper, visited an Orthodox mikveh in Boston for the conversion of her soon-to-be second husband, Jim, during the two hours a week set aside for non-Orthodox visitors; she was horrified that liberal Jews were confined to such narrow times and forced to wait outdoors in extreme heat or cold. At the peak of her influence from *The Red Tent*, her reimagining of the secret lives of women in the Bible who gather in a "red tent" during menstruation, childbirth, and illness, she wrote a column called "Why I Want a Mikveh."

"I want a mikveh" where converts will be welcomed with "hugs and champagne"; brides and grooms ("gay and straight") will be greeted with chocolate and henna; those healing from chemotherapy or pregnancy loss will learn that "water can soothe"; and those trying to get pregnant or suffering loss will find nourishment and inspiration.

Lots of people loved the idea; no one wanted to fund it. Finally, a rabbi told her, "If you want this to happen, you have to do it yourself."

Anita outlined her vision at a speech in New York City; Aliza Kline was in the audience. "Actually, I was a seat filler," Aliza told me. The daughter of Jewish professionals from Colorado, Aliza was in the process of relocating to Boston. She proposed that she work all but free for three months and see if she could raise money to cover her salary; she stayed for the next ten years as the founding executive director.

"From the beginning, the trick was to mix the needs of tradition with the needs of modernity," Aliza said. By law, a mikveh must contain two hundred gallons of water, but not just any water; moving water is required. Mayyim Hayyim uses Newton tap water, which is considered unmoving; multiple architects burned through multiple plans before settling on an outdoor moat that catches rainwater. A pipe then channels the living rainwater into the nonliving tap water, which each person briefly opens, creating the obligatory "kiss of living water."

The modern touches proved even trickier. "We had what I called our bricks-and-water plan," Aliza said. "What temperature should the water be? How do we get natural light? What happens if someone needs a wheelchair?" Answers: 90 degrees Fahrenheit, high windows, a lift. Nakedness was especially thorny. "There are so many body issues today. What if someone just had a double mastectomy, struggles with obesity, or is dealing with anorexia? Robes don't fit every body shape; you can't make yourself vulnerable if you're feeling exposed." Answer: giant sheets.

The biggest challenge was addressing the many unexpected reasons people wanted to immerse. "I convened a poet, a rabbi, and a psychologist," Aliza said. "They kept coming up with different situations—freezing your eggs, adopting a foster child, finishing your dissertation, getting a clean scan." The initial list included fifty-five different ceremonies.

"Years later I got exposed to design thinking in Silicon Valley. It's exactly what we were doing: define the problem, empathize with your customer, ideate, iterate, keep refining until you get it right. If someone's not coming to your ritual, it's not their fault, it's yours.

"And that really is the larger point," she continued. "If ritual is going to survive, we have to trust the end user. Millennials and Gen Z are far less inhibited about saying exactly what they need. Instead of lecturing people on what they *should* want, we need to listen to what they *do* want."

What they want is a moment of hope.

Among the Indigenous tribes of the Pacific Northwest from Alaska to Washington, a popular origin tale tells how a mythic raven tricks a greedy tyrant who keeps the sun locked in a box. Raven steals the sun, permanently scorching his wings from white to black but generously placing the sun in the sky, where everyone can bask in its blessings.

This story of selflessness became the foundation for one of the more extraordinary life rituals ever conceived by human beings. The bear-filled forests and salmon-packed streams of this region mask the challenges of surviving in a terrain where access to a full diet is limited; close cooperation among clans is essential. Tribes reinforce that mutuality by turning major life rituals—births, marriages, deaths—into occasions for mass redistribution of wealth.

Potlatches are carefully orchestrated gift-giving occasions where firearms, blankets, hides, canoes, food, and jewelry accumulated for years by high-ranking individuals are given away to low-ranking individuals. In just one potlatch in the twentieth century, a chief fed hundreds of guests for two weeks, then handed out eighteen thousand blankets, seven hundred silver bracelets, a dozen canoes, sewing machines, onboard motors, pots and pans, even copper.

Generosity is central to these tribes, explains Stanley Walens of the University of Virginia, because they "envision the world as a place of constant flux and motion." Potlatches were specifically scheduled around moments of transition, when society was at risk of falling apart. "At these times, the order and control of the ceremony, with its reassurance of mutual dependence, was meant to reestablish order" by reaffirming "the centrality of ritual."

Potlatches were so effective that they were banned by the Canadian government in the 1880s as a threat to Christian values. But as we've seen time and again, archetypes are too powerful. When the ban was lifted in the 1950s, a modern potlatch reemerged, with T-shirts and laundry baskets replacing cedar blankets and bentwood baskets.

Potlatches thrive because they're a testament to the final element of all life rituals: They are living examples of the world we'd like to see, prototypes of an alternative social order.

Thcy are mini utopias.

Coined by the English humanist Sir Thomas More in the sixteenth century, *utopia* is a combination of the Greek words for *good place* and *no place*. Utopias thrive in times of uncertainty, explains the Polish sociologist Zygmunt Bauman, because old routines start showing their age "and rituals their seediness." Uncertainty is exhausting. "The stubbornness of the blows, their irregularity, their nasty ability to appear from any direction." Uncertainty breeds fear.

Rituals provide relief from uncertainty in the form of unconditional support. Just think of all the improvised communities we've seen at work in life rituals—the gaggle of supportive ladies around the tooth-filing bed, the scrum of motorcyclists at the wake, the cow-counting uncles at the lobola. They're ambassadors of support. "Ritual is a means of performing the way things ought to be in conscious tension to the way things are," writes the American historian Jonathan Smith.

Ritual is an essay of what's possible.

The thesis of that essay is simple: The best response to fear is hope. At first glance, hope sounds flimsy—*I hope you feel better, I hope she likes me*—but in reality, it's substantial. Hope is not a thing with feathers; it's a thing with science. Optimism is the belief that good things *will* happen; hope is the mindset to *make them* happen. As Jerome Groopman, the chair of Harvard Medical School, writes in *The Anatomy of Hope,* his bestselling account of how he overcame his skepticism toward hope in healing, "Hope is the elevating feeling we experience when we see—in the mind's eye—a path to a better future."

Faith Brigham Leener learned this lesson firsthand. In her twenties, Faith and her three best friends started a grassroots organization in Brooklyn designed to create "a new type of religious community for ourselves and our millennial peers." Similar to Aliza's end-user approach, Faith had "thousands of coffee dates" with young people to learn what they needed.

"I heard so many heartbreaking stories—losing a job, losing a romantic partner: 'I spent my whole life trying to be in finance and now I hate it'; 'I want to be in love but I'm too afraid of rejection.'"

Faith started creating gatherings to meet these needs—dinners where people confessed their insecurities with complete strangers, ceremonies where neighbors offered support.

"My friend Denise asked me to create a ritual on the eve of her mastectomy. We invited a group of friends to her living room. People are always uncomfortable around new things, so I began by setting expectations: 'Our role is to give Denise space to share her feelings. We're not here to fix her or give her advice. We're here to listen.'"

Denise spoke; Faith led a reflection; guests shared candles, crystals, and soft clothing for her recovery. Then Faith closed the circle. I asked her what makes homegrown rituals succeed.

"I'm always listening for two things," she said. "The highest hope and the biggest fear. For a ritual to gain traction, the fear must recede and the hope emerge. The purpose of the ritual is to turn fear into hope."

Mayyim Hayyim's welcome area is designed to feel like a living room. It has sofas and chairs, a throw rug, and depending on the time of day, singing, clapping, flowers, and tears. To the left is an oak sideboard with an acrylic stand holding laminated copies of all sixty-seven ceremonies the center now offers. The ceremonies are divided into genres like a card catalog, a Dewey decimal system of existential metamorphoses: *birthing, healing, reproduction, relationships, transitions.*

Seth flipped through the deck looking for ones that might apply to me. *Finalizing a Divorce*: no. *Affirming the Moment*: maybe. *For a Challenging Life Transition*: definitely. He asked my intention, and I shared all the reasons I had gone on this journey—homesickness, grief, fear.

"Sounds like you're more at the end of a transition than the beginning," he said. Then he offered a gift: "You don't have to pick just one ceremony. These cards are laminated so we can mark them up." He whipped out a dry-erase marker. "I call it Frankensteining."

For the next twenty minutes we riffled through the cards, selecting passages, culling others, consulting Google. Julie poked her head in to say we were about to miss our time slot.

"We're writing our own ceremony," I said. "Least surprising news of the day!"

"You're certainly not the toughest case I've had," Seth said. "I once helped a guy do twenty-four immersions."

I settled on five, with readings for each one:

1. *Here I Am*—to capture my readiness
2. *For a Joyous Life Transition*—to appreciate the moment
3. *For Inscribing a Scroll*—to honor a new chapter
4. *The Traveler's Prayer*—to acknowledge the journey
5. *In Gratitude*—to celebrate the end

Seth led me to Changing Room 1, "Wave," to begin my preparation. Inside was a sitting area, a toilet, a sink, and a shower. Every surface was covered with baskets that overflowed with bath-and-beauty supplies—exfoliator, pumice bar, nail polish remover, dental floss. A placard offered guidance.

Take a minute and think about the transition you will mark today. In traditional language, you are transforming from ritually unready to ritually ready.

I began to undress. I also tensed up. Nagging rules written thousands of years ago are my least favorite part of religion. Here, I felt surrounded by them.

Remove all clothing, eyeglasses, contact lenses, dental plates, hearing aids. Each person enters the mikveh as naked as on the day of their birth. Simply a human being.

Taking off my wedding ring was the most surprising part; it felt like shedding part of who I am.

Remove all jewelry as well as makeup, paying special attention to the eyes. Remove nail polish on fingers and toes. (Acrylics may stay on if they have been on for more than a month.) There should be no physical barriers between the body and the living waters.

I stepped into the shower. Normally I'm a fast bather, but I found myself moving slowly. I scrubbed under my nails, used cleanser on my face, noticed nooks and crannies in my body that I hadn't thought about in years. I even washed between my toes.

Shower with thoughtful attention to the miracle of your body. Wash yourself head to toe; shampoo your hair, lather your shoulders, back, arms, belly, and genitals. Scrub elbows, knees, and heels. The water of the mikveh will feel even sweeter after this cleaning.

I dried myself carefully and looked in the mirror. I brushed and flossed my teeth; there was a nail clipper, so I removed a cuticle. There was also a pair of tweezers, which I didn't know what to do with. I worried that I might be ruining my prep, so I decided to shave. That's when I cut my chin. I panicked for a second that I would have to miss my slot. Bleeding in the mikveh is neither kosher nor polite.

A knock came at the door; I dabbed Kleenex on my chin, wrapped the sheet around my body, and stepped toward the pool.

As you enter the mikveh do not rush. Walk slowly. Count the seven steps into the water. In the mikveh, every body is a sacred vessel.

Hope is also a thing with choices.

Time and again in my conversations with ritual entrepreneurs, I was amazed by how people found the hope they needed in a ritual they created that few would have imagined.

Aimi Hamraie was born in Nebraska to refugee Iranian parents, moved to Atlanta, earned a PhD in design and technology at Emory, and became a professor at Vanderbilt University, specializing in the study of rituals in the disabled community.

"My parents had such homesickness," Aimi said. "I don't relate to that so much, but as a disabled person, I relate to the idea of wanting to feel grounded in a community that does ritual together."

Aimi runs a lab that uses design thinking to create rituals for marginalized communities, hosts a podcast on disability, and cocurated *#CripRitual*, a multisite exhibition of twenty-five disabled artists reimagining rites of passage for atypical bodies.

"We had people celebrating getting fitted for a new wheelchair, moving out of their childhood home and into community living, gaining access to a place they had been cut off from.

"Rituals are transformative," Aimi said. "They change our private world but also the public world. The disability rights movement began with people leaving behind their wheelchairs and crutches and crawling up the steps of the federal building in San Francisco to occupy it for a month. Now we're doing the same for everyday life, taking micro-moments that have meaning to us but are unknown to other people, and turning them into rites of passage."

Colleen Thomas also suffered in silence. Colleen was born in Ohio, earned a master's degree in spirituality in Colorado, and then spent decades working in secondary schools in California, until her relationship with her boss turned toxic. "He was very emotionally abusive to any woman who threatened him. I felt a deep sense of shame that I hadn't listened to my inner voice and left earlier."

Finally, Colleen sought out counseling, where she learned about exposure therapy, a cognitive behavioral technique in which individuals gradually confront their deepest fear. "*I need shame exposure!* I thought. The therapist recommended that I do it in the confines of a ceremony because the biggest antidote to shame is disclosure. So I threw myself a ritual."

Colleen and her husband invited a small group of friends to their home.

"When you work someplace, you get all these T-shirts and sweatshirts with logos on them; I had seven. I decided to identify seven areas of shame and write them out on each piece of clothing—'I wish I had spoken up for myself'; 'I wish I had been a better role model.'"

Colleen read aloud each piece of clothing in front of her guests, then donned them. "By the end I felt so bulky I couldn't even move. Then of course I had a hot flash because I'm in that phase of life." She had ordered a pink-and-green donkey piñata from Amazon, which she filled with candy and affirmations. Her husband hung the piñata over a wall; Colleen grabbed a broomstick.

"And I froze. I had just bared my soul to my closest friends, who were nice enough not to run away, but I was paralyzed by fear. Eventually this little voice inside me said, *Believe in yourself.* It grew louder and louder, moving from my feet to my body to my arms. Finally, I started swinging."

With the piñata in pieces, everyone took a treat, read an affirmation, and danced to Taylor Swift. Within a month, Colleen had two job offers and started a podcast. She called it *Shame Piñata: Creating Rites of Passage for Real-Life Transitions.*

In Lagos, I met Pastor Ituah Ighodalo, the head of one of the fastest growing churches in Nigeria, the five-thousand-seat Trinity House. Like many in this polyglot country, Ituah was born into a family with Christian, Muslim, and tribal roots.

"I grew up with rituals from all over the world."

An accountant by training, Ituah joined Africa's continent-wide embrace of Pentecostalism because it offers a more robust ritual tradition that stresses direct encounters with the divine, hands-on spectacles like full-immersion baptism and speaking in tongues, and what he calls a crisis-responsive approach to miracles and healing. Ituah knows a thing or two about lifequakes; his wife and copastor, Ibidunni, died of COVID-19.

"On Friday nights, I host an all-night healing and deliverance service that begins at 11 p.m. and continues to 4 a.m.," Ituah said. "People come for almost anything—romantic problems, illness, mental health, poverty. The services are so crowded I had to start another on Wednesdays."

One issue came up so frequently that it threatened to overwhelm the others—infertility. Ituah and Ibidunni had also struggled to get pregnant before adopting two children, so he added a monthly ritual called Fruit of the Womb that includes chanting, laying on of hands, and anointing with oil. I asked him the purpose of the ritual.

"Hope. Hope is having the deep belief that something will happen, even if you can't figure out how it will happen. When you give someone hope, you encourage them to be honest about the risks, but you give them the willingness to work for the best even while preparing for the worst.

"A main reason Pentecostalism has become so popular," he continued, "is that we create rituals that give you something to hold on to. Science can't answer everything. Sometimes you need belief."

The first thing I noticed about entering the mikveh is that I was moving downward. So much of spiritual geography involves escalation—scaling, climbing, ascending. The mikveh requires the opposite—immersing, submerging, descending.

Once on level ground, I located the pipe on the back wall, turned the red handle, and felt the crisp kiss of living water. I approached the front of the pool, where Seth had laid out my five prayers on the tile. The display looked like a bad joke come to life: *three laminated sheets, one laptop, and one placard walk into a bath.*

The mikveh involves dunking first, then blessing. I took a breath, hoisted myself on my toes, and then plunged into the water. I was so busy making sure that every part of me got wet that when I stuck my head above water, I was startled to hear a human voice. It was Seth shouting from behind his own sheet, "Kosher!" meaning that I had met the legal requirements of full immersion. We had agreed that he would witness my first three plunges, then leave me unattended for the final two.

I stand here today to affirm this moment, ready to conclude this life

Figure 20: The mikveh at Mayyim Hayyim in Newton, Massachusetts, laid out with my prayers.

transition. I recognize the lessons and losses of the past and open my heart to the future.

I slowed down long enough in the second plunge to notice the warmth of the water but also feel the twinge of a charley horse in my left hamstring. My legal concerns were fading; my body was reclaiming center stage.

Here I stand on my way to acceptance. Knowing that I can create a full life for myself. Knowing that I have a circle of loved and loving ones who will celebrate my endeavors.

I was largely freestyling the words at this point—beginning with the script, adding my own thoughts. The same with the immersions, where I started experimenting with my own choreography—torquing and twisting my torso, crossing and uncrossing my legs, even opening my eyes underwater to notice the blinking red, yellow, and pink lights, a display originally intended to delight children, though maybe we all become children in water.

Behold, I am writing for the sake of writing. Acknowledging the sanctity of the story I inscribe on my aging, recovering, healthy body. Every word that I record is a blessing.

I was beginning to understand why descent was so important. With each dip, I felt like I was being pulled into a whirlpool of memories—that morning at my bar mitzvah when the particles suspended in midair; that evening at our wedding when I hopscotched across generations; that afternoon I came home on crutches and watched my daughters crumble to the ground; that dawn I lay awake on Mount Nebo in Jordan and felt the birth of day on the spot where Moses died of a broken heart. A string of moments, flashbulbing across my life, when I wasn't in total control and, as Mahina suggested, had no choice but to let the story come to me.

May we go forth in grace, may we venture in awe, may we return in wisdom. May we evade every enemy, elude every agony, avoid every ambush. Blessed be the traveler who reaches the end.

I started to cry. Not tears of sadness so much as tears of recognition. "The only thing I could say," wrote the spiritual leader Ram Dass of his first arrival in India, "was that it felt like home. The journey was over."

Then I started to chuckle. Could it be that the ritual that felt the least *like* home is the one that made me feel the most *at* home? Maybe because I made it my home. I overlooked certain rules and messed up others; I wrote my own script then forgot half of it; I shaped the ritual into precisely what I wanted it to be only to find that it took me to places I had no idea I wanted to go.

And maybe that improvisation is the point, after all.

There's a moment in the Passover seder, my favorite Jewish ritual, when the liturgy instructs, "In every generation, a person must see themselves as if they personally came out of Egypt." We are not called to lionize our flawed and fragile ancestors; we are not told to idolize our epic and messy narratives; we are asked to re-inhabit them, to re-create them.

The purpose of ritual is not to revere; it is to relive.

The Hebrew word for *Egypt* in that passage, מצרים, *mitzrayim*, has multiple meanings. The *-ayim* makes it plural, which suggests that the word refers to the "two lands" of Upper and Lower Egypt in common use at the time of the Exodus. Jewish mystics later interpreted *mitzrayim* to mean "tight places," as in the narrow straits of financial difficulty, failing health, or other life challenges that continue to plague us. The Passover ritual offers us the opportunity to immerse in our most threatening waters in order to find a way out. It is the original misogi.

I chose to chant the final blessing in Hebrew: *Shehecheyanu, v'kiy'manu, v'higiyanu laz'man hazeh. Blessed be the spirit that keeps us alive, sustains us, and brings us to this special place.*

I fell back into the water, kicking and splashing. For the first time all morning, I was having fun. The mikveh felt like a playground, where as long as you stay within the borders, you can write your own experience. For me, that protean adaptability captures what I appreciate about Judaism. It's why for half a century my family has time shifted bar and bat mitzvahs so that each child can read the same story of Abraham going forth inspired by my mother's maiden name, Abeshouse; it's why for forty years we have moved Hanukkah to the one weekend of the year we know we can be together, Thanksgiving, creating our own hybrid ritual, "Thanukkah." It's why I've hosted Jewish-style mourning gatherings for close friends who've lost their parents, even if they're Muslim, and why I backed my mother's desire to toss yellow roses on her husband's grave, even if it's Christian.

And I'm clearly not alone. I witnessed the same spirit of openness in the labyrinths of Episcopal cathedrals, the baptisms of offspring of unwed parents in the Vatican, the weddings of LGBTQ+ Hindu couples, the humanist funerals of suicide victims in Ireland, as well as the post-denominational tribes of forest bathers, grieving weavers, and hoʻoponopono prison forgivers.

Thousands of years after we settled into a pattern of HUMANS → RITUAL → RELIGION, we have settled into a new pattern: HUMANS → RITUAL → COMMUNITY. For some that community is religious; for others it's spiritual; for still more it's based in something else entirely. For nearly everyone it's a world where ritual comes first, then community grows from there. As more than one religious leader told me, "My institution has become a rite of passage factory."

And no wonder. As I experienced firsthand in Mayyim Hayyim, ritual has the nimbleness, the expansiveness, the commitment to the end user, and the willingness to welcome however much or little tradition as that user demands. Ritual is living water. It is mikveh, a word that also has dual meanings in Hebrew. In Genesis, *mikveh* is the place where God gathers the waters of creation; in Jeremiah, *mikveh* is the hope that a homeless people can feel at home in God.

"To be a prophet is to find a vestige of hope in the wreckage of despair," writes my friend Lord Jonathan Sacks, the onetime chief rabbi of Britain. The Passover story, he adds, plays an outsize role in human imagination because it is "the supreme narrative of hope." Ritual plays an outsize role in human imagination because it is the supreme embodiment of hope.

Just as a mikveh is a place to assemble and imagine, a ritual is a place to gather and dream—to conjure passing through the tightest place you've ever faced and experience what it's like to reach dry land on the other side.

Conclusion

A RITUAL STATE OF MIND

How to Turn Any Gathering into a Life Celebration

Here's what happens when everything goes wrong at the start of a family ritual.

The wind was blowing atop Pilgrim Hill just off Fifth Avenue and Seventy-Second Street in Central Park on the first Friday of spring when my family tried to find a location to put down a picnic blanket. It was a horrible day for an outing—temperatures peaked in the forties; ripples were visible on the pond in front of the *Alice in Wonderland* sculpture; the ground was wet.

We had come at the tail end of spring break because Linda had the ambitious idea that we should host a twenty-four-hour family ritual to mark the girls' twentieth birthday. The idea was to take inspiration from my travels to revisit milestones in our family's life—relive traditions, make a few new ones, reset for the decade ahead.

"I've been thinking of this ritual as a kind of memory palace," I said.

We settled on a spot. I was prescient enough to have grabbed an off-white blanket before leaving the house; I was stupid enough to now put my muddy shoes in the middle of it. To avoid replicating my blunder, everybody turned their backs on one another to keep their shoes on the ground. I was flunking Ritual Design 101.

To get us back on course, I asked everyone to offer their intention.

Tybee: I like framing my life as a beginning. Being nineteen seemed old, because we were the oldest children. Being twenty seems young, because now we're the youngest adults.

Eden: With less direction imposed on us, I've been trying to take more agency over my life. I hope you'll see us less as children and more as adults.

Linda: My goal is to remind you that we'll always be home for you, that you'll always be individuals and a pair, and that we're also individuals and not just parents.

We chose to start this ritual in Central Park because in February 2005, the artists Christo and Jeanne-Claude unfurled seven thousand five hundred three saffron banners on massive orange gates across twenty-three miles of the park. Linda was in the final months of pregnancy, and we used to marvel at *The Gates* on our way to the doctor. She nicknamed the girls Cinnamon and Saffron.

Inspired by the moms I met who went public with their birth stories, Linda shared a warts-and-all version of the day the girls were born. She even brought cinnamon rolls, though the girls chided her for not picking the proper bakery from TikTok. I was reminded of my friend Marshall Duke, the psychologist from Emory, whose research found that children who know more about their family history—including their birth story—have a greater belief that they can overcome setbacks. Knowledge of family history is the number one predictor of a child's emotional well-being.

Even with the halo effect of revisiting that milestone day, things quickly veered back offtrack. We had chosen this spot because the park was hosting a special augmented reality experience for the twentieth anniversary of *The Gates*. If you pointed your cell phone at the path, you were supposed to be able to see the orange banners come to life, but the technology didn't work. We tried to light Shabbat votives at the hour of the girls' birth, but the wind was too strong. Toasting wine from a mason jar seemed forced; saying the blessing over bread using leftover cinnamon rolls made nobody happy except the muddy mutt who bolted from his owner, leapt on the blanket, and began licking the icing.

It was time to go. As we hurriedly packed, I suggested we play our Friday-night "noticing game." Tybee noticed that hills don't have a lot of grass this time of year; Eden noticed that dogs, unlike Gen Z, have low social anxiety; Linda noticed that you have to check windchill even in March.

I noticed that life rituals, no matter how much you plan them, still have the ability to surprise.

I set out on this journey with four questions. I'd like to answer them now.

WHY DO WE NEED LIFE RITUALS?

At the 1893 Chicago World's Fair, which popularized the Ferris wheel, the dishwasher, the brownie, and Cracker Jack, the biggest cultural sensation was Irish American painter Thomas Hovenden's *Breaking Home Ties*. A massive canvas depicting a family holding a farewell ritual as a son leaves home for greater opportunity, the artwork attracted mobs of weeping visitors, was voted the most popular painting of the exposition, and spawned thousands of duplications. Hovenden captured a world poised between past and future, writes the historian Susan Matt, a time when "Americans who moved far from home and grappled with homesickness began to express a longing not just for the home they had left, but for a home they had permanently lost."

When I first walked through my front door and felt homesick in my own home, I was embarrassed. Homesickness was for the weak, the young, the coddled. In the exalted individualism of today, one is not supposed to be too bound to family.

I now believe my instincts were misplaced. Not only is homesickness not a sign of weakness, it's a sign of strength, of health, of confidence, and of the universal human urge to belong. Homesickness is the affliction of our age, one that comes closer than any explanation I've read to capturing the deep cultural vein of loneliness, alienation, nostalgia, and longing that plagues people of all generations who worry about the future of our tech-saturated, cruelty-infatuated, compassion-emasculated world.

Homesickness is our invisible epidemic.

And we're not the first to feel this way. From the moment the Pilgrims landed on Plymouth Rock, writes Susan Matt in her wonderful book *Homesickness: An American History*, through nearly five centuries of trauma brought on by war, migration, enslavement, urbanization, secularization, and digitization, "Americans took homesickness seriously—as did their doctors." Only in this century, when the threat has become more insidious, have we begun to ignore it.

Homesickness is a universal emotion. The German word *Heimweh* and French expression *mal du pays* describe a painful longing for home; the Welsh *hiraeth* and Portuguese *saudade* capture a more melancholic longing for lost time. The English word *nostalgia* emerged in the late 1600s from the Greek *nostos*, meaning "return home," and *-algia*, or "pain."

The word *homesickness* first appeared in Britain in the 1750s and leapt to America in time for the Revolution. George Washington complained that ripping soldiers from "tender Scenes of domestick life" brings "sickness in many; impatience in all, and such an unconquerable desire of returning to their respective homes." A quarter of volunteers deserted. By the Civil War, five thousand soldiers were medically diagnosed with homesickness and seventy-four succumbed to it. Army bands were banned from playing "Home, Sweet Home."

But here's where a remarkable pattern emerged. Whenever an outbreak of homesickness occurred, it was met with an equally strong outpouring of ritual remedies. In the mid-1800s, holidays like Thanksgiving and Christmas, which had been times for families crowded into small homes to visit friends, became times for families who were dispersed to reunite; family reunions were invented in the 1870s; New England towns began hosting Old Home Week festivals in the 1890s to lure back former residents.

The twenty-five million rural Americans and twenty-five million immigrants who flooded into cities at the turn of the century changed the meaning of homesickness; suddenly, homesickness was less about missing a place, because improved transportation made it easier to return home, and more about missing a bygone time, a misty golden age when families were together and everyone got along. As before, a host of rituals popped up to balm this need, from new communities (fraternal organizations, burial societies) to new traditions (supper clubs, sewing circles). Back-to-back world wars produced one of the most successful anti-homesickness initiatives in history, the United Service Organizations, or USO, which have since reached fifty million service members in thirty countries with care packages, home-cooked meals, and performances by everyone from Bob Hope to Marilyn Monroe to Drake. As one official explained the rationale in 1942, "Nine out of ten of these boys are desperately homesick."

Homesickness waned in the fifties, as moving to the suburbs and moving for your job became national priorities. (IBM, the joke went, stood for "I've Been Moved.") Harry Truman insisted that family had to be subordinated to country; psychologists stressed that family had to yield to corporations. Homesickness was deemed a "threat"; "momism," assailed; "independence training," encouraged.

The ploy didn't last. By the 1960s, psychologists observed that Americans "suffered from a deepening condition of 'homelessness'"; scholars wrote of a "nostalgia wave"; the Beatles swooned of "yesterday." By the twenty-first century, technology created a crisis of "boredom, screens, and homesickness"; artists organized shows like *A Homesick World*; columnists cheered the end of "radical individualism" and the return of nostalgia for a "simpler, more connected world." Everyone was calling for the rise of communal experiences to push back on the tide of social disintegration.

Rituals, as they've done for hundreds of thousands of years, answered the call. From life to death to everything in between, people found new ways to celebrate, commemorate, and come together. They voted with their feet, their voices, their placentas, their cremains. They discovered, yet again, that togetherness is the only force strong enough to push back against homesickness.

Rituals connect us; they correct imbalances among us; they celebrate our loftiest moments; they chronicle our deepest aspirations. But mostly they make us feel at home. As Thomas Hovenden captured in another moment of national crisis, they replace our grief over broken home ties with a vision of ties that bind.

Day two of our round-the-clock ritual began where day one left off, with the girls questioning my design skills.

"I don't think this is a memory palace," Tybee said.

"Yeah, those are mnemonic devices," Eden added.

"But we're creating a mnemonic device of our family!"

An odd sidebar of my life is that I played a minor role in the history of the 5 Love Languages. My Baptist bookkeeper in Savannah gave me a copy of Pastor Gary Chapman's church-published book when Linda and I got married. It sat unread on my shelf for years until I happened upon it one day and discovered that it perfectly nailed a conflict we were having. Linda's love language is acts of service; mine is quality time. I wrote a profile of Chapman in *The New York Times*, his first national publicity.

I've since learned that individuals are not the only ones with a love language; families have one, too—whether spaghetti and meatballs, Scrabble, the Chicago Cubs, or the Appalachian Trail. Our love language is Sondheim lyrics. We are a family of words—show tunes, Mad Libs, dad jokes, the alphabet game. In designing a family ritual, I knew that words had to play a central part. I called my friend Catherine Burns, the longtime artistic director of the Moth, who recommended something that she did at her wedding, create a quilt of our favorite sayings. It was the perfect idea.

At our dining room table, I handed out four clipboards and notebook paper. Linda printed out a document that she started when the girls were young with their cutest musings (*Just remember, you can be an entrepreneur for a short time, but you're a mommy forever*). We brought up keepsake boxes from the cellar, and I spread out quilting squares and fabric markers.

What followed was as blissful a two hours as I can remember in our family—a feast of squeals, giggles, *I can't believe I said that*s, and *that's so cringe*s. None of the final entries would be remotely comprehensible to anyone outside our family: *Don't drop your potatoes on the* *floor, George Washington Bridge, Baseball and Pickles.* What felt universal was the collective negotiation: *That's funny! That's boring! Write that down! Don't you dare!*

Why did you ask for your allowance in euros?

Because you were the cheapest tooth fairy in history and gave us foreign currency worth five cents when all our friends got five dollars.

I have no idea what you're talking about; I wasn't your tooth fairy.

Da-aad.

When the girls were young, I wrote a sort of anti-parenting book called *The Secrets of Happy Families* that questioned many orthodoxies. One of those gospels was the importance of family dinner. Few things have been more studied than family dinner; tens of thousands have been videotaped, every *you know*, *um*, and *like* analyzed. The number one finding: There's only ten minutes of shared conversation in any meal; the rest is taken up with *pass the ketchup* and *take your elbows off the table.* If you can spend those ten minutes at family dinner, great! But if you're among the 70 percent of us who don't, you can get many of the same benefits by time shifting those ten minutes to, say, late-night snacks or breakfast games.

The same holds for family rituals. There is abundant research that rituals improve family well-being—they reengage members, reaffirm traditions, reinforce values. They also reinvigorate relationships—between parents and children, children and children, even parents and each other. As three Harvard Business School professors and a colleague at the University of Minnesota wrote in the study "Family Rituals Improve the Holidays," family gatherings can be stressful, "from family members wondering why the turkey is not prepared the way

Grandma always did to children complaining about giving up their bedroom for Grandpa." Rituals reduce that stress; they "serve as a buffer to such potential downsides by increasing family closeness and involvement."

But as these scholars stressed—and I observed repeatedly in my travels—the precise nature of those rituals doesn't matter. If your rituals are around the dinner table, great, but if they're around the ping-pong table, the campfire, the tackle box, or the soggy picnic blanket, also great.

You can be a tooth fairy for a short time, but you're a ritual designer forever.

WHEN DO WE NEED LIFE RITUALS?

When my father died, I debated how to begin my eulogy. I settled on one of his most endearing habits: teaching every child he met how to shake hands: *Stand up straight, firm grip, look them in the eye.* His message: handshaking is more than just a utilitarian act; it's a statement of who you are, an expression of your values, a means of conveying that you're open to relationship. It's a ritual.

The biggest change I underwent on this journey is rethinking how frequently we need life rituals. At the beginning, I was consumed with the academic debate around what is a ritual; what categories do they fall in; what distinguishes a life ritual from a civic ritual, a daily ritual, and so on? All these questions have value, but I have come to believe they have been rendered obsolete by the pace of change around us.

People need life rituals whenever they need them, from donating an organ to adopting a child, from the eve of surgery to the death of a pet. Today, in the absence of obvious leadership, people are taking matters into their own hands. As one millennial ritual entrepreneur told me, "The pushback with my generation is that we don't want rites of passage when our parents tell us; we want them on our own timeline. We're saying, 'Let me tell you what passage I'm going through and let's design a rite for that. And by the way, I'm going to create it, I'm going to name it, and I don't care if you think it deserves a ritual. I don't need your validation.'"

Given this free-for-all, can we at least agree on some guidelines that individuals, families, and even institutions can use to create a new ritual calendar?

To answer that question, let's do one final mathematical thought experiment. If we start the clock at adolescence and continue to the mid-eighties, we can set the denominator at seventy-two years. For the numerator, we're not looking for every disruptor; we're looking for occasions that rise to the magnitude of import and instability that they would benefit from a shared experience.

Drawing on a decade of data I've generated, I would benchmark the numbers like this:

Milestones (major birthdays, anniversaries, graduations)	8
Work (starting or ending a job or business)	5
Love (marriage, divorce, childbirth, adoption)	4
Loss (death of a loved one, loss of a home, natural disaster)	4
Body (illness, surgery, aging)	3
Total	24

Divide the number of years (seventy-two) by the number of life ritual opportunities (twenty-four) and you get one opportunity every three years. This figure alone proves the absurd inadequacy of speaking about a mythical "big four" life rituals.

But even this number doesn't capture the reality. If you use a conservative estimate and say that each of us needs a life ritual every four years, then each family of four would need four rituals in that time span, or one a year; each extended family would surely add one ritual every year, as would each friend group and each social network. Add these numbers together, and the average person experiences the underlying circumstances that would benefit from a life ritual *four times a year*—that's once every three months or nearly three hundred times in our adult lives.

Even if we merely aspire to this frequency and each of us takes micro-steps to imagine, plan, and organize; contribute to, RSVP to, and bring a gift to; laugh, hug, and cry during; then send a thank-you note, share photos, and trade gossip after even a fraction of this number of life rituals, we will reverse the loneliness epidemic in one generation.

How do we advance this ambitious goal? By developing a ritual state of mind.

The first step is to retire the idea that ritual is a string of fixed events on fixed timelines with fixed scripts and replace it with the idea that ritual is *an approach to human interaction* and a *commitment to human connection*. I learned this lesson from my children. Now that I see them less regularly, I can't sit back, harrumph, and say, *Sorry, according to a study written in Paris by oil lamp, we're not scheduled to have our next family ritual for another seven years.* Instead, I have to lurch at any opening that presents itself. Sometimes I even have to create an opening.

Ritual is not a fixed mindset; it's a frame of mind—a frame we must open whenever we can.

To achieve this goal, we must also move beyond another dated concept. Rituals are not just rites of passage—sprawling, multiday events requiring months of planning and bags of cash; they're also bites of passage—smaller, more targeted nibbles of connection requiring far less planning and sometimes no money at all. What psychologists call social snacking are brief interactions that promote happiness—with a neighbor, a barista, a friend on the street. Bites of passage are the ritual equivalent of social snacking—the wedding dress fitting, the tombstone unveiling, the divorce paper signing, the grieving and weaving circle. They're morsels of empathy and noshes of compassion that reinforce the larger message of rites of passage.

The aim of a ritual-anytime-anywhere attitude is to create more opportunities to beat back loneliness and homesickness. Those of us who care about empathy, unity, and belonging must face the reality that hate, division, and social unraveling are not just strengthening, they're also quickening. In 2025, researchers set up fake social media accounts of teenage boys; it took under eight minutes for divisive, corrosive content to appear in their feeds and under twenty-three minutes for violent content to surface. Within two hours, 78 percent of recommended posts were "toxic in nature."

When the poison is spreading this rapidly, the response must mobilize even more rapidly. As the algorithms of our newest human inventions divide us, our oldest human inventions must save us.

The hardest part of designing our family ritual was coming up with stakes, something that added gravitas and urgency to the experience. I called my friend Casper ter Kuile, the cofounder of the Sacred Design Lab, who recommended a ritual that he had done at a failed startup. Based on the Jewish tradition of tashlich, when individuals cast off their sins by throwing breadcrumbs into water, Casper asked his colleagues to write out regrets and then toss them into a plastic bag.

After lunch, Linda and I invited the girls to our deck. "There are many wonderful things about our family," I said. "But like all families, we have conflicts, bad habits, and things we can do better." I pulled out a Gertel's one-pound challah, which we passed around the circle, taking turns pulling off chunks, sharing something we wanted to leave behind, then tossing the bread into a salad bowl.

Fights about food.
Comparing every element of our lives.
Starting mornings off on the wrong foot.
Coming late to dinner.

Gradually the answers grew more abstract.

Lack of gratitude.
Not picking our battles.
Forgetting to elevate others.
Rarely trying new things.

And ultimately more profound.

Not maximizing joy.
Not doing random acts of kindness.
Not making art together.
Taking our ancestors for granted.

When the bread was finished, we stuffed the pieces back into the bag to take down to the river later. In the meantime, we went downstairs. Every Sunday for fifteen years, we gathered around our kitchen table for what we called our agile family meeting, where we asked three questions: *What's going well in our family? What's not going well? What will we work on in the week ahead?* Today we were here to mark a new phase.

I told the story of my eighteenth birthday, when my paternal grandfather, a country lawyer from Mississippi who wore suspenders and bow ties and liked to be called "Colonel," brought a will for me to sign before I had breakfast. It was a rite of passage without the right of refusal.

Linda pulled out a package that the girls cooed must be a gift; it contained two pink fireproof document bags. Linda explained that we have a black one with our important documents, and each of the girls needed to start their own, with their birth certificates, social security cards, passports, and the like. She then handed them each a will, which we discussed, they reviewed for grammatical mistakes, and then they signed.

The girls' linguistic persnicketiness proved nettlesome minutes later when we approached Pier 4 in Brooklyn Bridge Park to toss out the bread. A police officer was ticketing a fisherman; the girls eyed a sign that said it was against the law to *discard anything* into the East River. I promised that a challah was exempt, but they refused to take the risk. We searched around for a secluded spot, hurriedly dumped Gertel's best into the water, mumbled a prayer, then sped away from our low-stakes, high-comedy flight from the law for the last ritual of our day.

Crossing the Brooklyn Bridge.

HOW DO YOU CREATE A LIFE RITUAL?

The first step to crafting a meaningful life ritual is giving yourself permission to do so. You don't need a fancy degree, a good singing voice, or the perfect cake; you don't need a miter, a stole, or a mace. "Simply by virtue of being a human being, one is an authority on creating ritual," writes Malidoma Patrice Somé, the influential West African healer and teacher. “If people know the problem that they are confronting, they are capable of devising a ritual that will handle this problem.”

One thing I learned in my travels, though, is that while cultural differences are decreasing, generational differences are increasing. Minding these generational gaps is essential to a successful life ritual.

Silents (1928–1945) value formality and tradition; they like to honor established forms and include symbols of continuity. Boomers (1946–1964) crave meaning and legacy; they appreciate backstory and nods to the past. Gen X (1965–1980) prefers autonomy and independence; they look for customization with mix-and-match options. Millennials (1981–1996) seek framework and direction; they welcome flexibility but want the *why* behind each *what*. Gen Z (1997–2012) demands clear steps and structure; they want specific instructions with social media–style to-do lists.

These differences can be boiled down to a simple rubric:

Silents → Reverence
Boomers → Context
Gen X → Options
Millennials → Pointers
Gen Z → Instructions

Building off this model, I devised a 1-2-3-4-5 blueprint for how to design a life ritual: one act of reverence, two pieces of context, three options, four pointers, and five instructions.

1. Reverence: Do what makes you feel at home.

The single most important thing that a life ritual can do is make you feel at home. In an age of endemic homesickness, ritual is our best route to home-wellness.

But feeling at home is not objective; it's subjective. It's not a physical place; it's a psychological state. As the psychologist Geoffrey Cohen reminds us, "When crafting situations to nurture belonging," the physical features of the situation matter less than "the way the situation is being perceived, felt, and experienced." Thus, identify what you're most missing from home—whether that's safety, empathy, love, or joy—and design a ritual with that goal in mind.

2. Context: Identify your tension; define your intention.

For a ritual to be more than a passing distraction, it must fulfill two objectives: address the underlying uncertainty, fluidity, and instability in the group; and provide comfort, relief, and support for that volatility. The best way to achieve those twin goals is to first ask, "What is our pain point? What is the tension, transition, or turbulence that we're experiencing?"

Then, "What intention matches that tension? What do we hope to get out of the experience, what purpose do we hope to fulfill, what meaning do we hope to take away?"

Another rubric might be helpful here: the ABCs of Meaning. One of my favorite takeaways from all the life stories I've absorbed is that each of us has three primary pillars that bring us meaning. The *A* is *agency*—what we do, make, or create; our *me story*. The *B* is *belonging*—our relationships, friends, loved ones, and colleagues; our *we story*. The *C* is *cause*—a calling, mission, or purpose; our *thee story*. To set your intention: choose an A, a B, and a C—something for yourself, something for those around you, something for the larger community.

Missy Holliday, to cite just one example, created the honor walk to give herself a purpose following the death of her sister (her A); to serve the needs of the grieving families she worked with (her B); to help everyone involved in organ donation (her C). One ritual, three ABCs.

3. Options: Off-the-shelf or do-it-yourself, big or small, sacred space or third space.

Designing a successful ritual means considering three options:

One, off-the-shelf or do-it-yourself? Follow someone else's script or write your own?

Two, big or small? Whom do you want inside the circle, whom do you want to exclude?

Three, sacred space or third space? Sacred spaces already exist but come with restrictions; third spaces offer a blank slate but take more work to feel special.

As a rule: DIY, micro, third-space life rituals are gaining; off-the-shelf, macro, sacred-space life rituals are fading.

4. Pointers: The four somethings.

Whether you like pointers or not, do the four somethings—old, new, borrowed, you. In order. Start with something old, maybe from your religious upbringing or cultural heritage; in our family ritual, something old was *The Gates*. Then do something new, maybe drawn from a work retreat or a yoga class; our new was the quilt poem. Next do something borrowed, maybe from a friend or that trip to Spain; our borrowed was the challah tossing. End with something you—your brandy ceremony or "You'll Never Walk Alone"; our you was our Brooklyn Bridge tradition.

5. Instructions: Boundaries, stakes, compromise, empathy, hope.

If you like a TikTok to-do list, here are "five things you gotta try": Draw a boundary that defines the sacred space, articulate the stakes, compromise-rehearse on something important, create an atmosphere of empathy, and end with a moment of hope.

Whatever you do, your ritual should invoke others but ultimately be your own.

When I had cancer, the Brooklyn Bridge loomed large in my imagination. I would cross it on my way to chemotherapy appointments and came to view it as a bridge to the future. "Heaven looks at you from the Brooklyn Bridge," Sinatra sang. On Father's Day at the end of my treatment, when the girls had just turned four, I proposed that we walk across it for the first time as a family.

"Can we bring a compass!" Tybee cheered.

"Can we have a picnic!" Eden squealed.

Two hours, four changes of clothes, two squirts of sunscreen in the eyes, and one crying fit later, we were out the door. The girls flanked Linda ahead, practicing their four-year-old rock star poses. I followed on crutches. The girls made up a song:

> We're walking across the Brooklyn Bridge
> Our daddy has stitches and a scar
> We're walking across the Brooklyn Bridge
> Don't worry, it's not that far!

Looking back, I see now that I spent that year trying to ritualize everyday moments. I coined phrases—*Always learn to juggle on the side of a hill; the Council of Dads*. I spent a week glue gunning plastic Easter eggs onto poster board for twin Halloween jelly bean costumes. I asked Linda to bring *Curious George Goes to the Hospital* and yellow MetroCard cookies with the missing upper-right corner for when the girls visited me in intensive care.

I put myself in a ritual state of mind hoping that one of these memories might live in their minds, even if I did not. At the summit of the bridge that day, we laid out plastic cups and M&M's and held a tea party overlooking New York Harbor.

This time we brought the wedding china. And because the girls remembered, a family-size bag of M&M's. I asked everyone to share a dream for our family.

Tybee: I hope we continue to travel and see the world together but also come home to things that are familiar.

Eden: I hope we can continue to return home to one another—looking out for everyone's best interest even if it's not our own.

Linda: I hope that we will continue to be the first call on the good days and the first call on the bad days—and remember that family is our superpower.

I mentioned that the first time we walked across the bridge, I had to walk slower than everybody else. And that later I learned about flaneurs, pedestrians in Paris in the 1800s who strolled the arcades in leisure. As a symbol of their status, flaneurs would take turtles for walks and let the reptile set the pace. That idea inspired my line: Take a walk with a turtle. And behold the world in pause.

I hope we continue to pause as a family. Go fast, you get where you're going quickly, but you get there alone; go slow, you get there later, but you get there together. I hope we always get there together.

We passed around the M&M's, poured water into our cups, and toasted the future.

As we stood up to go, I was a little sad. The girls scooted ahead; Linda took my arm. Our twenty-four-hour ritual had some Keystone moments, she said, but it had been a smashing success. I wondered, though, if I had pushed too hard, wanted it too much.

The next morning, we gathered in the same foyer where my journey began. I kissed the girls goodbye as they headed back to college. An hour later a message appeared in our family group chat. It was a photo of Tybee and Eden, together on the train, each holding a yellow MetroCard cookie with the missing upper-right corner. Underneath was a message—those girls I worried had not been listening, claiming the last word:

Finishing the ritual!

CAN RITUALS SAVE US?

From time to time, ideas pop up that seize the imagination of the world. They capture what German philosophers called *Zeitgeist*, the "spirit of the time." In the 1920s, that idea was the lost generation; in the 1950s, it was domesticity; in the 1960s, freedom; in the 2010s, identity.

I believe that ritual captures the zeitgeist of our time. It's a vessel for the post-pandemic backlash against digital saturation, rampant isolation, and growing decivilization; it's an antidote to widespread confusion, anxiety, and stress; it's a conduit for authenticity, intentionality, and intimacy. It's a word that everyone seems to love. No matter where I went or whom I talked to, when I said that I was writing a book about ritual, a smile broke out, an exclamation erupted: *I love ritual!*

The fluid, protean nature of ritual almost certainly contributes to its popularity. Everyone loves ritual because ritual means something different to everyone. This ecumenicism is a major factor in why, of the three options I laid out at the start of this journey—we're permanently turning away from ritual; the ritual recovery is a dead-cat bounce; we stand at the dawn of a ritual renaissance—the evidence clearly points to the third. If anything, like other shifts of this magnitude, the ritual revival has been underway for some time and we're just getting around to naming it.

My experience points to why.

Rituals work in times of change because they titrate change. They work in times of social upheaval because they modulate social upheaval. They work in times of religious flux because they bridge the religious, the irreligious, the spiritual, and the *I'm not religious but I'm spiritual.*

Rituals work because they are *acts*. They are values lived out loud. As the old adage goes, it's easier to act oneself into a new way of thinking than to think oneself into a new way of acting. A genius of ritual is that it's an old way of acting that leads to a new way of thinking. By bringing our bodies into alignment with others, we realign our we-I axis. We assert the primacy of IRL over the tyranny of URL.

Rituals work because they are *shared.* Our earliest ancestors shouted, waved sticks, and stamped their feet in unison to signal to predators that they were more powerful together than they were apart; our latest brain researchers have shown that when we sing, dance, eat, or work together, not only do our bodies synchronize, but our feelings do, too. To be in union is to become a union; to be in a group is to become a groupkeeper.

Rituals work because they are *unnecessary.* We live in a stranglehold of necessities, with deadening schedules, dulling routines, and draining obligations. Rituals are the unnecessities that unyoke those necessities—they upend schedules, disrupt routines, sideline obligations.

They force us to focus on what Keats deemed our "negative capability," the ability to be in "uncertainties, Mysteries, doubts" without reflexively grasping for reason or explanation. Only by tapping into our negative capability can we fulfill our positive capacity. Only by embracing the unnecessary can we escape the unfulfilling.

Finally, rituals work because they are portable, replicable versions of *home*. "The ache for home lives in all of us," Maya Angelou said, "the safe place where we can go as we are." Today we need that safe space more than ever—for morale making, for meaning making, for memory making.

On my last day in Ireland, I decided to treat myself to a play. The only thing running was *Dancing at Lughnasa*, Brian Friel's memory play set in 1936 rural Ireland that centers on five unmarried sisters struggling with deprivation, repression, and longing. It won top play at both the Tony and Olivier Awards and was turned into a movie starring Meryl Streep. At the climax of act 1, the sisters hike up their dresses, let down their hair, and break into spontaneous, ecstatic dance in a cathartic ritual of release. At my performance, the dancing went on for ten minutes and received a mid-show standing ovation.

In the final scene, the adult narrator and son of one of the sisters, Michael, wistfully recalls that emotional night: "What is so strange about that memory is that everybody seems to be floating on those sweet sounds, moving rhythmically, languorously," he says. "Dancing as if language had surrendered to movement—as if this ritual, this wordless ceremony, was now the way to speak, to whisper private and sacred things, to be in touch with some otherness. . . . Dancing as if language no longer existed because words were no longer necessary."

When the lights came up, I—and everyone else in the theater—wiped away tears.

Ritual is the wordless, whispered language of memory. It is the act of surrendering and the art of imagining. It is the languorous, sacred sweetness of communion in a world bespoiled by division. For a culture on the brink of collapse, ritual is the remedy we crave.

It is a time to weep and a time to laugh.

A time to mourn and a time to dance.

A time to scatter stones and a time to gather them.

Our greatest spiritual leaders presented us with choices. For Moses, it was life or death; for Krishna, freedom or suffering; for the Buddha, enlightenment or delusion; for Jesus, idolatry or truth. What these pairings have in common is the choice between narrowness and openness, between bondage and freedom.

Today we face a similar choice.

We can succumb to the prison of I, or we can aspire to the promise of we.

We can submit to the phantom of aloneness, or we can strive for the fathom of togetherness.

We can bow to the darkness of virtual, or we can rise to the beacon of ritual.

Ritual is not perfect. It can be abused, it can inflame, it can flop. Ritual is fragile, its recent victories unwound. But ritual works. It offers a path along a three-hundred-thousand-year trail, from the red ocher cave burials of our earliest ancestors to the purple-glazed baptisteries of our greatest cathedrals, from the black-and-white cows of tribal brides to the cinnamon-and-saffron sarongs of teeth-chattering island teens, from our densest, greenest forests to our deepest, bluest pools.

Ritual may not be our last hope, but it may be our best hope.

I set before you a choice: social decay or ritual cure.

Choose ritual.

The way home.

Acknowledgments

I would like to express my profound gratitude to the scores of people who appear by name in this book—for opening your hearts, your homes, your lives; for inviting me to your weddings, your funerals, your tooth filings, and every other ritual imaginable; and for allowing me to witness the many exceptional ways that you are creating connection, intimacy, and meaning in a world that desperately needs it. As I hope these pages make clear, I am in awe of your dedication, exalt at your inventiveness, and believe with all my being that your example will illuminate a path for the rest of us to follow.

A journey of this magnitude is never taken alone. I am immensely appreciative of the many people who raised their hands, opened a door, or otherwise pointed the way. A small sampling includes James Martin, S.J., Anthony SooHoo, Pietro Sella, Marco Rampazzo; Joss Kent, Karen Richards, Lotus Khoza; Jeffre Joe; Amy Cunningham, Ida Benedetto; The Edge; Roger Barnett, Melina Baxter, Cris Juna; Susan and Rory Guihan; Lan Ahn Nguyen; Ireayo Oladunjoye, Bolaji Balogun, Kayode Adegbola; Ezra Bookman, Vanessa Ochs, Betty Ray, Bruno Wauters, and Charles Vogl.

Inspired by events in my own life, this book was nurtured through a series of conversations with Scott Moyers of Penguin Press, who pushed me in new directions, encouraged me to follow even my quirkiest instincts, and welcomed each successive draft with encouragement, discernment, and a commitment to the highest standards of storytelling. In a world that increasingly favors the caustic and abrupt, Scott insists on the slow and elevating. I am graced by his guidance.

Countless other professionals of peerless skill and uncompromising dedication at Penguin Press helped guide this book into the world. Thank you to the best in the business: Ann Godoff, Sarah Hutson, Darren Haggar, Matt Boyd, Danielle Plafsky, Helen Rouner, Mia Council, Colleen McGarvey, Elijah Rey-David Matos, and Ximena Gonzalez.

The publication of this book marks thirty years that David Black and I have shared plentiful life moments, life milestones, and life rituals. I am keenly aware of how rare such a relationship is.

I am uplifted by my association with Craig Jacobson; Alan Berger, Bruce Vinokosur, and Katie Maloney at CAA; Johannes Eichstaedt, who invited me to be a fellow at the Stanford Computational Psychology & Well-Being Lab; Suzy Welch and Dustin Liu at NYU Stern School of Business; and Chip Conley and Kari Cardinale at Modern Elder Academy.

I was joined in my own lab by superbly dedicated and bright young talent. I am thrilled to recognize the contributions of Michael Valladares, Irene Westfall, Eli Cuomo, and Lila Dominus. Special thanks to Kirk Benson, Caroline Stephenson, and Megan Johnson.

Boy am I lucky to go through life with the council of Ben Sherwood, Joshua Ramo, Max Stier, and Jeff Shumlin—always at my back, in my ear, by my side.

Writing is said to be lonely; for me it overflows with friends and colleagues who answer the call, improve the idea, dampen the doubts, return the favor. Thank you for being inside the circle with me: Kaja Perina, Sunny Bates, Lauren Schneider, Catherine Burns, Robert Wright, Esther Perel, Adriana Trigiani, Jennifer Aaker, Jodi Kantor and Ron Lieber, Campbell Brown and Dan Senor, Neri Oxman and

Bill Ackman, Casper ter Kuile, Gretchen Rubin, A. J. Jacobs, Karen Essex, David Kramer, Charlie Greene, Florence Pan, Sharyn Rosenblum, Jessi Hempel, and Marshall Duke.

The Rottenbergs are ritual people dedicated to tradition and reinvention alike—I am grateful for the many ways that we are building communal stories together.

Andrew Feiler is my brother, my partner, my sharpest critic, and my biggest booster; our sister, Cari, has been using creative gatherings to connect Philadelphians for three decades. I am overjoyed that our mother, Jane Feiler, was able to read this book and that during its final months of completion, we were finally able to publish Ed Feiler's memoir, *A Professional Savannahian*, which he finished just weeks before his death.

Linda Rottenberg is known around the world for her ability to assemble people seeking to make their dreams come true into communities of collaboration and meaning. She is as brilliant a ritual designer as anyone profiled in these chapters. The single biggest reason this book exists is her support at every turn, her unrivaled global network, and her formidable chorus of underlines, smiley faces, and *ABSOLUTELY NOTS* on each and every draft.

Eden and Tybee: This book began with your absence; it ended with your presence as we found thrilling new ways to connect and be together as a family. My deepest wish is that you cultivate a ritual state of mind and continue to be beacons of togetherness and collective effervescence in an increasingly atomized world. If you do, you will have fulfilled your mother's and my greatest dream for you—and the words of the dedication of this book. You will always feel at home.

Sources

All interviews quoted in this book were recorded and transcribed. My general philosophy is to respect, consider, and honor people's life stories, accepting that they contain certain events that others might interpret in a different way. I also drew on the wide literature around ritual. In this chapter-by-chapter accounting, I offer sources for all the quotations and academic references included in the book.

Introduction. The Ritual Renaissance

My research into lifequakes is detailed in *Life Is in the Transitions*. On organ donation, see Nicholas Tilney, *Transplant*. My history of ritual draws on Catherine Bell, *Ritual*; Ronald Grimes, *Deeply into the Bone*; Barry Stephenson, *Ritual* and *Excursions in Ritual Studies*; and Harvey Whitehouse, *The Ritual Animal*. "Social act:" Roy Rappaport, *Ritual and Religion in the Making of Humanity*.

"Ritualization": Julian Huxley, "The Courtship Habits of the Great Crested Grebe" appears in *Proceedings of the General Meeting for Scientific Business of the Zoological Society of London*. "Panting": Hjalmar S. Kuhl et al., "Chimpanzee Accumulative Stone Throwing," *Scientific Reports* 6. "Basic unit": Leslie A. White, "The Symbol," *Philosophy of Science* 7, no. 4. "No human": Rappaport. "Widest": Edmund Leach, "Ritual," *The International Encyclopedia of the Social Sciences*. "Sanskrit," in Rachel Reed, *Reclaiming Childbirth as a Rite of Passage*. "Doing": Stephenson, *Ritual*.

On types of rituals, see Arnold van Gennep, *The Rites of Passage*. Norbert Elias discusses the we-I axis in *The Society of Individuals*. "Every century": Stephenson, *Ritual*. On "celebration recession," see Mircea Eliade, *The Sacred and the Profane*; Robert Bellah, *Habits of the Heart*; Robert D. Putnam, *Bowling Alone*. "Gradually," Ernest Hemingway, *The Sun Also Rises*.

My article about YouTube was "Lights, Camera, We're Having a Baby!," *The New York Times*, 2016. "Viral video": "When Love Builds a Family," Watson Wedding Videography, Instagram, 2024.

"Ceremony else?": William Shakespeare, *Hamlet*, act 5, scene 1. "Fifty donors": Missy Holliday interview. "The problem": Feiler, "Should Your Spouse Be Your Best Friend?," *The New York Times*, 2017. "Groupishness": Whitehouse. "Primary takeaway": Feiler, *Life Is in the Transitions*; see also Zygmunt Bauman, *Liquid Times*. "Abandonment": Malidoma Patrice Somé, *Ritual*. "Urge": Novalis, *Philosophical Writings*, ed. and trans. Margaret Mahoney Stoljar.

1. Welcome With Joy

My history of the Vatican, including the obelisk, draws on R. A. Scotti, *Basilica*; "maternally": Franco Mormando, *Bernini*. More on my visit to Mount Ararat in Bruce Feiler, *Walking the Bible*. "Startling" in Andrew Curry, "Last Stand of the Hunter-Gatherers?," *Archaeology Magazine*.

SOURCES

"Big bang," see Jean-Marie Chauvet, Eliette Brunel Deschamps, and Christian Hillaire, *Dawn of Art*. "Lion Man": "Cave Art Movement Overview," theartstory.org; "python": "World's Oldest Ritual Discovered—Worshipped the Python 70,000 Years Ago," *ScienceDaily*, 2006; "loud": Sheila Coulson et al., "Ritualized Behavior in the Middle Stone Age," *PaleoAnthropology*, January 2011; "Sulawesi": Nell Greenfieldboyce, "Indonesian Cave Paintings As Old As Europe's Ancient Art," NPR, 2014; "Neanderthal": Jo Marchant, "A Journey to the Oldest Cave Paintings in the World," *Smithsonian* magazine, January 2016. "Ritual site," in Curry; "How things" discussed in Martin Puchner, *Culture*.

More on Brother Agnello in Christina Deardurff, "The Joyful 'Parish Priest' of St. Peter's Welcomes 'Jagged Humanity,'" *Inside the Vatican*, 2024. On the Axial Age, see Karl Jaspers, *The Origin and Goal of History*. "Opposing" in Ori Tavor, "Xunzi's Theory of Ritual Revisited," *Dao* 12, no. 3. "Hindu": *Bhagavad Gita*, 3:10.

"Why": Hans Hillerbrand, "Martin Luther," *Encyclopedia Britannica*, 2025. "The Reformation," quoted in Bell. "Less personal" discussed in Grimes, and Arthur Magida, *Opening the Doors of Wonder*. "Announced" in "Transsexual and Homosexual Persons and the Sacraments," *Vatican News*, 2023.

"Axis mundi" et al.: Mircea Eliade, *The Myth of the Eternal Return*. "Peak-end": Balca Alaybek et al., "All's Well that Ends (and Peaks) Well?," *Organizational Behavior and Human Decision Processes* 170. On wows, see Byung-Chul Han, *The Disappearance of Rituals*. "Race": Laura Mason, ed., *Food and the Rites of Passage*. "Ndembu": Victor Turner, *The Ritual Process*; "tablet": Grimes; "cakes": Mason.

2. The Lobola Connection

"Somewhere": Chinua Achebe, *Things Fall Apart*. Lobola details from "South Africa's Mandela 'Paid' 60 Cows for Graca," Reuters, 1998, and "King Mswati to Pay Hefty Price for Jacob Zuma's Daughter," Nehanda Radio, 2024. "Calculator": "Robert Matsaneng Tells Us How His Lobola App Works," Soundcloud/Premedia Broadcasting, 2015. "Embrace": Janet Hinson Shope, "'Lobola Is Here to Stay,'" *Agenda* 68.

My account of Diderot draws on Andrew Curran, *Diderot and the Art of Thinking Freely*. "Sneer": Stephenson, *Ritual*; Bell. On definition, see Talal Asad, "Toward a Genealogy of the Concept of Ritual," in Andrew Strathern, *Ritual*. "Hated": Bjorn Thomassen, "The Hidden Battles that Shaped the History of Sociology," *Journal of Classical Sociology* 16, no. 2 , and David Kertzer, in *The Rites of Passage*, 2nd ed. Émile Durkheim quote in *The Elementary Forms of Religious Life*; Van Gennep quote is in *The Rites of Passage*. Turner quotes from *The Ritual Process*.

"Widely" and "Ironically": David Sloan Wilson et al., "Multilevel Selection Theory and Major Evolutionary Transitions," *Current Directions in Psychological Science* 17, no. 1. "Sense": Jonathan Haidt and Selin Kesebir, "Morality," in Susan Fiske et al., eds., *Handbook of Social Psychology*, 5th ed. "Formidable": Harvey Whitehouse, "How Ritual an Animal?," *Journal for the Cognitive Science of Religion* 8, no. 2. "Team": Whitehouse, *The Ritual Animal*. "Firewalking," in Dmitris Xygalatas, *Ritual*. "Sweep": Rosaleen Nhlekisana, "Honey, Let's Waltz the Day Out," *Muziki* 4, no. 1.

3. The Taylor Swift Divorce Party

My account of South Dakota's divorce laws draws on April White, *The Divorce Colony*. "Elegance": White. "Turned out": Stephanie Coontz, *Marriage, a History*. "Cruelty": Eric Renshaw, "Looking Back," *Argus Leader*, 2016. "Kicked": Doree Lewak, "Divorce Registries Help People 'Getting the S—t Kicked Out of Them,'" *New York Post*, 2022.

"Length": Coontz. "Celebrations": Zara Stone, "The Legendary, Lavish Dinner Parties of South Dakota's Divorce Colony," *Atlas Obscura*, 2019. "Flying cars": Martin Chilton, "10 Things You Didn't Know About Chitty Chitty Bang Bang," *Independent*, 2020. "Toothbrushes": Bill McLouglin, "Prince Charles' Strict Rule for Camilla Wedding After Prior Diana Embarrassment Revealed," *Express*, 2019.

4. Skin in the Game

"Lexicon": Clifford Geertz, *Negara*. For more on tooth filing, see Fred Eiseman, *Bali: Sekala & Niskala*. "Hurry" et al.: John Gneisenau Neihardt, *Black Elk Speaks*. Adolescent rituals taken from Mircea Eliade, *Rites and Symbols of Initiation*, and J. S. LaFontaine, *Initiation*. "Rigorous" in Yehudi Cohen's *The Transition from Childhood to Adolescence* and Grimes, "Promotion": Grimes.

"Must have": Eiseman; "stupendous": Geertz; "pomp": Geertz. "Ritual learning": Anthony Wallace, "Revitalization Movements," *American Anthropologist* 58, no. 2. "Unforgettable": Grimes. "Dysphoria": Whitehouse, *The Ritual Animal*. "Stimulate": Robert McCauley and E. Thomas Lawson, *Bringing Rit-*

ual to Mind. "Worthless": Elliot Aronson and Judson Mills, "The Effect of Severity of Initiation on Liking for a Group," *The Journal of Abnormal and Social Psychology* 59, no. 2.

"Early Mayans": Gloria Hernández-Bolio et al., "Organic Compositional Analysis of Ancient Maya Tooth Sealants and Fillings," *Journal of Archaeological Science* 43. "Grills": Courtney Larocca, "Justin Bieber Flashed $25,000 Diamond-Encrusted Grills in a New Wedding Photo with Hailey Baldwin," *Business Insider*, 2019. "Bronze Age": Angelina Atienza, "Early Aesthetic Dentistry in the Philippines," *Acta Medica Argentina* 48, no. 1. "Cockfight" et al.: Clifford Geertz, "Deep Play," *Daedalus* 134, no. 4.

5. House of Correction

"Ambition" in "A Brooklyn Treasure Since 1838," The Green-Wood Historic Fund, green-wood.com/history. "Cooperation": Nichola Raihani, *The Social Instinct*. "Magical": Grimes. "Something": Thomas Lynch, *The Undertaking*. "Parliament" quoted in Raihani. "Drumming": Stephenson, *Ritual*. "Grove": Turner, *The Ritual Process*. "Overall": Geoffrey Cohen, *Belonging*.

"Intervention": Kathryn Berg, "Ritual as Clinical Intervention in Groupwork with African American Women," master's thesis at Loyola University Chicago (2012). "Violence": Anneliese Singh and Danica Hays, "Feminist Group Counseling with South Asian Women Who Have Survived Intimate Partner Violence," *The Journal for Specialists in Group Work* 33, no. 1. "Rites of Passage": Karen Marie Allen and Danielle Wozniak, "The Integration of Healing Rituals in Group Treatment for Women Survivors of Domestic Violence," *Social Work in Mental Health* 12, no. 1.

For more on forced adoptions, see Karen Wilson-Buterbaugh, *The Baby Scoop Era*, and Caelainn Hogan, *Republic of Shame*. "Parliament": "Julia Gillard Apologises to Australian Mothers for Forced Adoptions," *The Guardian*, 2013. "Third place," see Ray Oldenburg, *The Great Good Place*. "Code Grandma": Erich Schwartzel, "Disney World's Biggest Secret," *The Wall Street Journal*, 2018. "Diana": Blake Morrison, "Saying It with Flowers," *The Guardian*, 2005.

6. Jumping the Broom

"Mitchum": Frank Hotchkiss, "Filmed in Georgia," *Savannah Morning News*, 2022. My history of broom jumping draws on Tyler D. Parry, *Jumping the Broom*. "Journey": Parry. "Kunta": Alex Haley, *Roots*. "Pythagoras": Parry. "Bryde" et al.: Parry. "Forty-one": Parry. "Anything": Parry.

"Spooked," see "Queen Victoria's Funeral (1901)" at youtube.com/watch?v=t9yiG3EUz_A. David Cannadine's "The Context, Performance and Meaning of Ritual" appears in Eric Hobsbawm and Terence Ranger, eds., *The Invention of Tradition*. Corn shucking is discussed in Roger D. Abrahams, *Singing the Master*. "Breaking": Abrahams. "Ingenuity": Parry.

7. The Four Somethings

"To be married": Joan Didion, "Marrying Absurd," *The Saturday Evening Post*, 1967. "Slouching": Michael Cox, "On Two Published Versions of Joan Didion's 'Marrying Absurd'," *Assay* 8, no. 2. "Occasion" and other examples of weddings, Grimes. "Dearly beloved": Coontz. "Forever": Rebecca Mead, *One Perfect Day*. "Washing machine": J. Courtney Sullivan, "How Diamonds Became Forever," *The New York Times*, 2013. "Spectacle": Elizabeth Freeman, *The Wedding Complex*.

For a history of weddings in Las Vegas, visit weddings.vegas. "Vietnam": Michael Toole, "The Vietnam Wedding Rush," *Las Vegas Weekly*, 2005. Wedding numbers are at clarkcountynv.gov. "Little White": Cassidy George, "Why Won't Anyone Buy the Most Famous Wedding Chapel in Las Vegas?," *The New York Times*, 2019.

"Sweat": Grimes. "Resources": Puchner. "Handfasting": Freeman. "Barstow": Cox.

8. Celebration Trail

"Two worlds": Sarah Johnston, *Hekate Soteira*. "Bonds": Eliade. My history of time travel draws from James Gleick, *Time Travel*. "Winged": William Blake, "Eternity." "Free": Gleick. "Eradicates": Victor Turner, *Drama, Fields, and Metaphors*. "Useless": Mircea Eliade, *The Myth of the Eternal Return*. "Concrete": Eliade. "Dreamtime": Bruce Chatwin, *The Songlines*.

On *shinrin-yoku*, see Qing Li, *Forest Bathing*, and Dacher Keltner, *Awe*. "Indoors": Neil Klepeis et al., "The National Human Activity Pattern Survey," *Journal of Exposure Analysis and Environmental Epidemiology* 11, no 3. "Ponders": Chorong Song et al., "Physiological Effects of Nature Therapy," *International Journal of Environmental Research and Public Health* 13, no. 8.

"Climate grief": Rebecca Randall, "Do 'Forest Funerals'—and Other Rituals—Help Climate Anxiety?" *Sojourners*, 2023. "Glacier": Agence France-Presse, "Iceland Holds Funeral for First Glacier Lost to

Climate Change," *The Guardian*, 2019. "Rainmaking": Alex Martin, "As Climate Extremes Intensify, Japan Embraces Ancient Weather Rituals," *Japan Times*, 2024. "Siamese": "Get to Know Thailand's Unique Rain-Making Festival That Involves Cats," Asia News Network, 2025. "Pope": "Encyclical Letter Laudato Si' of the Holy Father Francis on Care for Our Common Home," The Holy See, 2015. "UN": "Only One Earth," 1990.

"Band-Aids": Placemaking Lab, "Curativos Urbanos," Medium, 2017. "Drum circles": "Drumming for Peace," URI.org, 2022. "Cubes": "The Artist Gunter Demnig," Stolpersteine.eu. "Bridge": "Longest Table Setting," guinnessworldrecords.com. "Chelsea": Scott Stiffler, "In Short, the Longest Table Was a Feast of Much-Needed Neighborhood Fun," *Chelsea Community News*, 2022.

"Stubborn": Mary MacGregor-Reid, "The Finnish Sauna," Mary MacGregor-Reid, personal blog, 2017. "Children": June Pelo, "The Sauna," 2020, Swedish Finn Historical Society.

My history of the Mapuche draws from Ana Mariella Bacigalupo, *Shamans of the Foye Tree*. "Exogenous": Javier Guido Puntieri, "Effects of Artificial Damage on the Branching Pattern of *Nothofagus Dombeyi*," *Annals of Forest Science* 63, no. 1. "Easy": Robin Wall Kimmerer, *Braiding Sweetgrass*. "Universe": Abraham Maslow, *Religions, Values, and Peak-Experiences*.

9. Bless the Broken Road

"Consultants": Nellie Bowles, "God Is Dead. So Is the Office. These People Want to Save Both," *The New York Times*, 2020. For a history of labyrinths, see Charlotte Higgins, *Red Thread*. "Trafficking": Kathleen Toner, "Unique Program Helps Women Escape Streets, Transform Lives," CNN, 2017. "Transition" et al.: Lauren Artress, *Walking a Sacred Path*. On "Bless the Broken Road," see Dave Paulson, "Story Behind the Song" *The Tennessean*, 2017, and "Marcus Hummon," Nashville Songwriters Hall of Fame." "Energizer": Artress.

"Gold Award": Ben Freda, "Girl Scout Earns Gold Award with Her Labyrinth," *The Abington Journal*, 2023. "Quinn": Douglas Quenqua, "The Labyrinth Revival," *The Atlantic*, 2015. "Indiana," see "Professor Awarded Half-Million Dollar Grant for Labyrinth Research," *IU South Bend News & Events*, 2024. Location data from labyrinthlocator.org.

10. A Time to Hold

On *Nineteen Eighty-Four,* see Robert McCrum, "The Masterpiece that Killed George Orwell," *The Guardian*, 2019. "Macabre": Jessica Mitford, *The American Way of Death*. "Thanatology": Grimes. "Daughters": Reddit, r/askfuneraldirectors, "How to care for my daughter's hair." For mourning rituals, see Peter Metcalf and Richard Huntington, *Celebrations of Death*, and Joanne Cacciatore, *Bearing the Unbearable*. "Compassion": Cacciatore. "Comfort": George Bonanno, *The Other Side of Sadness*.

For the history of Irish funerals, see Kevin Toolis, *My Father's Wake*, and Ann Marie Hourihane, *Sorry for Your Trouble*. "One percenters": Mark Tighe, "What's Behind the Motorcycle Murder?," *The Times*, 2017. "Don't": Freewheelers MC, freewheelersmcireland.com. "Walk": Oli Platt, "YNWA," *Goal*, 2023. "Synod": Hourihane; "peasant": Hourihane. "Tense" et al.: "The Story of RIP.ie Plus Support for Grieving Parents," *Aftering* podcast, soundcloud.com/aftering_podcast.

"Holding": Heather Plett, "What It Means to 'Hold Space' for People," heatherplett.com, 2015. "Squeezes": "About Us," Mount Jerome Cemetery & Crematorium, mountjerome.ie. For more on potato blight, see Pauline Lomax, "Irish Government Needs to Stop Using Famine Word to Describe the Great Hunger," *Irish Central*, 2015.

11. The Placenta Chronicles

An especially good source for the history of Rapa Nui is Steven Roger Fischer, *Island at the End of the World*. For childbirth, see Sonya Charles, "Ethical Issues Concerning Pregnancy and Childbirth," *Reference Module in Biomedical Sciences* (2014); Moira Donegan, "More Than a Natural Function," *The Nation*, 2023; and Laura Helmuth, "The Disturbing, Shameful History of Childbirth Deaths," *Slate*, 2013. "Attended": "A Brief History of Midwifery in America," OHSU Center for Women's Health. "Backlash": Jessica Grose, "Here's Why We Won't Say 'Natural Birth'," *The New York Times*, 2019.

"Tons": Fisher; "remarkably" et al.: Fisher. "Suicide": Jared Diamond, *Collapse*. "Conclusive": Mara Mulrooney et al., "Empirical Assessment of a Pre-European Societal Collapse on Rapa Nui (Easter Island)," in Paul Wallin and Helene Martinsson-Wallin, eds., *The Gotland Papers*. "Ricin": Peter Rogers, "Rapamycin," *Big Think*, 2023. "Love": "Analola Tuki," moevarua.com, 2019. "Strategy": Fisher. "Birth narratives": Lynn Callister and Inaam Khalaf, "Culturally Diverse Women Giving Birth," *Journal of*

Obstetric Gynecologic & Neonatal Nursing 33, no. 4. "Cornell": Maria Antoniak, David Mimno, and Karen Levy, "Narrative Paths and Negotiation of Power in Birth Stories," *Proceedings of the ACM on Human-Computer Interaction* 3 (2019).

"Cultures": William Ober, "Notes on Placentophagy," *Bulletin of the New York Academy of Medicine* 55, no. 6. "Navajo": Sarah Hollister, "Placenta Burial Rituals," Placenta Risks, placentarisks.org. "Investigated": Sharon Young and Daniel Benyshek, "In Search of Human Placentophagy," *Ecology of Food and Nutrition* 49, no. 6. "Hawaii": Emmie Siebert, "Fighting for Tradition," *Ke Alaka'i*, 2024. "Celebrities": Heather Saul, "Kim Kardashian West 'Eats' Placenta after Birth in a Bid to Ward Off Postnatal Depression," *The Independent*, 2015. "Yummy": Kourtney Kardashian, Instagram, 2015. "DIY": Annie Daly, "4 Ways to Eat Your Placenta," *Women's Health*, 2015. "Golden hour": "Capturing the Magic," *Life Laid Bare*, 2023. "First bath": Celia Shatzman, "Pregnancy and Birth Traditions Around the World," *The Bump*, 2017.

"Craving": Peter Berger, *The Sacred Canopy*. "Obvious": Rappaport.

12. The Garden of Lost Children

Jan Chozen Bays shares her story in *Jizo Bodhisattva*. Howard Carter's commentary appears in "Tutankhamun," available at griffith.ok.ac.uk. "Twins": see Jarrett Lobell, "The Pharaoh's Daughters," *Archaeology Magazine*, September/October 2022; Geoffrey Chamberlain, "Two Babies That Could Have Changed World History!," *The Historian* 72, 2001; and Zahi Hawass and Sahar, "Mummified Daughters of King Tutankhamun," *AJR* 197, no 5. "Athens" et al.: Stephanie Jo Fox, "Mortuary Practices on Children," *UNLV Retrospective Theses & Dissertations* (1996). "Nonevents": Marilyn Field and Richard Behrman, eds., *When Children Die*. "Maimonides": Stephanie Dickstein, "Jewish Ritual Practice Following a Stillbirth," *Responsa of the CJLS, 1991–2000*. "Church": "Catechism of the Catholic Church," Catholic Culture. "Child mortality": Saloni Dattani, et al., "Child and Infant Mortality," Our World in Data. "1960": Chozen Bays. "Fathers": Hourihane.

"Pregnancies": see Mansureh Yazdkhasti et al., "Unintended Pregnancy and Its Adverse Social and Economic Consequences on Health System," *Iranian Journal of Public Health* 44, no. 1; and Susheela Singh et al., *Adding It Up*, Guttmacher Institute and United Nations Population Fund, 2009. "Disenfranchised": see Kenneth Doka, *Grief Is a Journey*. "#IHadaMiscarriage": Erin Bunch, "Why We Need a Ritual to Cope with Pregnancy Loss," *Well+Good*, October 1, 2018.

"Sands": see sands.org.uk/history. "Months": "Proclamation 5890—Pregnancy and Infant Loss Awareness Month, 1988," Ronald Reagan, October 25, 1988. "Irish": Eileen Murphy, "Children's Burial Grounds in Ireland (*Cillíní*) and Parental Emotions Toward Infant Death," *International Journal of Historical Archaeology* 15, no. 3. "See": Christine Henneberg, "A Modest Proposal to Save Mothers' Lives," *The Atlantic*, 2023.

"Plunged": Tristin Hopper, "How Canada Forgot about More than 1,308 Graves at Former Residential Schools," *Ottawa Citizen*, 2021; and Alison O'Reilly and Sean Murray, "Exhumation of Babies at Tuam Mother and Baby Home to Begin in February 2025," *Irish Examiner*, 2024. "Laundry": Blane Bachelor, "These Public Spaces Honor the Private Grief of Pregnancy Loss," *National Geographic*, 2021. "Hart": Corey Kilgannon, "A Million Bodies Are Buried Here. Now It's Becoming a Park," *The New York Times*, 2023. "Star children" et al.: Bachelor. "Haggard": nowilaymedowntosleep.org/about-us.

13. A Moment of Hope

My history of mikvehs draws on Joseph Telushkin, *Jewish Literacy*, mayyimhayyim.org, and Jessica Steinberg, "Northern Community Successfully Transfers Ancient Ritual Bath to New Home," *The Times of Israel*, 2020. Details on water rituals from "Celebrating the Water Communion," Unitarian Universalist Association; Dave Bohon, "Dozens Baptized at Ohio State Event as Football Players Continue to Bear Fruit for Christ," *The Lion*, 2024; Anugrah Kumar, "Over 2,000 Students Respond to Jesus at Ohio State Campus Revival, Group Says," *The Christian Post*, 2025; and Ruth Graham, "Horse Troughs, Hot Tubs and Hashtags," *The New York Times*, 2021.

The history of misogi is described in Michael Easter, *The Comfort Crisis*. "Rite": Michael Easter, "Four Lessons from Misogi," *Two Percent*, 2024. "I Want a Mikveh": Anita Diamant, *Pitching My Tent*.

"Potlach": Stanley Walens, "The Weight of My Name is a Mountain of Blankets," in Victor Turner, *Celebration*. "Utopias": Bauman. "Elevating": Jerome Groopman, *The Anatomy of Hope*. "Felt": Ram Dass, "Mushrooms Gave Me What I Could Have Had at My Bar Mitzvah," in Magida. "Prophet": *The Jonathan Sacks Haggadah*.

SOURCES

Conclusion. A Ritual State of Mind

"Duke": Bruce Feiler, "The Stories That Bind Us," *The New York Times*, 2013. My history of homesickness draws on Susan J. Matt, *Homesickness*. "Social": W. L. Gardner et al., "Social Snacking and Shielding," in K. D. Williams et al., eds, *The Social Outcast*. "Toxic": Liz Dunphy, "Children Fed Toxic Content by Social Media Algorithms, Study Finds," *Irish Examiner*, 2024. "Simply": Patrice Somé, *The Healing Wisdom of Africa*. On generations, see Jean Twenge, *Generations*. "Crafting": Geoffrey Cohen. "Sing": Barbara Ehrenreich, *Dancing in the Streets*. "Negative": John Keats, "Selections from John Keats's Letters," Poetry Foundation, 2009. "Ache": Maya Angelou, *All God's Children Need Traveling Shoes*. "Dancing": Brian Friel, *Dancing at Lughnasa*.

Index

INDEX

INDEX

INDEX

INDEX

INDEX

INDEX

INDEX